Rocky Colavito

9/4

Rocky Colavito

Cleveland's Iconic Slugger

MARK SOMMER

McFarland & Company, Inc., Publishers
Jefferson, North Carolina

ISBN (print) 978-1-4766-7397-4 ∞
ISBN (ebook) 978-1-4766-3729-7

LIBRARY OF CONGRESS AND BRITISH LIBRARY
CATALOGUING DATA ARE AVAILABLE

LIBRARY OF CONGRESS CONTROL NUMBER: 2019018230

Printed in the United States of America

McFarland & Company, Inc., Publishers
Box 611, Jefferson, North Carolina 28640
www.mcfarlandpub.com

Table of Contents

Acknowledgments

Writing a book takes a village.

A special thanks to all who helped along the way, with apologies to anyone who may have been overlooked:

Gary Mitchem, McFarland's senior acquisitions editor, for his guidance and support.

Bob DiBiasio, Cleveland Indians' senior vice president for public affairs, for his early support and valuable assistance.

Bill Flynn, retired *Buffalo News* city editor and lifelong Colavito fan, for his careful proof-reading and helpful suggestions.

Tom Grace, historian and union representative, for his early reading of the manuscript and research assistance at the Hall of Fame in Cooperstown.

Marc Bono, Cleveland.com reporter; Frank DiLeo, City Honors School (Buffalo) English teacher; and Mark Goldman, author, historian and Dylanologist, for their early reading of the manuscript and valuable suggestions.

Colavito collectors Steven Pierce and Harvey Weber for their generous assistance.

Mike Billoni, former general manager of the Buffalo Bisons when the team was the Cleveland Indians' Triple A affiliate, and Tim Tielman, executive director of the Campaign for Greater Buffalo History, Architecture & Culture, for their insightful suggestions and encouragement.

William Barrow, head of special collections, and Donna Stewart, digital production unit, at Cleveland State University's Michael Schwartz Library; Pamela Dean, curator for Italian-American history at Western Reserve Historical Society; Ruth Flannery, project manager for Playhouse Square Archives; baseball historian Bill Jenkinson; reference librarian Cassidy Lent and manuscript archivist Claudette Scrafford of the National Baseball Hall of Fame and Museum's Giamatti Research Center; researcher Bill Lucey; and Leila Zetchi, distribution manager for *Memphis* magazine, for their generous research assistance.

Mark Dehem of the Athlete Collection; Michael Margolis, director of baseball information and public communications for the New York Yankees; Alex Trihias, communications assistant for the Major League Baseball Players Alumni Association; and writer Jonathan Eig for their helpful assistance.

Basil Russo, president of the Italian Sons and Daughters of America, for his valuable insights.

Sabermetricians Brian Heise and Adam Darowitz for generously analyzing Colavito's career.

Topeka Men's Group members Tom Averill, Frank Barthell, Mahasen Desilva, Byron Fry, Rick Frydman, Jim Kleiger, Steve Lerner, Tom Murphy, Leigh Myers, Ty Petty, Tom Prasch, Eric Rosen and Radu Teodorescu for their encouragement and support.

Buffalo News co-workers for their encouragement, as well as graphic artist Leah Samol, columnist Sean Kirst, reporters Bob McCarthy and Matt Spina, and sales assistant Brian Mann for their valuable assistance.

Writer and former Yankees public relations director Marty Appel and New York sportswriter George Vecsey for their valuable insights.

Baseball-Reference.com and Baseball-Almanac.com for their handy online resources.

Ryan Becker and the Society for American Baseball Research's Luke Easter Chapter in Rochester for their helpful assistance.

The Buffalo & Erie County Public Library for its baseball collection and valuable resources.

Former Indians teammates Joe Altobelli, Max Alvis, Joe Azcue, Gary Bell, Larry Brown, George Carver, Tito Francona, Vern Fuller, Sam McDowell, Sonny Siebert, Duke Sims, Ralph Terry and Luis Tiant; former Tigers teammates Paul Foytack, Willie Horton, Al Kaline and Jake Wood; former Athletics and Indians teammate Jim Gentile; former White Sox teammates Ken Berry and Tommy John; former Yankees teammate Joe Pepitone; and pitcher Jim Kaat for sharing their memories.

Nancy Score, Herb Score's widow, for sharing memories of her husband and his friendship with Colavito.

Jerry Muro for generously sharing childhood memories and insights about growing up with Colavito.

Colavito fans who shared their memories and reflections, and sometimes photographs and memorabilia, too: Lawry Babitt, Tom Baker, Gregory Bartone, Bob Fitzpatrick, Sheldon Green, Susan Grimm, George Hupcej, Bill Jonke, Brent Kecskemety, Dale McMillin, Randy Marks, Jerry Michalak, Ida Pocci, Mark Potthoff, Stan Raskin, Kent Reinker, Allen Richardson, Tom Rudar, Jr., Larry Russ, Gary Stromberg, Frank Weiss, Christine Williams.

Gerry Nemeth, who teaches a class on the "Glory Days of Cleveland Professional Sports" at Cuyahoga Community College, for his valuable assistance.

Indians fan Brian Berg for his enthusiasm and assistance.

Margaret Reardon, administrator of the Baseball Heritage Museum in Cleveland, for her unbridled enthusiasm and support.

Rocky Colavito Fan Club (1956) co-founders Emily (Fitzgibbons) Toth and Barbara (O'Connor) Warny; and Rocky Colavito Facebook Fan Club founder Phyllis LaVietes, for generously sharing their memories.

Baseball I Gave You All the Best Years of My Life, edited by Kevin Kerrane and Richard Grossinger (North Atlantic Books, 1977), for inspiration.

Every beat reporter, writer, columnist, photographer, author and cartoonist who covered or wrote about Colavito as a player, broadcaster and coach for newspapers, magazines and books cited in the endnotes.

Anne Sommer for her encouragement and support.

Laura for her consideration and support.

Johanna and Nathan for their patience and understanding while their father was anchored to a computer.

Bethany for being there every step of the way.

The Colavito family—Rocky's wife, Carmen; their children, Rocky, Marisa and Steve; and of course, Rocky Colavito for graciously and generously sharing his life with me.

Preface

I was 13 when I read *Don't Knock the Rock: The Rocky Colavito Story*. The book was paid for with bar mitzvah money without my parents knowing, which still triggers a tinge of guilt. I didn't grow up in Cleveland and root for the Cleveland Indians, but Rocky Colavito was one of my favorite players anyway. I liked his cool name, the way he looked, and the home runs he hit, but there was something intangible, too. Like a lot of kids, I mimicked Colavito's batting stance with bat held high, which I saw on Major League Baseball's "Game of the Week" that aired Saturday afternoons. Since I was a displaced New Yorker living on the West Coast and a Yankees fan by inheritance, Mickey Mantle and Roger Maris were also among my baseball idols. Willie Mays and a few others were in that select group, too. I grew up listening to the Angels and Dodgers on the radio and learned the nuances of the game through Vin Scully's incomparable play-by-play.

Baseball was in its last days as the uncontested national pastime when Colavito retired in 1968. The game was also different then. Divisional play, the designated hitter, free agency, interleague games, and steroids were still in the future. So were cable TV, the internet, and social media. The wave of cookie-cutter ballparks hadn't occurred, nor had the retro-designed stadiums that came after, since many teams still played in their original ballparks. There were one-third fewer teams, and the top salary was $125,000, with most ballplayers needing second jobs in the off-season. The World Series was played in the daytime, leading kids everywhere to smuggle transistor radios into school or fall suddenly ill.

The idea for this book came in early 2017, while randomly searching Colavito's name online. I knew a lot about his major-league career, but little about his life afterward. I wondered about what appeared to be Colavito's strained relationship with the Cleveland Indians, the team he was most associated with, after his playing days were over. It was during my search that I was shocked to learn that *Don't Knock the Rock*, which came out in 1966, when Colavito had three more seasons to play, was still the only biography

1

written about him. I wondered how that could possibly be, since more than a half-century had passed since the book's publication. After weeks of consideration, I concluded that a comprehensive examination of Colavito's career was long overdue. That included delving into the controversial trade after the 1959 season that saw Colavito, the American League's reigning home-run champion, sent to Detroit for Harvey Kuenn, the batting champion. The prospect of tapping into my knowledge and love of baseball while revisiting the baseball era of my youth appealed to me. Plus, Colavito seemed like a fascinating subject.

"The Rock," as Colavito's fans called him, was a star in two of major league baseball's most colorful periods and played with and against many of the sport's greatest players. He played professionally through all but two years of the 1950s and 1960s and was a coach or color commentator during a good portion of the 1970s and early 1980s. But despite being a six-time All-Star and fan favorite, Colavito seemed to have fallen through the cracks. Perhaps it had something to do with playing most of his career in Cleveland, followed by Detroit and Kansas City, cities not known for their limelight. Colavito also never played in the World Series, denying him the national exposure that came with it. Statistically, his career measured closely with many peers and players after him who gained admittance to the Hall of Fame, yet his vote totals barely registered a pulse. I wondered why.

It was apparent even from Buffalo, a fellow Rust Belt city a three-hour drive from Cleveland where I work as a journalist, and whose Bisons for a time were the Indians' top minor-league affiliate, that Colavito remains one of Cleveland's most beloved sports stars. Telling his story, it was clear, required hearing from fans of his generation. In interviews conducted in Cleveland, I found that the mere mention of Colavito's name typically brought fond and adoring memories, which turned bittersweet over the trade and the team's flailing fortunes that followed for decades afterward.

With the help of the Indians' front office, I got in touch with Colavito, started taking notes that first day, and didn't stop. After several hundred hours of interviews, I found Colavito to be the admirable and upright person fans have believed him to be. He is humble, down-to-earth, grateful to his supporters, and fiercely loyal to Cleveland. A strong sense of right and wrong is informed by his Catholic faith. Colavito also has an incredible memory, which proved to be an incalculable help in telling his story. Here's one example: When I reminded Colavito that a hotel employee in 1956 had alerted him to a photograph in the *Cleveland Plain Dealer* of his wife, Carmen, holding newborn Rocco Jr., he told me I was partly wrong. "It wasn't a hotel employee," Colavito corrected me, "it was an elevator operator. Her name was Lillian," he added. "Rocky, that was 63 years ago," I said. "Nobody remembers something like that." But I was wrong. He does.

Presenting a balanced view of Colavito was one of the biggest challenges in writing this book. He was 83 when this project began, and several people known to have been critical of him at one time or another were no longer alive. That was especially true of managers, general managers and sportswriters Colavito clashed with. He also played in a time when sports journalism generally portrayed athletes in more glowing terms, even serving as gatekeepers to hide a ballplayer's personal failings and to avoid embarrassing the teams they covered. This made it difficult to offer first-person perspectives of Colavito that could have stood in contrast to the accounts that mostly appear in the book.

To research Colavito's career, I scoured back issues of *The Sporting News*, "the Bible of Baseball," from 1951 to 2002, comprising 1,465 pages and 5,588 mentions. I read past issues of the *Cleveland Plain Dealer* that spanned his playing career and post-retirement years, back issues of other Cleveland newspapers, and dailies from around the country. Decades of *Sport, Baseball Digest, Sports Illustrated* and other periodicals, and books on baseball and the City of Cleveland, proved invaluable. Interviews with 21 former teammates, including 14 who played with Colavito in Cleveland between 1965 and 1967, offered revealing insights, as did the contributions of others who knew him or followed his career.

To say I've been on a journey sounds like a cliché, yet that's what it feels like. It's my hope that in shedding new light on Rocky Colavito's life and career, this biography will spark renewed interest in his accomplishments on and off the playing field, and what he meant to Cleveland and to the game of baseball.

Note to the Reader: Except where other sources are cited, quotations attributed to Rocky Colavito are taken directly from interviews conducted with the author between February 2017 and August 2018.

Introduction

No. 23.

That's the ranking Rocky Colavito was given in *The Sporting News Selects 50 Greatest Sluggers*, a glossy, coffee table book published in 2000. Joe DiMaggio, Colavito's idol and role model, was listed one behind him at 24.

Colavito wasn't aware of the book or his high standing until informed over the phone in March 2017, shortly after interviews for this book began. He was dumbfounded and couldn't wait to tell his wife the news. "Carmen, you're not going to believe this," Colavito said in his still-faint Bronx accent to his wife of 63 years, in their home near Reading, PA. After filling her in, he directed his words back to me. "I would have said are you out of your mind? That's how much I thought of Joe DiMaggio," Colavito said. "I'm just being honest. I'm complimented tremendously, and I really do appreciate it. But there must be some kind of mistake. That's just wrong." Colavito doesn't like to toot his own horn. This book could just as easily have been titled, "I Say This in Modesty." It's a phrase he regularly uses before recalling an accomplishment with his razor-sharp memory, whether crushing a ball into Cleveland Municipal Stadium's upper deck in left field, throwing a runner out at third with his rocket of an arm, or hitting four home runs in one game in the American League's toughest home-run park.

The Sporting News wasn't suggesting Colavito was a better ballplayer than DiMaggio or St. Louis Cardinals star Stan Musial, ranked right behind the Yankees great in its list of greatest sluggers. Nor was it claiming that Colavito was better than the 14 other Hall of Famers named after him. The staff's conclusions—before today's reliance on advanced metrics—came after sorting through statistics such as total home runs, slugging percentage, home runs per at-bat, and total bases, as well as a perception of the players as sluggers.[1] The ranking was a heady placement for Colavito, who hadn't played a game in 32 years. Though no plaque of Colavito resides in Cooperstown, it served as a reminder of his star-studded career between 1955 and 1968, most of those years with the Cleveland Indians.

Colavito, a feared home run hitter, was the second-fastest big-leaguer to reach 100 homers, and the fifth-quickest to attain 300 round-trippers. Though his career lacked the longevity of many of his peers, he had the third-most career home runs among right-handed batters in American League history and ranked 15th all-time when he retired. He was also a model of consistency.

Baseball, more than any other sport, values statistics, and Colavito's were formidable. He had 11 seasons in a row of 20 or more home runs. He hit 30 or more seven of those times, and more than 40 three times. He led the league in home runs once and finished in the top five on seven occasions. Colavito was also a fierce run producer. He had more than 100 RBIs six times, leading the league once and finishing in the top five seven times. "The Rock" also played in nine All-Star Games, and the three home runs he hit are tied for third all-time. He never won a Most Valuable Player Award, but he finished in the top five three times.

The right fielder also had a cannon of an arm that scared baserunners and awed fans. Colavito threw a ball 435 feet in a throwing exhibition, and his 16 assists one year led the American League. In 1965, he became the first outfielder in the league to play every game and not make an error, extending that streak the following season to 234 games.

But Colavito's career is also marked by something else: He was at the center of arguably baseball's most controversial trade. Colavito was the American League's best slugger over the 1958 and 1959 seasons, and at age 26 was just entering his prime as a ballplayer. His home runs were matched by his striking appearance and contagious enthusiasm, which made him the team's most popular player and an Italian-American icon. But before the start of the 1960 season, Colavito was traded to the Detroit Tigers by General Manager Frank Lane for batting champion Harvey Kuenn. The trade was a crushing blow to Colavito's fans and proved to be a disaster on the field and at the turnstiles.

Colavito returned to the troubled franchise five years later, leading the league in runs batted in and causing attendance in Cleveland to surge. But the Indians slugger's return didn't have the storybook ending that first season seemed to foretell. He was reduced to part-time status two seasons later and then traded in mid-season. Colavito continued as a reserve player over the next year and a half, closing out his career with his hometown New York Yankees. He is enshrined in the Cleveland Indians Hall of Fame, and fans still cling to the hope that he will one day be voted into the Baseball Hall of Fame in Cooperstown, and that a statue of him will be erected outside the Indians' ballpark. Whether either happens, Colavito remains one of Cleveland's and the Italian-American community's most beloved and revered figures, and one of the most iconic ballplayers of his era. This is the story of how he got there.

1

The Trade

Inside Cleveland's downtown Loew's State Theatre, moviegoers settled into velvet-cushioned seats to watch a matinee of *Please Don't Eat the Daisies*, a new comedy starring Doris Day. Ten-year-old Sheldon Green of Mayfield Heights, a suburb east of Cleveland, and his grandparents were among them.

It was Easter Sunday, 1960, and in a holiday tradition long observed by Jews, Sheldon was looking forward to Chinese food after the movie. Sitting in the theater also allowed him to press the pause button on a plan he was concocting to convince his parents on Tuesday morning that he was too sick to go to school. This was a matter of some urgency, since the Cleveland Indians were playing their season opener that afternoon against the Detroit Tigers, and anticipation for the team ran high. The Indians had made their first pennant run in several years the previous season, only to stumble the last month and finish five games behind the Chicago White Sox. Still, the team had finished ten games ahead of the New York Yankees, whom the Indians were used to trailing in the standings.

The biggest reason for the team's success was Rocky Colavito, a power-hitting outfielder with movie-star looks and all-star talent who was at once an Italian-American and baseball icon. Local sportswriters had already proclaimed Colavito, at 26 years old, one of the most popular ballplayers ever to play in Cleveland. Fans of all ages embraced him for his earnestness and friendly disposition. They liked the gratitude he expressed and the joy he embodied, whether tipping his hat to applause as he headed back to the dugout following a home run, rushing headlong to his position between innings, or signing autographs after the game. They were also captivated by the home runs the pull-hitter launched to left field and the long throws made from right field to gun down runners on the base paths. Sheldon could go on endlessly about who was the better player, Mickey Mantle or Willie Mays. But Rocky Colavito had hit more home runs and scored more base runners over the past two years than both. This was no small source of civic pride, considering Mantle and Mays were stars on the East Coast and West Coast, respectively, while Colavito played in the Midwest.

Sitting inside the State Theatre, Sheldon stared up at the giant screen, enjoying the antics of the four sons tormenting their mother, the Doris Day character, until a commotion began in the front of the cavernous theater. A few minutes later, the carbon arc movie projector located high above the balcony came to a sudden halt, the screen went dark, and the house lights came on, casting a spotlight on the 1921 movie palace's Italian Renaissance grandeur. All eyes were on the theater manager as he emerged from the wings and walked to the middle of the stage. Sheldon's grandfather, an immigrant from Ukraine, braced himself for an announcement that the United States was going to war with Russia amid mounting Cold War tensions. What was about to be said had nothing to do with global affairs, but for young Sheldon the next 17 words detonated with the same kind of earth-shattering force. "I regret to confirm that Rocky Colavito has been traded to the Detroit Tigers for Harvey Kuenn," the theater manager said tersely, adding only that the movie would restart in five minutes. The stirring inside the theater returned, only louder, with angry comments rising above the din. "I remember looking up at Grandpa, and I began to cry," Sheldon said. "He shot off a few choice words in Yiddish." They didn't stay for the rest of the movie, and there would be no Chinese food that night. Sheldon was inconsolable, and his grandparents took him home. Nor would he listen to the Indians game that Tuesday, or for a good while longer. "And so began an era of awful baseball in Cleveland," he would say years later.

Looking back as an adult, Green realized that he idolized Colavito for many reasons. There was the way he pulled the bat behind his shoulders and stretched in the on-deck circle, how he set himself in the batter's box and slowly pointed the barrel of the bat at the pitcher, and then held his bat up high, waiting for the pitch. There was also the way Colavito gravitated toward kids like him. "My dad used to make a point of taking me to Municipal Stadium at least once a month, and I'd look down on the field and Rocky would be talking to kids in the first row before the game," Green said. "Many of the players didn't seem to care about doing that, but Rocky was different. He seemed genuine." Green also liked the confidence the muscular, 6-foot-3, 185-pound ballplayer projected. "He just knew what he was doing. When he was at bat or in the field, you knew he was going to do something spectacular." The charismatic Colavito was frequently described as a "matinee idol," a term usually reserved for stars of the silver screen. "He was probably the most handsome guy ever to play baseball in Cleveland," Green said. "Look at the old black-and-white photographs. In my neighborhood, which was 70 percent Italian and maybe ten percent Jewish, the girls also loved him, even if they hardly knew anything about baseball. He had such star power."[1]

The Loew's State Theatre in downtown Cleveland (Parade Studio).

The trade stung adults but became seared in the memories of kids like Green, who had not experienced such heartache before. Gary Stromberg was listening on his grandfather's Philco radio when he learned of the trade from Jimmy Dudley, the voice of the Indians. "Tribe fans younger than me were perhaps too young to fully comprehend the magnitude of the trade. Older fans would eventually move on," Stromberg said. "But for all of the ten-year-olds, we were burdened forever with the horror of losing Rocky that terrible day."[2]

Thomas Rudar, Jr.'s father took him aside after Easter dinner to break the news. "I didn't cry, but I sat in the living room away from the rest of the family and had that sinking feeling in my stomach," Rudar recalled. "Having grown up in Little Italy, all of us loved Rocky Colavito. He was my idol—he was everybody's idol. All my family was heartbroken. We were never going to see No. 6 in his pinstripes in right field, and we wondered if he would ever visit the neighborhood again." Rudar remembers some kids crying the next day, and older boys using words he had never heard before about General Manager Frank Lane, who had traded Colavito away. "We all pledged to never see another Indians ballgame again," he said. The next day, Rudar delivered the afternoon paper, with the trade splashed across the front page. "I was not only sick over the trade, I was a *Cleveland Press* carrier and had to deliver the news to 60 customers, 90 percent of whom were Italian," he said.[3]

Italians in Cleveland

Italians first appeared in Cleveland's census in 1870, when 35 residents were counted out of a population of 92,829.[4] But Cleveland was multi-ethnic before that. More than 25 percent of its 6,071 citizens were believed to be foreign-born in 1840, four years before Cleveland began calling itself a city.[5] By 1870, 42 percent of its residents had come over from other countries, led by the Germans and the Irish. In 1890, some three-fourths of Cleveland's 261,353 residents were considered immigrants or the children of foreign-born parents.[6] Poles, Russian Jews, Hungarians, Czechs, Slovaks, Slovenes, Croats, Serbs, and Greeks joined Italians as part of a large-scale migration fleeing poverty or difficult social conditions.

The city's Italian population continued to climb from just over 3,000 in 1900 to nearly 11,000 in 1920. Many of the new immigrants were unskilled farm workers from Italy's rural south, where Colavito's parents emigrated from that year.[7] The first Italians settled in the lower Central-Woodland district, finding work in the produce markets in an area that came to be known as Big Italy along Woodland and Orange Avenues, on the city's east side from E. 9th to E. 40th Streets. By the late 1920s, several Italian communities had sprouted around St. Marian Church at E. 107th St. and Cedar Avenue. Another community would later form in the Woodland and E. 110th St. area. An Italian-American footprint also rose on the west side, near Clark and Fulton Avenues and on Detroit Avenue near W. 65th St. But the most enduring neighborhood would prove to be Little Italy, centered at Mayfield and Murray Hill roads, between E. 119th and E. 125th Streets. Holy Rosary Church and Alta House, a settlement house, were there. A dense commercial district included small groceries, fruit stands, bakeries, pizzerias, and a movie theater.

Churches and hometown societies—many associated with the Sons of Italy that organized its first Cleveland chapter in 1913—were focal points of the Italian-American communities. Cleveland's Italians, who identified more with the village they came from than the country they left behind, retained their dialects, traditions, and patron saints in the new country they now called home. Italian-Americans were 10.3 percent of the city's 900,429 residents in 1930, the third-largest immigrant population in the nation's sixth-largest city.[8] Many found work on bridges, sewers and streetcar tracks as Cleveland was expanding its streets and city services. Some worked on the railroads and provided cheap labor in factories, while others got jobs in the embroidery and garment trades or as gardeners and stonecutters. Italian artists produced frescoes, mosaics, and sculptures in cemeteries, churches, public works, and private homes. Some 80 percent of Cleveland's barbers were from Italy and 70 percent of the cooks, who prepared meals at swanky Cleveland hotels and the Shaker Heights Country Club. Sicilian produce importers brought oranges, olive oil, bananas and figs to Cleveland, while Joseph Russo & Sons became Ohio's largest macaroni company by 1920, the same year Roma Cigar Co. was shipping 20,000 cigars a week.[9]

Cleveland during the early 20th century was also becoming an industrial powerhouse, with steel, chemical, and automotive industries and paint manufacturers providing Italian-American immigrants and non-immigrants steady work, including union jobs. Cleveland was also gaining a reputation as one of the country's most attractive and progressive cities to live in. A parks system established in 1917, which followed the growth of public parks in cities such as New York, Boston and Buffalo, encircled Cleveland with a chain of green space and boulevards. The world-class Cleveland Museum of Art was erected. A new public auditorium, main library, music hall, airport, and multipurpose stadium were all built in a ten-year period between 1922–1931. A half-dozen motion picture theaters and vaudeville houses rose in Playhouse Square, and Cleveland Union Terminal, boasting a new railroad station, opened in 1930, one year before the unveiling of Terminal Tower, the tallest building outside New York City until 1964.[10]

Cleveland was also making its mark in popular culture. Superman, who fought for "truth, justice and the American way," and alter ego Clark Kent were created in 1933 by Clevelanders Jerry Siegel and Joe Shuster. Youngstown confectioner Harry Burt developed the Good Humor bar in the early 1920s, and Italian immigrant Ettore Boiardi established the Chef Boyardee brand in 1928.[11] Comedian Bob Hope grew up in Cleveland, and Prohibition agent Eliot Ness, who brought down Al Capone and later ran for mayor of Cleveland, moved to the city in the 1930s. Actor Paul Newman was from nearby Shaker Heights.

But life in the United States was difficult for Italian-Americans, who had darker complexions, curlier hair, and a Catholic background. They were subjected to bias and discrimination in employment, education, and housing, making it hard to assimilate. Italians were stereotypically portrayed as organ grinders, fruit peddlers, and knife-wielding criminals, and referred to as "dagos" and "wops," occasionally even in daily newspapers.[12] Some of the ill treatment was notorious. Lynching used in the South to terrorize African Americans didn't spare Italians, with 11 immigrants strung up on a single day by an armed mob in New Orleans in 1891. Italian-born anarchists Nicola Sacco and Bartolomeo Vanzetti, in a 1921 trial that received world-wide attention, were railroaded into the electric chair despite recanted testimony, sparking protests in major cities throughout the United States and Europe. The ascent of the Mafia, which had a foothold in Little Italy for decades, and of fascist dictator Benito Mussolini in Italy from the mid–1920s to the 1940s, also made Italians suspect to many. Despite comprising the largest ethnic group to serve in the U.S. military during World War II, Italian-Americans, along with Japanese- and German-Americans, had to register as "enemy aliens" with the U.S. government under Executive Order 9066, signed by President Franklin Roosevelt in February 1942. It called for the compulsory relocation of 10,000 Italian-Americans and curtailed the movements of 600,000 nationwide through travel and curfew restrictions.[13]

That's where baseball came in. The country's national pastime played a key role in helping Italian-Americans feel accepted in the country. The sport provided national heroes they could be proud of and who enhanced their own sense of self-worth. Joe DiMaggio, who came up to the New York Yankees in 1936, was baseball's first Italian-American icon. "DiMaggio's success allowed Italian immigrants to feel they were being accepted in America, and that their children could succeed here," said Basil Russo, who grew up in Cleveland's Italian community. "DiMaggio became a national hero during his 56-game hitting streak, and that did wonders for Italian-Americans. After DiMaggio retired, Rocky Colavito assumed that role among the greater Cleveland Italian-American community."[14]

Russo, a retired judge and attorney, and national president of the Italian Sons and Daughters of America, said it's impossible to overestimate how important Colavito was to Italian-Americans in Cleveland and throughout Northeast Ohio.

> During the late–50s and mid–60s, Rocky was the best player on the Indians and arguably became the most beloved player in team history. But Rocky was much more than that to the Italian-American community. Rocky was a class act. He comported himself both on the field and off the field in a very professional manner and in a very dignified manner. That was one of the reasons why the immigrant generation became so attached to him. They admired him, and felt he created a favorable image for Italians throughout the country.

Dan Gugliotta, who grew up outside of Cleveland in Mayfield Heights, looked up to Colavito. "He was Italian, and I was Italian. I wanted to be a

Colavito batting at Yankee Stadium in 1957 (Baseball Hall of Fame).

baseball player, and he was my idol," Gugliotta said. "Everyone did the bat stretch and pointed their bats at the pitcher. And he had such a cool name—Rocco Domenico Colavito. It was straight out of central casting."

Allen Richardson, who is part-Italian and grew up in Elyria, outside of Cleveland, also worshipped Colavito.

Rocky fit in Cleveland, which was a multi-ethnic town where everyone was basically from families in Eastern Europe. The Italians especially loved him. Rocky was beyond a hero. He was a god, especially to the kids, but also to the fathers and the grandfathers who had followed Cleveland baseball. I grew up on stories of the 1948 and the 1954 World Series from my father and grandfather, and the stories of Satchel Paige, Larry Doby, Lou Boudreau and Bob Feller. I didn't remember them, so when Colavito came along, not only did he offer new hope for the team, but Rocky was my guy—and he was their guy, too. He was the first baseball hero in my generation, and I embraced him completely. The words that come to mind with Colavito are grace and modesty. It was one of the things that endeared Cleveland to him. We knew he loved the city and that he loved us. He was a star, but he didn't act like one, and he deserved that status. He had matinee-idol looks—I remember my family saying that—and he had that one flaw that endeared him to everyone. He was kind of like Achilles—he was a great warrior, but he had flat feet.

Trading Colavito broke Cleveland's collective heart, but it was felt strongest by Italian-Americans, Russo said. "As upsetting as it was to the average Clevelander, I can't even begin to describe how devastated Italian-Americans were. They were angry and felt betrayed. Someone had taken their hero and sent him away." Colavito's name still resonates strongly a half-century later, Russo said. "He has a special significance to our community and remains a very big name in Northern Ohio. Any of the older generation will readily identify him as the most popular ballplayer ever to play in Cleveland."[15]

Igniting an Inferno

Frank "Trader" Lane, the Indians general manager who sent Colavito away, may be—along with former Cleveland Browns owner Art Modell—Cleveland's most vilified sports figure. Lane was like a gunslinger with an itchy trigger finger and a bullet in his chamber when he arrived in Cleveland. He took over the Indians in 1957, his third team in what was his tenth consecutive season as a GM. He had a reputation for re-engineering the teams he took over through trades—lots of them. Over the course of Lane's career in the front office with five teams, Lane made 414 transactions involving nearly 700 players. He never won a pennant.[16] As ballplayers and fans alike knew, no player was safe from his whims. With the Cardinals, Lane's second team, he considered trading all-time great Stan Musial before ownership intervened. In Lane's three-plus seasons with the Indians, he traded all but two players he inherited on the major league roster—and in the third year even swapped managers in the middle of the season, sending the Indians' Joe Gordon to Detroit for Jimmie Dykes. Lane traded Roger Maris to the Kansas City Athletics, giving up on the young slugger two seasons before he won back-to-back Most Valuable Player Awards with the New York Yankees and broke Babe Ruth's hallowed mark for most home runs in a season. But the most controversial trade Lane made—the one he was most assailed for, hung in effigy in Cleveland neighborhoods over, and branded with another moniker, Frank "Traitor" Lane—was sending Colavito, the American League home run champion, to the Detroit Tigers for batting champion Harvey Kuenn.

Colavito helped propel the Indians in 1959 to a second-place finish, boosting attendance at Cleveland Municipal Stadium from 663,805 in 1958 to 1,497,976—a whopping 834,171 increase. The revolving turnstiles also put an end to concerns that poor attendance could send the Indians packing to another city. Lane, nine months before the trade, even predicted Colavito would be the biggest star in the American League. "With Ted Williams nearing the end and Mickey Mantle apparently leveling off far below what was expected of him, Rocky should easily become the greatest single gate attraction in the league," Lane said.[17] But that didn't prevent him from putting

Colavito down during the off-season and floating the possibility of trading the face of the franchise. Lane was compulsive and combative, belittled others, and was prone to contradictory statements. He wondered aloud that off-season about swapping Colavito for Mantle, which the Yankees made clear they had no interest in doing. He also raised the possibility of trading him away for Kuenn. Lane had expressed a preference for singles hitters in the past, favoring batters who consistently made contact and got on base over home-run hitters like Colavito, who were streaky and, in Lane's opinion, stranded too many base runners.

Harvey Edward Kuenn, Jr., couldn't have been more different from Colavito. He wasn't the best hitter to emerge from Milwaukee—that distinction belonged to Hall of Famer Al Simmons—but he may have been runner-up. Kuenn hit .303 over a 15-season career, while Colavito would hit .303 in a season only once in 13 years. Kuenn led the league in hits four times, where Colavito never got closer than third. But Colavito had the advantage in run production. He hit more than 20 homers 11 seasons in a row, including three seasons of more than 40, while Kuenn reached double figures twice with a career high of 12. Kuenn had more than 71 RBIs once in his career. Colavito did it ten times.

The two ballplayers differed in other ways, too. Colavito had black hair and was lean, muscular, and handsome. Kuenn wore a crew-cut, kept a bulge of tobacco stuffed in his left cheek, and had a pot belly. Colavito signed for a small bonus and didn't attend college, while Kuenn was given a contract for $55,000 after being an All-American shortstop at the University of Wisconsin. In Kuenn's first full season with the team, he hit .308, was the near-unanimous pick for the Rookie of the Year Award and married Dixie Sarchet, winner of the Miss Wisconsin beauty pageant. Kuenn finished among the league's top half-dozen hitters in batting average in five of his first six seasons and won the batting title in his seventh. His .314 career average going into the 1960 season was second in the league only to Ted Williams' .346 among active players. But it hadn't been all smooth sailing. After being named the Tigers' team captain in 1957, Kuenn proceeded to slump in the field and at bat. His average dropped 45 points, and his fielding percentage at shortstop went from best to worst in the league, exposing his limited range and ineffectiveness at turning the double play. The team took away his title after the season, believing the added pressure contributed to his poor play. Switched to the outfield, Kuenn rebounded the following two seasons, resulting in a career-best .353 average in 1959. But the Tigers had played only .500 ball over the past three seasons, and the team's brass concluded that more power was needed in the lineup. Kuenn was expendable.

While Lane coveted Kuenn, something else also seemed to be driving his recurring interest in trading Colavito. Perhaps it was the contentious contract negotiations they had over three successive off-seasons, Lane's penchant for trades, or maybe jealousy over Colavito's popularity, as the ballplayer suspected. But it could also have been an aversion to Colavito's squeaky-clean persona. "It is possible that Lane likes Kuenn because he chews tobacco and doesn't drink chocolate sodas," one reporter speculated. "Lane doesn't like 'chocolate soda' players,'" noting that "Lane had complained the club had too many 'chocolate soda kids.'"[18] Colavito enjoyed ordering chocolate egg creams—chocolate syrup, seltzer and milk—at soda fountains while growing up in the Bronx. Sometimes he had a scoop or two of ice cream added to make a chocolate ice cream soda. But he was perplexed over why Lane referred to him that way. Whatever the reason was for Lane's determination to trade Colavito, he pulled the trigger on April 17, 1960, two days before the start of the season.

The Indians were playing their last exhibition game of spring training that day in Memphis against the White Sox in Russwood Park, home to the minor league Memphis Chicks of the Southern Association. The nearly 60-year-old ballpark had earned a footnote in rock 'n' roll history a little more than four years earlier on July 4, 1956, when Elvis Presley played a concert there four months after his debut album. The stadium had also been packed eight months ago to the day to watch Sputnik Monroe and Billy Wicks wrestle for Monroe's state championship.[19] The afternoon baseball exhibition brought out more than 7,000 people for the rare chance to see major leaguers play in Tennessee.

Colavito provided early fireworks by hitting a 350-foot home run over the left-field fence leading off the second inning. It was his eighth homer of the spring in what had been a power-packed spring training for the Cleveland slugger. Colavito's home run helped the Indians to a 2–1 victory, but he wouldn't be around at the end of the game to celebrate. In Colavito's next at-bat, he hit a grounder that handcuffed the third baseman, reaching first base after the runner on first was forced out at second. When manager Joe Gordon came out of the dugout toward him, Colavito assumed he was being lifted for a pinch-runner so he could take the rest of the day off before the Indians flew north that night to Cleveland for the home opener. But Gordon had another purpose. "Rocky, that's the last time you will hit in a Cleveland uniform. You have been traded to the Detroit Tigers for Harvey Kuenn. I wish you all the luck in the world," Colavito remembered Gordon telling him. "I was so stunned, but all I could manage to say was, 'Same to you.'"

"I hate to leave Cleveland because the fans have been so good to me," Colavito told a reporter later that day. "I really love those people and always will. Nothing will ever change that." He added, "I had a terrific rapport with Cleveland fans. They just liked me. I don't know why, and I liked them because they always treated me fairly."[20] Kuenn learned of the trade while the Tigers were playing the Kansas City Athletics at Henley Field in Lakeland, FL, where the team trained. Manager Jimmie Dykes told him behind closed doors. "It's part of the game," Kuenn said afterward, as he puffed on a cigar. "I'll miss Detroit because I've spent so many years there, but I guess everything will work out for the best." As he spoke, his eyes "glistened with moisture and he spoke through lips tight with emotion," the *Detroit Free Press* reported.[21]

Local media in Northeast Ohio reflected the fans' outrage the following day. "TRIBE GETS KUENN IN COLAVITO TRADE," a headline in the *Cleveland Plain Dealer* announced that Monday morning, followed by, "FANS ENRAGED; EX-TIGER IS '59 BATTING CHAMP."[22] The lead story on the sports section, on page 33 read,

Colavito's trade to the Detroit Tigers was splashed across the front page of the *Cleveland Plain Dealer* on April 18, 1960 (Barcroft Media).

"COLAVITO STUNNED BY LANE TRADE: Regrets Leaving Indians." "No other Cleveland player in more than a decade has won and held the affection of the fans, and particularly the young fans, as he has," a Cleveland beat writer wrote. "No more than a half-dozen in the history of Cleveland baseball have been accorded the hero-worship he enjoys…. Kuenn may take his place in the lineup and fill in with distinction, but he cannot ever take the Rock's place in the hearts of the people."[23] The newspaper's sports department reported calls running 9–1 against the trade. "I'll never go to the ballpark again," the *Plain Dealer* quoted an angry Robert Intorcio saying. "Tie him to a boxcar and run him out of Cleveland," was William Scott's advice for Lane. "The trade stinks," added Gilbert Jansen, an Indians bat boy in the 1930s.[24]

Colavito went back to the hotel room to shower and flew that night with the team to Cleveland, where about 300 fans waited to greet the players at

Cleveland International Airport and to offer the departing player words of encouragement. By then, an inferno of another kind had been unleashed. Shortly after takeoff, the pilot told the team over the intercom to look out their windows. "As sure as could be, there was a big flame," Colavito said when he looked down on Russwood Park from thousands of feet in the air. The fire began 4½ hours after Colavito learned he had been traded. An employee at Baptist Memorial Hospital glanced outside around 7:30 p.m. and noticed smoke coming from the west side of the ballpark. Firefighters rushed to the scene but were quickly overwhelmed by escalating flames that began in the freshly painted bleachers and spread into a five-alarm fire. "I looked up and saw the heavy steel girders start to bend," Captain Gail Goforth said. "Then the bleachers started falling all around us."[25]

Patients from Baptist Memorial and the nearby maternity ward of John Gaston Hospital were evacuated, with no reported injuries to firefighters, patients, or bystanders. The wooden grandstands were reduced to rubble from the flames, and the 59-year-old ballpark never saw another pitch.[26] Although the fire was believed to have started in a trash can near the wooden stands, no one was able to say for sure. Was it due to "the Curse of Rocky Colavito," coined to describe the poor play that followed the Cleveland Indians for decades after he was traded away? Conspiracy theorists may believe so. An official cause of the fire was never determined.

2

Signing with the Indians

The Bronx was a melting pot of immigrants bustling with activity when Rocco Colavito, Jr., the youngest of five children of Italian immigrants, was born at home on August 10, 1933. It was a big day for the Colavito household, but New York City was too busy to notice.

The period following World War I was a time of rapid change in the northernmost of New York City's five boroughs. Jewish, Italian, and Irish immigrants were the most pronounced arrivals, followed by French, German, and Polish newcomers looking for a new start in the Bronx's 42 square miles of land surface.[1] The extension of the New York City subway system contributed to the growth of the borough, which by 1930 stood at 1.2 million residents, over one-third more people than just ten years before.[2] The large numbers of people created demand for a privately-funded housing boom in the Bronx despite tough economic times, leading to a proliferation of tenement-style buildings, many with Art Deco ornamentation.

At the time of Rocky's birth, the Bronx had something else going for it, even as the country was still in the grips of the Great Depression: More residents could count on private bathrooms, central heating, hot water, and electric refrigerators there than in New York City's other boroughs. The Bronx also had its share of parks and attractions, including the Bronx Zoo, New York Botanical Garden, and "The House that Ruth Built"—Yankee Stadium. The Bronx Bombers began playing at East 161st Street and River Avenue ten years before Rocco was born, about 20 blocks from the stadium.

The 1930 Census showed that 67,732 of the 1.2 million Bronx residents had emigrated from Italy. Rocco Colavito, Sr., came to the United States on a boat in 1920 after serving in the Italian army in the First World War. Future wife Angelina Spadafino also arrived from Italy through Ellis Island.[3] Both hailed from southern Italy's port city of Bari, located on the Adriatic Sea. The two had been acquaintances, but it was in New York that they became romantically involved. Rocco Jr., was born on the ground floor of a five-story tenement at 1701 Fulton Avenue, in the lower Bronx, next door to Public

School 4, where he would attend kindergarten through eighth grade. The family moved to an apartment building a half-block away when Rocky was an infant, and at age seven they moved again, two blocks to a six-story tenement at 544 Claremont Parkway, where he remained until he got married. The family's move to the first-floor apartment was necessitated by Angelina's Colavito's increasing difficulty in climbing stairs. In those days, before building codes required them, elevators were usually reserved for the apartments of the more well-to-do.

Ann, the oldest of Rocky's four siblings, was nine years older. Domenico—pronounced with the second "o" silent—was seven years older, followed by Vito, five years Rocky's senior. Clara, the closest in age to Rocky, was 15 months older. Rocky got along with all his siblings but was closest to Domenico, who went by "Dom." He was called "Rocky" by his family and "Rocco" by schoolmates. The Colavitos grew up in a lower middle-class section of the Bronx. There were a lot of Italians in the neighborhood, but also Irish and Jewish neighbors with whom Rocky was friendly. Their apartment had three bedrooms, with the boys sharing one bedroom and the girls another. There was also a dining room, kitchen, and bathroom.

Rocky was close to his mother, who was of average height with black hair that was starting to turn gray. She had a kind smile and was a welcome sight when he came home from school. "My mom was a terrific lady. She loved her family, and she made sure you had what you needed," Colavito said. "When I would come home from school, around 3 o'clock, she'd go to a store and bring us this fresh, big-sized Italian bread that was round. She'd slice a big piece and put butter on it to hold me over to supper. She knew kids should have something."

Angelina Colavito suffered from high blood pressure, and her health declined rapidly when Rocky was nine. She was admitted to Bronx Hospital, blocks from where they lived. It was there, at such a tender age, that Rocky's greatest heartbreak occurred. "She went to the hospital and she didn't come back," Colavito said. "I remember this: I kept saying to my father, who I called 'Daddy,' 'I want to see Momma, I want to see Momma.' I kept saying it, and I was crying, and they said you will, and finally they brought her in, but the hospital rule was that no children could be in the room. So, Vito, who was crying, took me for a walk in the park to keep me from seeing her." Angelina Colavito was only 43 when she died. Rocky remembers his family being close, but it was hard without the children's mother. Ann, 18, did her best to fill her shoes. Dom, the second oldest at 16, played a big role, watching over Rocky and keeping him in line.

Rocco Sr., who Rocky said was "a strong-minded, good man who worked hard," owned an ice business with his own route, making deliveries from an ice truck before refrigerators made his job, and ice boxes, obsolete. When that business ended, he went to work as a truck driver hauling salvage metal, which he did over the next 35 years for Bronx Iron & Steel Corp. He left for work at 5:30 a.m. to catch the elevated subway at Third Avenue, then transferred at 149th Street for a train to Jersey City. The long trip back meant he didn't get home most nights until between 7:30 and 8 p.m. Rocky and the other Colavito children didn't see their father until suppertime on weekdays for many years, until a transfer to the Bronx enabled him to get home earlier.

The family patriarch, who stood five feet, six inches tall, weighed 160 pounds and was well-built, was stern and expected to be obeyed. It was something the kids learned the hard way at one time or another. "My father was on the quiet side, but could have a pretty bad temper, especially if you got him riled up," Colavito said. "When supper, often involving pasta, was ready, your butt better be there. He wanted his family to eat dinner with him. My sister Ann was late once, and he threw a heavy, triangle-shaped glass ashtray at her that gouged the plaster wall when she ducked. She flew out the door and didn't come back until he calmed down." Rocky was on the receiving end, too.

> My father once told me to bring his pants to the dry cleaner. I said, "OK, Pop," but I forgot. I said, "I'll do it tomorrow." Second night he asked me again. I said, "Pop, I forgot." Now he's getting annoyed, but he didn't do anything that time. The third time, I came in and said, "Hi, Pop," and he backhanded me right in the mouth and I went flying backwards. I grabbed those pants and brought them to the dry cleaners. It was unusual for him to give me three chances, so I got what I deserved. I wouldn't say I got hit a lot, but you didn't step out of line. I got my share. Later, when I played ball, he'd say, "I never hitta you kids," and I'd say, "Yeah, right Pop," and he'd give you that shit-eating grin.

Colavito was a fair student, but often had other things on his mind. "Baseball, baseball, baseball and baseball," he said. He'd play anything that involved a bat and ball, including stickball, with broomsticks substituted for bats and light Spaldeen or tennis balls used on makeshift blacktopped ballfields, with sewer lids serving as home plate or second base. There was also stoop ball, box ball, and his favorite, punch ball, in which kids hit balls off tall buildings that fell in fair play. Touch football was played in the fall and winter between lamp posts, three boys to a team. But most of all, there was sprawling Crotona Park and its five ballfields that quickly became Colavito's home away from home. He played in pickup games during the week and organized games on weekends. Besides Colavito, two other all-time great home run hitters played there—one before and one after his career. Hank Greenberg, the Detroit Tigers slugger and Hall of Fame member, as well as general manager of the Cleveland Indians at the start of Colavito's career, lived at 663 Crotona Park North in the 1920s. Future Indians and Red Sox slugger Manny Ramirez played in the park in the early 1990s.

Board of Education
of the City of New York

Rocco Colavito

Has satisfactorily completed the course of study for Elementary Schools, has earned the approbation of the principal and teachers and is entitled to pursue a High School course in the City of New York.

In Testimony Whereof we have affixed our signatures hereto this twenty-fourth day of June 1947

Andrew G. Clauson
President Board of Education

John E. Wade
Superintendent of Schools

Sadye S. Reiss
Chairman Local School Board

Minnie Obermeier
Assistant Superintendent

Simon Hirdausky
Principal Elementary School
No. 4 Borough of the Bronx

ORIGINAL

CERTIFICATE OF ACCEPTABILITY

LAST NAME – FIRST NAME – MIDDLE NAME	PRESENT HOME ADDRESS
COLAVITO, JR., ROCCO DOMENICO	544 Claremont Pkwy, Bronx, NY

SELECTIVE SERVICE NUMBER				LOCAL BOARD ADDRESS
50	30	33	438	1910 Arthur Ave., Bronx, NY

I CERTIFY THAT THE QUALIFICATIONS OF THE ABOVE NAMED REGISTRANT HAVE BEEN CONSIDERED IN ACCORDANCE WITH THE CURRENT REGULATIONS GOVERNING ACCEPTANCE OF SELECTIVE SERVICE REGISTRANTS AND HE WAS THIS DATE:

☐ 1. FOUND FULLY ACCEPTABLE FOR INDUCTION INTO THE ARMED SERVICES.

☒ 2. FOUND NOT ACCEPTABLE FOR INDUCTION UNDER UMT & S ACT AS AMENDED.[1]

[1] Any inquiry relative to personal status should be referred to your Local Board.

(DO NOT USE THIS SPACE)

DATE	PLACE	TYPED OR STAMPED NAME AND GRADE OF JOINT EXAMINING AND INDUCTION STATION COMMANDER	SIGNATURE
8 May 52	NYC, R&IMS, NY4,NY	WILLIAM F. DONEGAN JR., Capt. Inf.	*William F. Donegan Jr.*

Colavito's elementary school certificate (Colavito's personal collection).

Vito and Dom were both outstanding ballplayers. Dom, a catcher, played later for the Hickory Rebels, a New York Giants affiliate in the Class D North Carolina State League. Before becoming discouraged and calling it quits, he advanced to the Class B Trenton Giants, the same team Willie Mays would later make his minor league debut with in 1950. Vito, whose range at shortstop earned him the nickname "the Octopus," was no slouch, either. "Vito could throw better than all of us, and he was a helluva shortstop," Rocky said. "A lot of people in the neighborhood thought he was the best athlete among us." But Vito's career aspirations led in another direction: commercial art. Rocky was even used as a model by Vito for several comic book illustrations, including a cover drawn for Heroic Comics, a popular comic book line.

Rocky grew up a devoted fan of the New York Yankees and the team's star center fielder. "Joe DiMaggio was my all-time favorite player. I was a Yankee fan, and Joe D. was it. He could do everything," Colavito said. "He was an outstanding outfielder; he played with grace and made things look easy that were difficult. He also had a good arm, ran the bases well, and was a clutch player and one of the best hitters ever. He carried himself with class, like a gentleman." Colavito wore Joltin' Joe's No. 5 from sandlot days through his early years in the minors and adopted DiMaggio's batting stance, with feet spread apart and hands held high. He also wanted to conduct himself on and off the field like his role model. Others noticed, and Colavito was sometimes called "Joe D." Colavito's other favorite Yankees included first baseman Lou Gehrig, Vito's favorite, and catcher Bill Dickey. Colavito never got the chance to see Babe Ruth play, since the "Sultan of Swat" played his last game in Yankees pinstripes when Rocky was a year old. "We all had teams we liked and rooted like hell for," Colavito said. "Every night I checked the back of the *Daily News* to see the line scores that would tell you the day's home runs, winning and losing pitchers and then the box scores. I was a Yankee fan through and through."

Colavito attended games at Yankee Stadium through a Police Athletic League program. Kids were given a button for ten cents, which allowed them to sit in the upper deck of the left field grandstand. One seat stood out. "There was a marker on the back of a seat that said Jimmie Foxx hit one there," Colavito said. "I couldn't believe any man could hit a ball that far." Colavito saw DiMaggio hit two triples in a game that each landed by the 457-foot sign in center field. One hit the wall on the fly, and the other landed where the ground met the wall, sending the ball straight up in the air. Colavito recalled that game years later, after crushing a ball to the same spot in Yankee Stadium for a long out. "Mickey [Mantle] caught one off me that would have hit the fence," Colavito said. "He laughed at me coming off the field. I thought, 'How did DiMaggio hit the two triples?'"

It didn't take long for people to notice Colavito's powerful throwing arm. As a child, he loved tossing rocks, and as he got older, his brothers would have him throw balls for distance, sometimes for wagers with other neigh-borhood kids. Colavito threw balls beyond the outfield fences in Crotona Park, past a playground fence across from his school, and over an elevated subway, with its three rows of tracks, onto Claremont Parkway, three-quarters of a block away. Sometimes, he would bet on himself against Jewish kids living on Fulton Avenue. While Colavito could toss the ball wildly, his throws in games were often low enough to reach the base or hit the cutoff man, and with enough velocity to get there quick. "God gave me the ability to throw the ball pretty hard, and on the line," he said. "I just loved to throw, I always did. It used to pass through my mind later how good I might have been if I was a pitcher, but I never dwelled on it." In contrast to his strong arm, Colavito ran slowly due to inverted arches. The decline became more apparent fol-lowing a growth spurt. Colavito's lack of speed plagued him throughout his career, making it hard for him to beat out infield hits or get a quick jump on the basepaths or in the outfield. "I grew fast, and that was the end of my speed," he said. "I ran too long in the same place."

Colavito's best friend was Jerry Muro, who lived three blocks away. The two Italian-American boys were virtually inseparable, though their person-alities were quite different. Colavito was outgoing, while Muro was quiet and shy around others. "Rocco was an extrovert and very popular," recalled Muro, a lifelong friend who calls Colavito by his given name, considering "Rocky" his "public name." The boys met in the summer of 1941, when they were seven years old, and became fast friends. Colavito called Muro "Bulski," a variation of Muro's nickname of Bull," given for his husky build. Rocco hung out in different neighborhoods and was well-liked by everyone, Muro said. "Rocky had charisma. Wherever we went, you'd hear, 'Hey Rock, how's it going?'" The boys spent a lot of time at each other's homes and would watch *The Milton Berle Show* at a neighbor's apartment. "That was before everyone had a television set," Muro said.

On a freezing December night in 1947, the 14-year-olds stood outside Archie's Tavern on 174th Street, near Washington Avenue, peering through the window to watch heavyweight boxing champion Joe Louis defend his title with a controversial 15-round decision over Jersey Joe Walcott. Colavito was given a weekly allowance, which he used to pay for Muro and himself when they were out. "If we went to a movie, I paid for my ticket. But if we had a snack, or went to play pool, he always paid," Muro said. He spent a lot of time with the Colavito family. "Dom was intelligent and could be generous, but he also had a tough side, which allowed Rocco to lead somewhat of a charmed life," Muro said. "Nobody would mess around with Rocco because of his older brother." Muro thought Vito was the best athlete in the Colavito family. "He was tall and lanky, and reminded people of Marty Marion, the Cardinals shortstop," Muro said. "But Vito didn't have Rocco's desire." Ann

Colavito was "the matriarch and the person who ran the household, and Clara and Rocco had a typical sibling rivalry," Muro said.

The boys played baseball in school yards, at Crotona Park or on Fulton Avenue, a wide street with little traffic. If parked cars were in the way, they were almost always unlocked, allowing someone to release the hand brake so the car could be pushed out of the way. Colavito ran around an empty ballfield wearing combat boots in the winter to stay in shape, and he kept a small black handball in his jacket pocket to squeeze for hand strength "He had forearms like iron," Muro said. Muro marveled at his friend's throwing arm. "I told Rocco that what you have is a gift from God. Nobody has an arm like you." Control, though, was a problem. "When he would throw his fastball, he didn't always know where it was going. Batters were afraid to dig in against him for fear of getting hit." During recess, Colavito would rush home just to put his baseball uniform on. "Rocco was destined to be an outstanding ballplayer," Muro said. "Everything was geared toward that. His whole life was baseball."

Because Colavito lost his mother at an early age, he learned to be self-sufficient sooner than most kids, Muro said. "I admired that Rocco became very independent and took care of himself. He was very resourceful. The kitchen had a Bendix washing machine in the middle, between the sink and the refrigerator, and he used it frequently. He washed his own clothes, and took his shirts to the Chinese laundry and to the dry cleaner."

Muro said his friend remained the same person he grew up with despite the fame baseball brought. "Rocco never changed—he remained very loyal, and he never let success get to him. I used to say, 'When you become famous you're going to forget about me,' and he would grab me in a headlock and say, 'No, I love you, Bulski.'" But despite the closeness—they still talk on the phone—things naturally changed as they raised families, lived apart, and Colavito's career took off. "At that point in his life, Rocco belonged to the world," he said. Muro also had his own successful career. He graduated from Fordham University, where his baseball prowess brought offers from scouts, and went on to be a vice president of Occidental Petroleum and chief financial officer of Hooker Chemical, a subsidiary. Muro said he was proud of his friend, and the feeling was mutual. "Rocco was always proud of me, and used to brag about me to others," he said.[4]

Colavito's first big moment in a baseball game came when he was a nine-year-old batboy for the Bronx Braves, a team of neighborhood teenagers Dom and Vito played for. Before a game in Coney Island, Rocky was enlisted to play right field when the team had only eight available players. He walked twice and struck out twice. Nervous and excited, Rocky had only one fielding opportunity, but it came at the biggest moment in the game. A batter lofted a high fly ball toward him with two outs in the last inning, with the Braves clinging to a 10–9 lead and the tying and winning runs on base. "I caught it, but I'll never forget the panic I felt while I waited for what seemed like hours for that ball to come down out of the sky," Colavito recalled. "I hardly had to stir out of my tracks, but to me it's still the most memorable catch I've ever made." He was mobbed and hoisted onto the team's shoulders.[5]

When Rocky was 12, Dom was drafted into World War II, where he was stationed in the European theater. To honor him, the proud youngster, at confirmation, adopted "Domenico" as his middle name. It was one of the ways Rocky held his brother close, though he never legally changed his name. "Domenico was fighting in the 106th Infantry, and I always prayed for him," Colavito said.

Besides baseball, Colavito liked basketball, but he stopped playing in early March each year to reduce the chance of an injury that could keep him away from his favorite sport. Baseballs and bats were often improvised. Damaged balls would be taped and broken bats repaired with small nails and tape. Colavito tried an experiment on a bat one day that failed miserably. He put rosin all over the baseball club and baked it in the oven to make it extra-

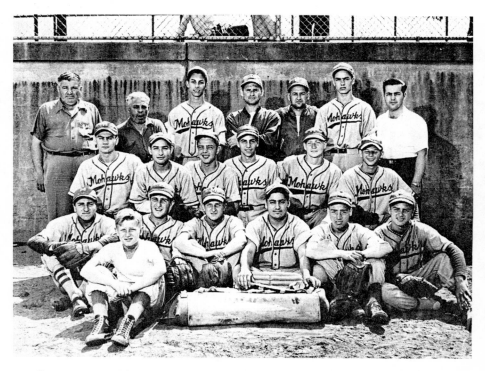

Sixteen-year-old Colavito, top row, second from right, with the New York Mohawks (Colavito's personal collection).

hard. He repeated the steps a second time, and when he took it up to bat, it broke, putting an end to the experiment. "Some big leaguers supposedly did this to help seal the bat," he said. "I wasted so many hours doing that, and I never did it again."

Baseball soon meant playing on the New York Mohawks, a team in the Federation League for boys 14 and under. The team had Italians, Armenians, Germans and Jews among its ranks. Colavito played center field, developing the habit of pounding his glove when the ball was in the air and coming toward him. "If I did that I knew I had the ball," he said. He liked playing the outfield and making use of his powerful throwing arm. Colavito also occasionally pitched, and he batted cleanup. Not to be outdone, he coached the team, too. Muro was also on the team, playing third base and left field. Each of the team's players paid weekly dues of 25 cents to pay for the umpires. When team members reached the league's cut-off age, the Mohawks moved up to the Tri-County League, with an adult sponsor taking over from Colavito as coach. Sunday games involved playing for a winner-take-all pot of money, with members of both teams contributing through allowances or part-time jobs. Colavito earned the money he bet working as a delivery boy for a pharmacy and sometimes hustling pool, which he had become skilled at playing.

In one memorable Mohawks game, the team was down 9–0 to the league's last-place team, Colavito remembered.

> Everything in the world was going wrong. Mr. Al Morgan, our beneficiary who put up the money for uniforms, balls and bats, was going bananas. I felt so bad for him because he was normally pretty quiet. I was always an optimist and said, "Don't worry, everything is going to be all right." When the score got to 9–8, Bobby Halpern, who didn't have a hit all season, was the batter with the bases loaded and two outs in the last inning. I called him over and told him, "Bobby, you can do it, you can hit this guy." Lo and behold, he hit a clean base hit up the middle and we beat them 10–9. Morgan went out of his mind. He was so happy that Bobby was the hero that I think he had tears of joy. That was one of the biggest moments of my life.

Joan Smith lived in Colavito's neighborhood and knew him mainly because he played baseball at school with her brother, Irwin Kranes, nicknamed "Sleepy" because his eyes drooped. Smith said people in the neighborhood knew that the young Colavito didn't have a mother, and he was shown more consideration because of it. The neighborhood was also proud of him for his athletic ability. "Everybody knew about Rocco and talked about him. He appeared very kind, very considerate and very shy. But when it came to playing ball, it was like somebody else emerged. He was an event in Crotona Park, and a lot of it was because of his attitude." Smith said it was obvious that Vito and Dom played a big role in his life. "You got the feeling they were protective of him," she said.

Smith, who was Jewish, said the neighborhood was poor and, in her opinion Italian families, such as Colavito's, were generally not as interested in education at that time as some other ethnic groups. "The Jewish people counted on kids going on to the City College of New York and graduating, and seemed to stress education more at that time," she said. "It didn't appear education was on the forefront for the Italians."[6] Colavito said education was not stressed in his household beyond passing his courses, nor was school something he excelled at. He liked English, history and some shop classes well enough, but didn't apply himself. Colavito attended Samuel Gompers Trade School, a public high school, and thought he might become an auto mechanic if baseball didn't pan out. Angry when auto mechanics classes weren't offered as advertised, he transferred to Theodore Roosevelt High School. Colavito considered going out for the baseball team, coached by Hank Greenberg's former manager, but it didn't prove enough of an incentive to stay in school. Instead, the 16-year-old high school junior dropped out. "I had a term paper and the teacher said if I turned it in I'd pass, but I dilly-dallied and didn't turn it in, so I quit," Colavito said. "I knew it wasn't a smart thing to do, even at that age." Colavito's siblings graduated high school, and he knew few kids his age who hadn't stayed in school. Colavito later wondered how his life would have differed if he had transferred to Cardinal Hayes High School, the private Catholic school Muro attended that, he observed, gave kids more individual attention than he received.

Years later, after Colavito was a big-league ballplayer, he admitted to sportswriter Ed Linn that he dropped out of high school with the under-standing that his admission would not be published in the *Saturday Evening Post*. "I never wanted sportswriters to know because I never wanted that for any kid," Colavito said. "He swore to me up and down that he wouldn't write it. I said give me your word of honor, and he did." Linn wrote about it anyway, to Colavito's regret, though at least five other articles appeared while he was in the minors that mentioned it.

Colavito found work at a slipper factory in lower Manhattan that paid 70 cents an hour. His job was to bleach slipper bottoms a pinkish color with a brush and then hang them on rickety racks to dry. He gave his father half of his week's pay, leaving enough to pay for his transportation and a sandwich, plus a little extra spending money. He was worried about the building's poor light out of concern that it could harm his eyes for hitting a baseball. "I was always cognizant of that kind of thing," he said. "I wanted nothing to hurt my chances." After six months, Colavito's pay rose $9 dollars a week to $37, but he needed to give his boss notice. Colavito was going to spring training as a professional ballplayer.

The Indians were the first to show interest in signing the lanky young man who, though only 16, had already reached his full 6'3", 185-pound frame, one inch shorter than Vito and three inches taller than Dom. Zip Zeoli, a "bird dog" scout reporting to Indians scout Hal Reason, who scouted players for Cleveland in the New York–New Jersey area, was high on Colavito's teammate Eddie Behrman, who also played the outfield. Zeoli suggested to Reason that he attend a Mohawks game at Crotona Park to watch him. On the day Reason was there, Colavito knocked in the winning run with a double past third base. Reason, though, didn't think much of Colavito's potential because of his lack of speed. But impressed by Behrman, he set up a tryout for him and another half-dozen boys in front of Mike McNally, general manager of the Wilkes-Barre Barons, the Indians' team in the Class A Eastern League. Lou Zacklin, who co-sponsored the Mohawks, convinced Reason to let Colavito try out, too. When McNally got a look at Colavito's cannon of an arm, his lack of speed quickly became an afterthought. "It was one of those cold, blustery autumn days when nobody can really hit," McNally said. "But I took one look at this baby-faced kid's arm, and I knew we should be able to do something with him."[7]

The Indians wanted to sign Colavito as an outfielder-pitcher, but there was a hurdle to overcome first. Major league baseball didn't allow teens to sign before graduating high school unless a waiver was granted. Rocky and his family, in a letter written by Dom, requested one for financial considerations, and Commissioner Happy Chandler agreed. His office issued a bulletin saying a special dispensation had been made for Colavito, and he could sign a contract beginning January 1, 1951, six months before his class at Roosevelt High School was to graduate.[8] The announcement from the commissioner's office worried the Indians. "To the best of my knowledge, we were the only people in baseball who had ever heard of a kid named Rocco Colavito, and now Chandler had alerted everybody that there was a youngster who might be worth their attention," McNally said.[9]

The Indians' fears proved well-founded. Five teams showed interest in Colavito—the Boston Braves, Brooklyn Dodgers, New York Yankees, Philadelphia Athletics, and Philadelphia Phillies. The Braves had Colavito try out with other players at Prospect Park in Brooklyn, where he got a triple in an intra-squad game. He also threw a player out as Vito was there to watch. But the Braves never made an offer. The Athletics had Colavito throw from the mound at Shibe Park, mostly to pitchers, and later dangled a $6,000 bonus along with a contract for $5,000. The deal collapsed when the A's scout phoned Colavito later to say the club had mortgaged its ballpark and was no longer able to sign him.[10] Dodgers scout Al Campanis expressed interest in Colavito without seeking a tryout. Campanis, who became the Dodgers' general manager after the team moved to Los Angeles, met with Rocky and Dom at the Colavito home. But his offer for Rocky to go to spring training with the team came without a financial guarantee. Phillies scout Fred Matthews also had Colavito attend a tryout, but didn't make a firm offer.

Colavito was particularly excited at the prospect of wearing Yankee pin-stripes. He auditioned in Yankee Stadium in front of head scout Paul Krichell, who had signed Lou Gehrig, Whitey Ford, Phil Rizzuto, and scout Harry Hess. Colavito and the other tryouts took batting practice and went through fielding, running, and throwing exercises.[11] "Without a doubt, trying out for the Yankees was a dream come true," Colavito said. In a game that day, Colavito pitched and clubbed a double. He also drilled a ball in batting practice that went over 400 feet into the left field bullpen.[12] The Yankees, intrigued most by Colavito's arm, offered $3,000, but none of the money was guaranteed. Hess came to the Colavito home prepared to wrap up the deal with Rocky and Dom, but things didn't go well.

> This guy with the long cigar is giving me this crap about how everybody wants to sign with the Yankees. I did not care for his demeanor or his attitude, and I loved the Yankees. That has to tell you something. Growing up in New York, you get pretty savvy. Playing pool, I also learned how to negotiate with money. I was a Yankee fan right up to the day when I first put on a Cleveland uniform, but I didn't like the way Harry Hess acted. I just thought he was a braggart who was full of shit and trying to buffalo me, plus he was a Johnny-come-lately. And there was cigar smoke all over the house.

In an interview years later, Hess said he never felt the Yankees were in the running for Colavito's services. "We liked him, but we never really had a chance. His older brother, Domenico, was handling the business and a close friend of his was a part-time scout for the Indians. I forgot what we offered, maybe $1,200 or so. But we knew we were just being used as a buffer, that the brother was trying to get us to set value so that Cleveland would have to top it. It wouldn't have mattered if we offered $5,000. The Indians were going to get him anyway," Hess said.[13] Colavito said that wasn't the case. He felt a certain allegiance to Cleveland because of the way the organization had treated him, but a better offer could have carried the day, since the Yankees were his favorite team.

The Indians did make Colavito feel wanted. The organization gave him the chance to see what playing in the minor leagues was like by letting him accompany the Wilkes-Barre Barons on a week-long road trip to Albany and Schenectady in the summer of 1950. Traveling with the team was only Colavito's third trip away from home on his own. The first two times hadn't gone well. He had gone to a week-long summer camp a few years earlier and was terribly homesick. Colavito won a swimming contest, played baseball and wrestled at camp, but wanted to go home. His sister Ann told him he had to stick it out. "I kept picturing my father looking out the window, as he often did when he came home from work," Colavito said. "For a kid, a week may feel like a half of forever." Colavito also played briefly in a league in Rutland, Vermont, before he went on the trip to Wilkes-Barre.

Dom took Rocky to the bus station for the 250-mile ride. Feeling homesick, he batted only six times before returning to New York. But being with the Indians farm team was different. This time, he was excited to be going away, and adjusted well to his surroundings. "I wanted to make the big leagues and make a good impression," Colavito said. "I was like one of the guys, and there were future big leaguers on that team. I sat on the bench, and I loved being there." The team's first baseman was Harlem Globetrotter Nathaniel "Sweetwater" Clifton, and Colavito bonded with him. "You want to talk about a nice man, he was a gem, a prince," he said. The Indians also provided Colavito with tickets to the 1950 World Series, where he watched Whitey Ford pitch the Yankees to a victory over the Phillies' "Whiz Kids" in the fourth game, with Joe DiMaggio getting two hits and Yogi Berra clubbing a homer. That gesture also meant a lot to Colavito.

Rocky and his family decided to take the Indians' offer of $3,000, even though it was a contingency contract. The Indians agreed to pay Colavito $1,250 up front, $750 if he stayed with the team 30 days, and $1,000 more if he remained for 60 days. His first-year Class A contract additionally called for $300 a month for the six-month minor league season. Rocky's father sealed the deal on December 28, 1950, after he and Dom negotiated details at the Colavito home, despite Dom holding out for more money. "The father was there, as nice and as dignified a man in an Old-World sort of way as you'd ever want to meet," McNally said.

What happened next is open to question and blurry over time. In one account, McNally claimed that Rocky's father turned to Rocky and asked, "Is this the man that sent you a Christmas card?" When Rocky said he was, his father nodded. "We sign the contract."[14] In another, Rocky's father said in Italian, "Sign before you don't get anything."[15] After a few short verbal exchanges, Colavito signed the contract. "My father never said to me, 'I'm so proud of you,' and it didn't have to be said. It was on his face," Rocky said. The day after the signing,

Indians General Manager Hank Greenberg with Colavito, 17, at ceremonial contract signing (Colavito's personal collection).

the Phillies scout called to say he was ready to sign the young slugger, but it was too late.[16] "If they had called when they were supposed to, I would have gone back to Cleveland and given them the chance to match the offer," Colavito said. The signing was announced on the Western Union ticker tape, just after the January 1, 1951, date the commissioner's office had set for the teen to be signed. A publicity photo reenacted Colavito inking his contract next to Indians General Manager Hank Greenberg, his left arm draped over the young ballplayer's shoulder.

With the money Colavito received up front, he gave $100 to Dom, who had to be talked into taking the money, used $150 to buy new clothes, and gave the remaining $1,000 to his father. "My father didn't know he was getting anything, but I always gave him money. I was grateful I had a place to live," Colavito said. After the season, Colavito used $275 to purchase his first car, a two-door, black 1941 Pontiac, which he later sold to buy a four-door, black 1941 Chevy for $350. In mid–February, Colavito headed south to the Indians' minor league spring training camp. When the 17-year-old stepped off the bus and into the hot Florida sun, it was as a professional baseball player.

3

Indianville

Visitors to the Indians' Daytona Beach spring training camp in 1951 could tell what teams the 400 ballplayers were assigned to by the color of their stirrups. Players heading off to Triple A wore dark blue, while Double A players showed blue with a white stripe. Class A players wore green, Class B players royal blue, and Class C players red. Rocky Colavito wore brown, the same as every other player in Class D, the lowest rung of the minor leagues. "All you had to do was look at the player to know what kind of contract they had," he said.

Each morning at Indianville, players checked a board to see what field they were assigned to and to get updates. For those trying to make a club, it was also the source of bad news, since that's where the names of the players cut by the Indians were posted. "At the end of every day, you'd see kids looking at the list," Colavito said. "You'd see some of them by the board, crying. I felt bad for the ones who were cut and had to turn in their uniform." The 17-year-old Colavito feared that had happened to him the first day. "I'm looking at all the outfielders, and I can't find my name," he recalled. "I'm wondering, 'Did I get cut before I even got here?'" Colavito marched into the office of Mike McNally, who had been promoted to farm director in the off-season. McNally, who signed Colavito to a contract as an outfielder-pitcher despite doubts about his speed, told the young ballplayer that he had looked in the wrong place. Colavito's name was with the list for pitchers. Colavito said he'd be willing to pitch every fourth day—the frequency with which starting pitchers took the ball in those days—but only if he could play outfield the other three days when he wasn't on the mound. McNally told him he'd be on the outfielder list the next day. Later that week, Indians General Manager Hank Greenberg went to bat for Colavito, defending the teen's desire to play the outfield despite his lack of speed. "I said, 'Hank, Rocky should be a pitcher or a first baseman because his feet are so flat,'" McNally recalled. "Hank told me, 'My feet were flat, too, and I was able to play the outfield. Let him play where he wants.'"[1]

Colavito stayed in touch with friends and family that spring. Jerry Muro, his best friend in the Bronx, received a post card with a one-cent stamp dated March 18, 1951. On one side were pictures of baseball fields and a beach, with the words "Cleveland Indian Farm System Training Base (Finest Camp in Baseball)." On the other, Colavito wrote, "Dear Jerry, I arrived here Sunday afternoon, and I am fine as I hope you and your family are. I will write again when things start happening. So long for now, Rock." When spring training broke, Colavito was ready to play his first official game as a professional ballplayer. He had little idea then of how rare it was to make the big club. Of the more than 200 first-time players who reported to Indianville in 1951, only Colavito and first baseman Joe Altobelli reached the majors.

Colavito didn't have to go far to report to his new team: He was assigned to the Daytona Beach Islanders in the Florida State League. Games were played at night because of the hot temperatures on Florida's Atlantic Coast, with the lone exception of Sunday afternoon games. The eight cities in the league were close enough for the team to avoid overnight trips. Colavito asked Islanders business manager Marion Troy if he could wear No. 5, the same number worn by his idol, Joe DiMaggio. He was also homesick at the start of the season and developed such painful shin splints that the teenager called Dom to tell him he was considering quitting, before being talked out of it. A salve prescribed by a doctor helped heal his leg condition. On April 30, Colavito hit his first home run as a pro, connecting in the sixth inning against Deland Red Hats pitcher Joe Repetz. Two more homers followed a week later.

Colavito also began his career-long practice of running quickly from the dugout to right field at the start of an inning and from the outfield back to the dugout when the inning was over. He did it to keep himself in good condition and avoid leg injuries. "I always felt that running firmly

Colavito, 17, began his professional baseball career in 1951 with the Daytona Beach Islanders, the Cleveland Indians' Class D team (Colavito's personal collection).

and pretty quickly nine innings in and nine innings out would keep me in good shape," Colavito said. Roger Maris, whom he played with in the minor leagues and major leagues, adopted Colavito's approach. "I never had a pulled leg muscle that I recall, and I remember Roger Maris, who I had explained my reasoning to, saying to me, 'Hey, Rocco Socko, I run out to my position and I run in, and I haven't had any problems with my legs.' I always felt it was a very high compliment that he would follow what I said."

Colavito roomed with Altobelli, who was also in his first year of professional ball, in an owner-occupied house that rented to ballplayers. The two went to a pool hall across the street to play snooker, a game in which the cue ball is used to pocket the other balls in numerical order. "We thought it was a good idea to split our money by living together because we didn't have much of it in those days. Rocky was a fine person, and a good roommate," recalled Altobelli, who would manage the Baltimore Orioles to a World Series victory in 1983. "Rocky was a fascinating hitter with the power he had. He could hit a ball a long way. He hit a bunch of home runs that first year."[2] Colavito liked playing for Mike Tresh, the Islanders' player-manager. He also found that hitting the long ball paid off in more ways than one. When Colavito and his teammates homered at home, a bucket was passed around the stands. At the end of the game, half of the money collected went to the batter, which Colavito said came in handy, and half went into a pool shared at the end of the season by all the players. In the season's final game, Altobelli pitched the first five innings and Colavito came on in the sixth inning to throw four scoreless innings the rest of the way.

Daytona Beach finished in sixth place, but Colavito, in his maiden 1951 season made the most of his opportunity. He led the league with 23 home runs, had 111 runs batted in, scored 88 runs, and batted .275 while playing in a league-leading 140 games. Playing mostly center field, Colavito had a league-leading 303 putouts to go with 19 assists, but also made 20 errors to lead the league. The slow-footed Colavito even managed to steal five bases and hit his only professional inside-the-park homer that season, circling the bases after the left fielder and center fielder collided in pursuit of his fly ball. Colavito was named to the Florida State League's All-Star team by sportswriters and managers and received his first mention in *The Sporting News* on August 22, 1951. "Rocky Colavito of Daytona Beach stole the show with his twenty-first and twenty-second homers of the season to drive in five runs and defeat Leesburg, 9 to 6," the article reported.[3]

Colavito was upset when he received a contract in the off-season for the same $300 a month he received for his first season. Muro, unbeknownst to Colavito, informed Hank Greenberg, who immediately raised the pay to $400 a month. Colavito was promoted to the Class B Cedar Rapids Indians in the Illinois-Indiana-Iowa League before the start of the 1952 season. But as

Colavito came out of spring training, he was notified by his draft board to fly home and take a physical exam. The Korean War was in full swing, and 18-year-olds were being drafted into the service. When doctors got a look at Colavito's inverted arches, they were ready to deem him 4-F, which would render him unqualified due to his physical condition. After a sergeant objected, Colavito was sent to Fort Jay on Governor's Island in New York Harbor for a second opinion. Once again, doctors examined his flat feet and classified him 4-F, this time without resistance from higher-ups.

Colavito joined Cedar Rapids a week into the regular season, and in his first game hit two home runs and knocked in six runs. A short time later, sidelined by the flu and a mouth infection, he was hospitalized for almost two weeks in Davenport, IA. Colavito lost 17 pounds in 15 days, dropping from 185 to 168. "I never felt that bad in my life," he said about his first-ever hospital stay. After regaining his strength, Colavito returned to the lineup to play in 32 games, hitting eight homers in 94 at-bats. But with just a .170 batting average, the team sent Colavito to a warmer climate in Spartanburg, SC, to regain his health and get a fresh start. He donned No. 15 because No. 5 wasn't available, and in 66 games for the Spartanburg Peaches, considered a better level of Class B ball in the Tri-State League, his playing improved. Under manager Pinky May, Colavito hit .252 with 11 home runs, including five in seven games, to go with 55 runs batted in. That year was also the first in which he primarily played right field and, improving on the year before, made just two errors. He also won several watches by hitting balls off a sign behind the left field fence, thanks to a ballpark promotion by a local jewelry store in the small Southern textile town. Colavito mailed the watches to family members. He was also under orders from Dom to buy a subscription to the local newspaper. "Domenico would give me hell if I didn't buy him a news-paper subscription in every place I played," he said. Dom cut the clippings and collected them in a scrapbook that would follow Rocky throughout his career.

Bob Talbert, a Spartanburg batboy who grew up to be a *Detroit Free Press* columnist, remembered how popular Colavito was with the fans. "When the handsome slugger hit Spartanburg, the girls went gaga," Talbert recalled. "I can't quite say the same for the Tri-State pitchers. Rocky was only 18, just three years older than me, but he was a professional baseball player and it made him seem older. The minute the Rock stepped into the batter's box you could tell he was a major leaguer. You could always tell."[4]

Spartanburg finished third in the standings but made it into the first round of the Tri-State League's playoff series. In the deciding fifth game, Colavito smashed a home run to tie the game with two outs in the ninth inning, then won the game in the 11th with another round-tripper to defeat the Gastonia Rockets. The night before, Colavito told first baseman Al Smith, his roommate (not to be confused with the player who later starred with the Indians and White Sox), that he was going to hit two home runs. Smith was anxious to have the season end so he could get home and told Colavito, in a serious tone, "Don't you dare do that." Colavito recalled, "And I did, even though I really wanted to go home, too." It was an exhilarating win, though the team lost in the next round.

Colavito played his third season in 1953 with the Reading Indians in Reading, PA, in the Class A Eastern League. In spring training, he roomed with Herb Score, a hard-throwing pitcher who set the rookie strikeout record two years later with the Indians, went on to become a broadcaster with the team, and became Colavito's closest friend in baseball. The manager was Kerby Farrell, whom Colavito would play for at his next minor league stop in Indianapolis, and later with the Indians. The outfield dimensions in Reading Municipal Memorial Stadium made it a pitcher's park, and Colavito got off to a slow start, failing to homer in his first month. Feeling down, he spoke on the phone to his father, who didn't understand baseball well. "I was hitting like .070, and he said, 'Looks-a like this a-year you a-hit a-no home runs,'" Colavito recalled, mimicking his father's broken English. "I was laughing my ass off."

Dom got mad at their father for not being encouraging. Colavito said he remained confident at the plate even when things weren't going well, and he never cut down on his swing, as some hitters did. "As a hitter, I tried to hit the ball as hard as I can, and as far as I can," Colavito said. "I never said I'm going to hit a home run, though I'd be lying if I said there weren't situations where a home run would be nice." He found that the slightest difference on where the bat made contact determined how far the ball would go. "I never believed it's a game of inches," Colavito said. "It's a game of a quarter-inch, an eighth-of-an-inch, and a sixteenth-of-an-inch. Sometimes a sixteenth-of-an-inch more and the ball's downtown." Farrell thought Colavito's poor start necessitated some changes at the plate. He wanted Colavito to alter his batting mechanics to avoid lunging toward the ball and striding too soon into the pitch. He had the 20-year-old change his wide and upright stance, adopted years earlier to emulate DiMaggio, by shortening it and batting from a slight crouch. The manager also changed Colavito's uniform number from No. 5 to No. 8. "Rocky was just trying too much to be DiMaggio. I just wanted him to be himself," the manager said.[5]

Colavito could be stubborn about doing what he was told, but he made the adjustments. "I wanted to play so I followed his orders," he said, harboring fears of being sent down to a lower rung of the minors if he didn't. The changes worked wonders when, several days later, Colavito hit three home runs in a game and narrowly missed a fourth when left fielder Jake Donaldson leaped against the left field fence to catch his long drive. Colavito continued to hit the rest of the 1953 season, leading the league with 28 home runs and 121 runs batted in to go with a .271 average. Reading won 101 games and clinched the pennant, with Colavito once again having an outstanding post-season. He hit six home runs and narrowly missed two others in 12 games. For his regular season efforts, Colavito finished third in the voting for the Eastern League's Most Valuable Player Award and was voted Reading's most popular player by the fans.

But what happened off the field that year had the most significance. Colavito and some of his teammates regularly ate at the Piccadilly restaurant in downtown Reading, an inexpensive eatery that wasn't generally celebrated for the quality of its food. It was there on a July evening that Colavito, 19, met Carmen Perrotti, a dark-haired, 16-year-old student at Central Catholic High School and a professional dancer with the Marie Shaw Dancers. Both were one month shy of their next birthdays. Carmen, who lived in the nearby town of Temple, was with Mary Attili, a teen who had a crush on Colavito and kept newspaper clippings of him in her wallet. The girls had been to a movie earlier that night. "Rocky came over to Mary and was talking to her. Then he said, 'Who's your friend?' and she introduced us," Carmen recalled.

> We ended up sitting in a booth just telling funny stories. He told a joke, and then all of a sudden we realized we had missed our last bus. It wasn't love at first sight, but he was very friendly. He offered to drive us home, and Mary got right in the middle of the front seat of the ballplayer's 1939 Buick. When Colavito asked where we lived, she told him where I lived first and gave him directions. The next day, I asked her how it went, and she said, 'All he wanted to do was talk about you.' So out came the pictures from her wallet.[6]

Carmen was asked by her cousin Sylvia a few weeks later to go on a double date with Colavito and a teammate after a game. But no one remembered to tell him. Colavito talked to her from outside the car she was sitting in and then left to go on a date with another girl. Carmen fumed, not realizing he was unaware of the situation. They didn't see each other for several weeks, until Colavito asked her out. After that night, he stopped dating the other girl, and he and Carmen quickly became inseparable. Carmen appreciated early in their relationship how family-oriented Colavito was. "He said, 'When I get to the big leagues—not if—I'm going to help my dad.' I thought that was admirable. Not too many guys his age had the foresight to say that," she said.[7] When the season ended, Colavito drove his next car, a 1948 Pontiac, every other weekend from the Bronx to see her. He also brought Carmen to New York to meet his family, where she stayed with his sister Ann. "When we got serious, I told my mom we wanted to get married," Carmen recalled. "We weren't poor, and they were hardworking people, but we didn't have much money. She said she had money set aside for college for not quite two years, and to please think it over. But I said no, I had enough of school. I probably would have waited longer except I knew Rocky wouldn't be in Reading the following year. He told me he was probably going to Indianapolis."[8]

That's what happened. For the 1954 season, Colavito was assigned to the Triple-A Indianapolis Indians in the American Association, the last rung before the major leagues. Farrell, his manager, was promoted with him. He got off to a fast start, earning his first mention in the *Cleveland Plain Dealer* on May 22, 1954. "The Indians haven't had a good Italian ballplayer in ages, but this drought will end soon if Rocky Colavito and Joe Altobelli of the Indianapolis farm club keep on their current pace," a columnist wrote. "Colavito, a 20-year-old outfielder, is leading the

Colavito warms up in the outfield before a game with the Indianapolis Indians in 1954. Roommate Herb Score is behind him (Colavito's personal collection).

American Association in home runs. Altobelli, a first baseman, is one of the league's top five hitters. Colavito, whose home is in the shadow of Yankee Stadium, became a batting terror when he stopped imitating Joe DiMaggio and found his own style."[9] That was followed two days later by an article about Colavito hitting three successive home runs in a 12–9 Indianapolis victory, the second time in two seasons he had done so. They were among his 11 hits in 14 at-bats that series, bringing the usually slow-starting outfielder's home run total to 17.

Colavito's cannon of an arm also attracted attention. His throw from right field in a game on June 12 in Toledo's Swayne Field went an estimated 360 feet on the fly into the catcher's glove, narrowly missing runner Kermit Wahl at the plate. The ballplayer took a lot of pride in getting assists. "If I threw a key runner out to save a game, it was like hitting a home run," Colavito said. "It was a thrill, and the people in the stands acknowledged it." Meanwhile, the local press also had fun with Colavito's name, calling him at turns "Socco Rocco" Colavito, "Rocco (the Socko) Colavito" and "Rock 'em Rocky" Colavito.

Colavito was on fire through July 10, 1954, hitting .327 with 28 home runs and 75 runs batted in. That included homers in six consecutive games and nine in a ten-game span. It was the best start he ever had as a professional ballplayer. One three-run clout clubbed by Colavito hit a billboard behind Victory Field's left field fence, entitling him to four steak dinners. Another cleared a sign atop the scoreboard in left field that landed on West 16th Street. An article in *The Sporting News* suggested that Colavito was a threat to Nick Cullup's all-time American Association home run record of 54 by a right-handed hitter, set in 1930.[10] Another noted he was four homers behind the pace set by the left-handed-hitting Joe Hauser, who slugged a league-record 69 home runs in 1933 for Minneapolis.[11] Playing in a doubleheader, Colavito hit three home runs and had five hits while playing in pain after being hit by a pitch following his second homer. "What nobody knew was that Rocky had been hit on his elbow," his roommate Herb Score disclosed. "After he played the doubleheader, I had to help him put on his shirt, button it and tie his tie for him because he couldn't bend his arm. But he never let it show in the games."[12]

Indianapolis took over first place in the American Association on April 22 and never relinquished their lead. They were ahead by 17 games on August 7 and finished 10½ games ahead of second-place Louisville. But Colavito couldn't maintain his torrid pace. He went into a sustained slump—the kind he would periodically combat throughout his career—that saw him drop to a .209 average with eight home runs with 33 RBI through Labor Day, a span of

Colavito, top row, third from right, in the Indianapolis Indians 1954 team picture (Colavito's personal collection).

66 games. The 1954 season was still a banner year for Colavito. With the same number of at-bats and hits as his previous season with Reading, he batted .271, knocked in 116 runs and led the league in home runs with 38, breaking the team record of 33 set by Wally Post the year before. It remained the team record going into the 2019 season. It was the third time Colavito led a minor league in home runs, and it was statistically his best season yet. Fans showed their appreciation by voting Colavito the team's most popular player. He wowed them in a throwing exhibition at the end of the season, tossing a ball from home plate over Indianapolis's left-center field scoreboard, some 380 feet away.

Rocky and Carmen became engaged in the summer of 1954, although Colavito never actually proposed. "We just assumed we were going to get married," he said. Word quickly spread to the local press, which ran a photograph of Carmen admiring her engagement ring with Colavito looking on, shortly after she arrived in Indianapolis. "Neatly attired in a white linen dress, Carmen settled herself comfortably into the box at Victory Field to watch her fiancé battle the Charleston Senators," a local scribe wrote. "When Rocky smiled up at her or tipped his hat, Carmen glowed like an electric light bulb. Brown eyes flashing, Carmen was as excited as Rocco must have been at his first home run."[13] When she was asked how long they had been apart, she said it had been 106 days. "I had every calendar in the house checked off," Carmen said. Reporters peppered them about a wedding date, which the couple was unequipped to answer because they hadn't discussed one. "The reporters said when are you getting married, and we just looked at each other and said in the fall," Carmen said. "That got in the paper, and Colavito's father had a fit when he read it. My father said, 'What do you want, to go down the aisle in a barrel?' In other words, they couldn't afford the wedding because they were already taking a trip to California."[14]

Rocky and Carmen Colavito were married on October 30, 1954, one year after meeting in a restaurant in Reading, PA, where Rocky played minor league ball (Colavito's personal collection).

The wedding was held in Reading on October 30, 1954. The groom was 21, the bride 18. Dom was the best man, and Attili was the maid of honor. After honeymooning in Miami, where they also visited Herb Score, the newlyweds made Reading their home. They didn't wait long to start a family of their own: Rocco Jr., their first child, was born nearly two years later. After marrying, the couple moved in with Carmen's parents in Temple, less than ten miles from where Colavito had played ball in Reading. The couple bought a house there in 1957 and moved to a larger one several miles away in 1962. "I wouldn't trade growing up in the Bronx for all the tea in China," Colavito said. "It was a great environment and I liked it, but you want to be with the girl you love, and I can't say I really missed it. I also got into hunting, and it was something I loved to do." Carmen didn't want to stray far from home, and she, Attili, and a second lifelong friend, Ilda Avanzato—"the Three Musketeers"—have remained inseparable for over 60 years.

For a wedding present, Indians GM Hank Greenberg gave the Colavitos tickets to the first two games of the 1954 World Series, between Cleveland and the New York Giants at the Polo Grounds. It's where Colavito had seen his first game as a youngster. They were in the stands in the eighth inning of the series opener when Willie Mays made "The Catch" in center to rob Vic Wertz of an extra-base hit. "I was going bananas, because he caught it over his shoulder," Colavito recalled. "That's Willie Mays. He was some kind of player." They also watched Dusty Rhodes' game-winning, three-run pinch-hit home run that barely cleared the right field fence, 257 feet away. "I can still picture Davey Pope, who I played with in spring training, going back on that big high fly ball and watching it just drop into the first row," Colavito said. "It would have been a pop fly in any ballpark, and easily caught." The Indians were swept in four games, a disappointing finish after a record-setting 111 wins during the regular season.

Colavito worked part-time that off-season and for the next few years with the Temple Mushroom Transportation Company. The owner was a friend of his father-in-law. The company picked up mushrooms during the off-season from growers, and Colavito helped load the truck and put mushrooms in the cooler before they were shipped northeast. He was also an occasional dispatcher. Later that off-season, Greenberg hired both Colavitos to come to Cleveland and sell season tickets for the 1955 season. "Rocky Colavito came to Cleveland and he likes the place so well he wouldn't mind sticking around say, 15 or 20 years," wrote Harry Jones, the Indians beat reporter for the *Cleveland Plain Dealer*. "'I sure hope I can make it,' Colavito said in awe, for this was his first look at the stadium. 'I'd really like to play here this year.'" The article noted that the Indians had three established outfielders in Al Smith and future Hall of Famers Larry Doby and Ralph Kiner, but suggested that if Colavito continued to hit like he had in Indianapolis, "one of the three regulars will have to give way to the boy from the Bronx."[15]

A photograph in the sports section the following day showed the Colavitos at Municipal Stadium, with Rocky gesturing toward right field, where he hoped to be playing in 1955.[16] The cavernous stadium, with yellow brick and art deco ornamentation, had opened just south of Lake Erie on July 1, 1931. It was built in 370 days by Osborn Engineering, which designed Yankee Stadium and Comiskey Park in Chicago and redesigned Boston's Fenway Park. Municipal Stadium was built as a multipurpose facility that was eventually home to the Cleveland Indians and the Cleveland Browns of the National Football League.[17] It was baseball's largest stadium, with some 78,811 seats, until Los Angeles Memorial Coliseum served as the temporary home of the Dodgers from 1958 to 1961. Municipal Stadium is where Colavito played the majority of games over his career and hit the most home runs.

In February, Colavito was featured in a two-page pictorial spread in *Sport* magazine titled, "Rookies to Watch in '55." The national attention put the baseball world on notice that Colavito's future looked bright. He shared the spotlight with Score, the Yankees' Elston Howard, the Dodgers' Chico Fernandez, the Braves' Ray Crone, and the Pirates' Bill Virdon.[18] Score went

A couple of admirers surround Colavito before an Indianapolis Indians game in June 1955 (Colavito's personal collection).

on to win the Rookie of the Year Award in the American League, while Virdon took top honors in the National League. Colavito, now wearing No. 38, found himself in spring training among future Hall of Famers Bob Feller, Early Wynn and Larry Doby, and all-star Bobby Avila. "It was like going to heaven," he said. "They were all big-time ballplayers I had seen in the World Series." Manager Al Lopez was looking forward to seeing the highly touted minor-league prospect. "I want to give Colavito a good shot," he said. "We seem to be pretty well fixed in the outfield, but if Rocky has developed as much as I hope he has he could take a regular job away from anybody."[19]

A photo in the next day's paper showed Colavito and outfielder Ralph Kiner holding bats as they looked at the camera. The headline read, "A Couple of Clouters—Kiner and Colavito." Kiner had led the National League seven consecutive years in home runs, but his first season in Cleveland was his last as a player, due to recurring back pain. "Rookie Rocky Colavito and veteran Ralph Kiner brandish big bats they hope are loaded with long distance clouts as they begin training with Cleveland's Indians in Tucson yesterday. Kiner rapped 54 homers for Pittsburgh in 1949. Colavito, also an outfield candidate, slammed 38 for Indianapolis last season."[20] An eager Colavito approached Bob Feller on the first day of spring training to ask if he would throw him curve balls. Colavito said he was having trouble hitting curves and wanted to get better. Feller said he would throw some to him when he was in shape to pitch.[21]

Colavito had a habit in the on-deck circle of clutching the ends of the bat with each hand behind his back to stretch his back muscles, a routine that was copied by legions of fans through the decades. That spring Colavito added another: he began planting his feet in the batter's box and slowly pointing his bat at the pitcher before getting ready for the pitch with hands held high. "We played an exhibition game against the New York Giants in Los Angeles at Wrigley Field, their Triple-A park," Colavito recalled. "Hoyt Wilhelm was pitching for the Giants, and I pointed my bat right at him and hit the next pitch for a home run. After the game, a friend said, 'Rock, did you realize what you did before you hit that home run? He said, 'You pointed the bat right at the pitcher.' I said, 'I kind of remembered it, and maybe I should just do it all the time,' and I did. I did it as a ritual for good luck." Countless kids would mimic those actions later. "It never occurred to me that anyone would follow in my footsteps," Colavito said. He didn't think pitchers minded him doing it, but years later, possibly out of amusement, Jim Bouton pointed a ball at Colavito before he wound up to mimic him. "I hit the ball deep to left center, and it was caught in front of the wall," Colavito said. "I wanted that home run so bad." Jim Kaat, a pitcher who won 283 games over a 25-year career, said he didn't think pitchers resented Colavito for pointing his bat at them. "Rocky very distinctively held the bat and pointed it, but it wasn't an intimidating thing. It was a timing thing, and I think we all recognized that," Kaat said. Nor was sneaking in a pitch while Colavito went through his routine an option, either. "We always thought there was a way that we could quickly deliver the pitch before he got back into position, but that never worked," Kaat said.[22]

Colavito tried to make a good impression in 1955 and avoid his typically slow start in the spring. During a March 6 intrasquad game, he brandished his throwing arm on two plays that caught the *Cleveland Plain Dealer*'s attention. "The highlight of the game occurred in the fourth round when 21-year-old Rocky Colavito, strong-armed graduate of Indianapolis, threw Al Rosen out at the plate from deep right field. Rosen was trying to score from second. Colavito gave fair warning an inning earlier that no one in their right mind runs on Rocky's arm. When Sam Dente looped a single along the right field line, Colavito quickly fielded the ball and returned it with bullet-like speed to first base."[23] On March 25, Colavito hit his first exhibition home run as the team, behind Feller's five innings of one-hit ball, defeated the San Francisco Seals. "After backing the left fielder against the wall 360 feet away in the third, he sent a pitch beyond the fielder's reach, almost 400 feet away," the *Cleveland Plain Dealer* reported.[24]

But despite those glowing moments, a crowded outfield limited Colavito's playing opportunities. At a luncheon held in the ballroom of a downtown Cleveland hotel the day before the season began, Lopez introduced him as one of the team's most promising rookies.[25] But later that day, Greenberg informed Colavito that the Tribe's manager felt he needed another season of minor league ball under his belt. Being optioned to Indianapolis was a big disappointment, but Colavito was banking on getting called up early in the season. Instead, another player got the nod. "I remember Red Ruffing, then a roving instructor for the Indians, telling me that if Mantle was in this organization, he'd probably still be at Triple-A," Colavito said. "They just didn't bring guys up early."

Back in Indianapolis, Colavito's statistics were similar but slightly down from the previous season, hitting .268 with 30 home runs and 104 RBIs. In Denver, a ball he crushed off Denver Bears pitcher Jack Urban was one of the longest home runs he ever hit. "If it went one foot past the fence, it went 200 feet, and over a light tower," Colavito said of the ball that carried out of Bears Stadium. Colavito reached 30 home runs with a flourish by blasting three in the season's last series. He led the American Association with 23 assists from right field, the most he ever had in a season, majors or minors. He was also voted the most popular player by fans for a third year in a row. But those weren't the only games Colavito played in 1955.

4

"Roomie"

Herb Score was a high school pitching phenom when Rocky Colavito first encountered the lanky southpaw. It occurred in an intrasquad game at Daytona Beach in 1952. Score was being scouted by Cleveland's Cy Slapnicka, who had signed Indians Hall of Fame pitchers Bob Feller and Bob Lemon. Score, a pitcher for Lake Worth Community High School, was invited by Slapnicka to the Indians' spring training camp to see how he would fare playing with and against some of the players on the Class A Reading squad. Colavito was in right field behind Score when he pitched that day. Even though Colavito was in his second year of professional baseball, the slugging outfielder was younger than the pitcher by two months and three days. "Herbie was a tall, thin kid with some acne on his face, and he could throw bullets," Colavito recalled. "I played every right-handed hitter close to the right-field line on the assumption they would swing late. I think he pitched two or three innings, and no one put the ball in play."

Score was born in 1933 in Rosedale, NY, a neighborhood in Queens. He moved to Florida in his early teens and excelled on the mound, throwing six no-hitters and leading his high school team to the state championship. On Score's 19th birthday, he signed a baseball contract for $60,000 with the Indians—a figure 20 times the amount of Colavito's—and was sent straight to the Triple-A Indianapolis Indians. But starting at that level proved to be a mistake. Score struggled in 12 games due to control issues, compiling a 2–5 win-loss record and 5.23 ERA. He only allowed 37 hits in 62 innings but averaged almost a walk per inning. Score was assigned in 1953 to the Class A Reading Indians, where he went 7–3 with a 4.68 ERA. Walks again were his major stumbling block, issuing 126 free passes in 98 innings. Colavito, meanwhile, led the Eastern League with 28 home runs and 121 RBIs.

That season, Score and Colavito, both 19, became close friends. Each had a roommate who played in a poker game that ran late into the night, and invariably woke them up when they returned. So halfway through spring training, it was decided to put the two poker players together, and for Colavito and Score to bunk in the same room. They only roomed together in spring training that year, but that marked the first of seven straight seasons they roomed together for some, if not all, of each season. "We just got kind of thrown together, and then we became really close," Colavito said. "Herbie wasn't overbearing, but he was a confident kid. He said things a lot like I did. On the road and off the road, we never, ever had a harsh word. He respected me, and I respected him. We talked about everything. We were inseparable. He was more like a brother than a friend." Both affectionately called the other "Roomie," and both liked to dress nicely, often with a suit and tie.

Colavito attended church growing up but went less frequently during his first couple of years in the minors. Score was a devoted Catholic, and Colavito resumed attending church on Sunday mornings and Catholic holidays with his friend. The two also observed Lent together during spring training. "I was never an altar boy, but I went to church regularly," Colavito said. "I think it's helped pull me through some tough times. I used to pray a lot. You're always looking for help when you're not doing well. I looked to God for help, and I got it a lot of times." The two also enjoyed shooting pool. But one thing they didn't do in the afternoon like some players was attend movie matinees. Colavito was concerned that watching movies could harm his eyes and affect his ability to hit a baseball.

Score was shagging fly balls in center before a mid-season game in 1953 when he made a shoestring catch, only to tumble over and dislocate the shoulder of his throwing arm. The fall ended his season. The next year, Score returned to Indianapolis and came into his own. The fire-balling pitcher went 22–5 with a league-leading 2.62 ERA, which was impressive enough. But Score also racked up a sensational 330 strikeouts in 251 innings, shattering the league mark of 264 that had stood for 48 years, while adding a changeup to his arsenal of fastballs and curves. The number of walks he issued was also way down. Score's performance in 1954 earned him *The Sporting News* Minor League Player of the Year Award. Colavito also had another outstanding season, clubbing a league-leading 38 home runs to go with 116 RBIs and a .271 batting average. That summer, the roommates bought a 1940 Chevy Coupe two-seater for $125, which they named the Black Demon. After unsuccessfully trying to teach Score how to drive a stick shift, Colavito wound up chauffeuring his roommate to and from dates. The car gave out at the end of the season, but they were still able to sell it for $35.

The Cleveland Indians had a banner season in 1954, setting the all-time American League winning percentage of .721 by going 111–43. But their four-game sweep at the hands of the New York Giants in the World Series put a damper on the team's incredible season. The team was in the middle of a period in which the franchise saw its greatest success. From 1948 to 1959, the Indians won two pennants and finished in second place six times, a record

Colavito, 6'3" and 185 lbs., checks out his Louisville Slugger bats (Colavito's personal collection).

second only to the Yankees. Making the team wasn't going to be easy, but the Indians organization had high hopes for its next generation of stars, led by Score and Colavito. Although Colavito was back with Indianapolis to start the 1955 season, Score made the Indians roster in spring training, cracking the team's starting rotation. "With a record like he had at Indianapolis, they had to make a place for him," Colavito said. Bob Feller was the greatest Indians pitcher of all time, with 266 victories despite missing nearly four full seasons in the prime of his career for military service in World War II. But he was at the end of his career. Feller won 13 games in 1954 and would win only four more before retiring. The staff in 1955 was led by 23-game winners Early Wynn and Bob Lemon, 19-game winner Mike Garcia, 15-game winner Art Houtteman, and Score.

Feller had enough in the tank in his 17th season to pitch the 12th one-hitter of his career against the Red Sox in the first game of a doubleheader in Cleveland on May 1, 1955. It was a tough act to follow, but in the second game Score proceeded to strike out 16 in just his third start, two shy of Feller's record for a nine-inning game. The first nine outs came on strikeouts. Two weeks later, the Indians went into Fenway Park, where the Red Sox would often stack right-handed hitters to take advantage of the left field wall's short distance from home plate. Score spun a three-hit shutout, striking out nine.

In Score's first season in the majors, he won 16 games, lost 10 and had a 2.85 ERA. He also struck out 245 batters in 227⅓ innings, topping the rookie mark set by the Phillies' Grover Cleveland Alexander in 1911, a record which stood for nearly 30 years. Score made the All-Star team and was named AL Rookie of the Year. Score was even more dominant in his second year, going 20–9 with a 2.53 ERA and 263 strikeouts, the most since Feller sat down 348 batters in 1946. His walk ratio was lower once again, and he allowed fewer than six hits per nine innings, setting a franchise record that lasted until 1968. For the second year in a row, Score was named to the American League All-Star team. In the off-season, Red Sox General Manager Joe Cronin offered the Indians the unheard-of sum of $1 million for Score. But Indians GM Hank Greenberg turned the offer down without hesitation. Score, Greenberg said, "may become the greatest pitcher in the game's history."[1]

Herb Score was a pitching star for the Indians before injuries took their toll. He later had a long broadcasting career with the team (Baseball Hall of Fame).

The 1957 season began with optimism, with no limit in sight for the 23-year-old. "If nothing happens to this kid, he'll be the greatest left-hander who ever lived," Indians' Hall of Famer Tris Speaker said.[2] But Score had already had a lifetime of unfortunate occurrences. When he was 2, he was hit by a bakery truck, damaging both of his legs and raising fears he might never walk again. He came down with rheumatic fever several years later and was bedridden for ten months. As a freshman in high school, Score fractured an ankle playing basketball, and while still wearing a cast underwent an emergency appendectomy. His middle name was Jude for the patron saint of hopeless causes, and he credited prayer with helping him to overcome the injuries and ailments that came his way. He would be tested again on May 7 in a game at home against the Yankees.

Gil McDougald, the second batter of the game, hit a low line drive that struck Score in the right eye, tearing the retina, breaking his nose, and causing severe hemorrhaging, with blood spewing from his eye, nose and mouth. McDougald, seeing what happened, ran straight to the mound rather than first base out of concern, as third baseman Al Smith fielded the ball and threw to first. Colavito raced in from right field to help.

> I looked toward center because you knew the ball was going up the middle, but I didn't see the ball. In a split second I looked back toward the mound, and Herb was toppling over and had not yet hit the ground. I lit out for the mound. When I got there, he was lying on the mound and you could see he was hit in the eye. I put my glove under his head to cushion him and waited for him to be taken off the field. When the inning ended, I went down the steps into the dugout, and then ran up the runway to the clubhouse, all in one motion. When I got into the clubhouse, he saw me. I said, "Roomie, how are you doing?" and he said, "What the hell are you doing here?" I said, "I came out to see how you are doing," and he said, "I'm all right," like get the hell out of here and get back to the team.

Colavito also felt bad for McDougald, who said after the game he would quit if Score lost his sight.[3] "McDougald was a good Catholic boy like Herbie," Colavito said. "He felt terrible." Ironically, McDougald had been struck in the ear two years earlier by a batted ball during spring training and would later go deaf from the injury.

Colavito was able to see Score for the first time six days after he had been hospitalized. "Rocky, I'm glad you finally hit a homer yesterday [one of four hits against the Athletics]," Score said. "I was making plans for you to join me here. I told the nurse to get a bed all set, because the way you weren't hitting I figured you'd soon be a hospital case, too." Colavito responded, "I'm glad to see you giving it to me, Roomie. It proves you're getting better."[4] An article in *Sport* magazine that August chronicled Colavito's and Score's close friendship. "It is one thing for roomies to like each other, but Score and Colavito worry about each other's playing, pray for each other and take care of each other. That is rare."[5]

The sight in Score's eye fully returned, but he sat out the rest of the season to heal and recuperate. There were high hopes for his full recovery early in the 1958 season, especially after he pitched a three-hit shutout against the White Sox and struck out 13 in a commanding performance. A week later, Score threw a pitch in Washington that bounced in front of home plate, and then a second that did the same thing, revealing a torn tendon in his left elbow. He returned to the pitcher's mound again in Washington about six weeks later and struck out five of eight batters, only to have the sharp elbow pain return. "Everybody you talk to says that the line drive was what ruined his career. It wasn't," Colavito said. "He hurt his arm twice on two visits to Washington. He hated that mound." Score also claimed that his arm troubles in 1958, and not the line drive off the bat of McDougald the year before, derailed his career. "The reason my motion changed was because I hurt my elbow, and I overcompensated for it and ended up with some bad habits," he said.[6]

Score was unable to return to the same pitching motion he used before he was hurt, and his pitches lacked the same velocity and movement. Score was devastated by the latest setback, but he never complained, Colavito said. "I never met anyone in my life who could handle adversity better than him. This guy never made any excuses about anything." Nancy Score, Herb's widow, said he never felt sorry for himself despite misfortunes that came his way. "He never talked about what could have been, and he never, ever complained," she said.[7] Score returned to the Indians in 1959, making changes to his pitching motion in a bid to avoid re-injuring his arm. In a 3–2 victory over the Tigers on May 24, he declared, "It's the best fast ball I ever had." He struggled through the first two innings, throwing 60 pitches and walking five, before settling down.[8] Score struggled throughout the season, and his once-feared velocity dropped. He finished with a 9–11 record, 4.71 ERA and 147 strikeouts. "Down deep I never thought he would be right again until he could pop the ball and not sling it," Colavito said. "I often thought he knew that it wasn't going to come around, too."

Herb Score, like Colavito, liked to dress with style away from the ballpark (Baseball Hall of Fame).

Score was traded by Indians General Manager Frank Lane for White Sox pitcher Barry Latman in April 1960, one day after he shocked Cleveland fans and the baseball world by trading Colavito to the Tigers. Score, though, looked forward to being reunited with former manager Al Lopez. "I don't think he was really mad about being traded from Cleveland," Colavito said. "He hoped Lopez would help him with his pitching and get him back on track. That's the feeling I had, too. Sometimes guys come up with another pitch and they get help with it. I was hoping for anything that would reinstate him as the type of pitcher he was." Coming on the heels of the Colavito-Kuenn trade, Score's departure "raised scarcely a ripple," a columnist wrote. "Had Score been traded away as recently as a month ago, it would have been press-stopping news. Yesterday, it was anti-climactic. The citizens still were so enraged over the departure of the popular Colavito that they hardly noticed the end of the Cleveland phase of a career that seemed destined three years ago to be one of the greatest in the game's history."[9]

No second act as a pitcher was in store for Score. He pitched parts of three seasons with the White Sox and was sent to the minors during two of them, going a combined 23–25. His final season in 1963 was with Indianapolis, the Triple-A team where he began his career. He lost all six decisions. Score continued to pitch, he said, because he needed to be convinced it was time to walk away. "I still believed my arm might come back," he said. "I was only 30. I didn't want to be sitting somewhere when I was 60 and wondering, 'What if I pitched one more year, would I have found it?' Now I know. I have no doubts."[10]

Score, who was on a Hall of Fame trajectory those first two seasons, won 55 and lost 46 for his career, with a 3.36 ERA, with an average of over nine strikeouts per nine innings and a lot of what-ifs to wonder about. "He would have been probably one of the greatest, if not the greatest, left-handed pitchers who ever lived," Feller said upon Score's death in 2008.[11] The only Cleveland starting southpaw to rival Score's strikeout prowess was Sam McDowell, who between 1965 and 1970 had strikeout season totals of 279, 283, 304 and 325. Score went on after his career to become the longest-running Indians play-by-play radio announcer, beloved for his unpretentious, low-key style and common man approach.

"Rocky and Herb were real close friends, and their personalities were similar," recalled Sonny Siebert, a former pitcher and teammate of Colavito's in the mid–1960s. "They were both kind of quiet and good guys."[12] As the years rolled on, Colavito occasionally picked up Indians games and listened to his friend when the reception at his Pennsylvania home permitted it. "Herbie was my best friend of all time," Colavito said. "We always kept in touch with each other."

Score retired from broadcasting after the 1997 season. "People will tell me I'm unlucky," Score said. "Me? Unlucky? I started with a great team in the Indians and played under a great manager in Al Lopez. Then I went from the field to the broadcasting booth at the age of 30, and 30 years later I'm still doing the games," he said, three years before he retired after the 1997 World Series. "If you ask me, that's not unlucky. That's a guy who has been in the right place at the right time."[13]

A year after retiring from the booth, Score was severely injured in an automobile accident when a tractor-trailer failed to stop at a stop sign. The truck struck the passenger side of Score's car. He suffered severe injuries to his brain, lungs and chest, and spent a month in intensive care. Colavito visited him and was optimistic about his friend's chances of recovery. Score recovered enough to throw out the ceremonial first pitch in Cleveland on Opening Day in April 1999. But when Colavito visited him at his home after Score suffered a stroke in 2002, his health had taken a turn for the worse. "It was night and day," Colavito said. "Something had happened. After that, it was downhill."

Despite Score's abbreviated career, the greatness he showed early on was recognized by the Indians when the team inducted him and five others into the Cleveland Indians Hall of Fame on July 29, 2006. Colavito was among them. It was the first time anyone had been added since the first 20 players were named in 1972. "I think putting him in the Hall of Fame was the right thing to do, and I know I appreciated it, and his family appreciated it," Colavito said. The stands erupted as Colavito walked onto Jacobs Field, pushing his friend, who could no longer speak after a series of strokes, in a wheelchair. "To see the love that day between Rocky and Herbie was pretty cool," Indians executive Bob DiBiasio said. "They were truly brothers."[14] Nancy Score said the fact that her husband allowed Colavito to push his wheelchair reflected the esteem he felt for him. "They were dear friends," she said. "They just were inseparable in their baseball careers and with what each other did. Both saw the world in black and white, without much gray and with strong convictions. Once you were their friend you were always their friend," she said. Their faith also helped bind them. "They were very devout and strong in their devotion," Score said, noting that a Catholic Man of the Year award her husband received in Cleveland was one of the honors that meant the most to him. She also said both men could be misunderstood. "I think some people thought they were aloof, but they weren't aloof, they were shy—at least until you got to know them."[15] Colavito and Score were named among the team's 100 greatest players in 2001, on the team's 100th anniversary. Score died on November 11, 2008, and Colavito gave one of the two eulogies.

The two friends squared off against each other once in a game. It occurred in 1960 in Comiskey Park, after Colavito had been traded to the Tigers and Score to the White Sox.

Herbie had a job to get me out, and I had a job to get a hit. I hit a ball way up in the upper deck that curved foul in the last few seconds, where it was 352 down the line. Herbie was standing on the mound with his hands on his hips and he hollers at me, "Hey, what the hell is this?" and I was laughing my ass off. I said, "Roomie, I'm just trying to make a living." He goes back to the mound and I hit this dribbler down the third base line that I beat out. He looks at me and puts his hand on his hips again and said, "Are you going to take that?" I laughed some more. "Roomie, what am I gonna do? I've got to."

5

Hit or Miss

Rocky Colavito had dreamed about being a big-league ballplayer for as long as he could remember. He thought about it from way up high in the Police Athletic League section of the left field grandstand in Yankee Stadium, watching his idol Joe DiMaggio in center field. He imagined playing under the big lights when scooping a ball off the hard outfield surface at Crotona Park and rifling a throw to home plate. He held onto that aspiration through five seasons in the minors and into his first Indians spring training, where he failed to make the cut. Now, at age 22, Colavito's life-long goal was on the verge of happening: The Tribe was calling him up to join the big-league club for the last three weeks of the 1955 season.

Colavito made his debut on September 10, 1955, at Fenway Park against the Red Sox as a pinch-runner. Given his lack of speed, it was an unlikely way for him to enter his first big-league game. Colavito scored as part of a five-run inning that put the team in the lead for good. He didn't get many chances to play over the next week, striking out twice in pinch-hitting appearances. Then, in the second game of a September 24 doubleheader against the Tigers in Briggs Stadium, Colavito was summoned in the first inning to pinch-run for Al Smith, who hadn't missed a game all year and started in the field just to maintain his streak.

In Colavito's first at-bat, he singled off Tigers pitcher Ned Garver. But he didn't stop there. Colavito proceeded to rack up four hits in four at-bats, scoring two runs. The first two hits were line drives off an extension fence in left field that would be removed the following season, narrowly missing home runs both times with doubles instead. Colavito also impressed with his glove. He "made two dazzling catches and one spectacular throw in right field," the *Cleveland Plain Dealer* reported. "In the fifth, after backing up against the right-field stands to catch a normal fly, Rocky made a 326-foot throw to third base on the fly, nailing Earl Torgeson, who later said he thought he would easily advance." Colavito also caught the last out with a flourish, running in to make a diving catch of a short fly ball.[1] He shared the spotlight with rookie Hank Aguirre, who threw a three-hit shutout. In Colavito's brief end-of-the-season call-up, he played in five games, with the four hits in nine at-bats.

Following the 1955 season, Colavito played winter ball in Venezuela, where he was paid $1,000 for the month. "It was supposed to be a part-time vacation," Colavito said. But it didn't work out that way. Games in Caracas started at 8:30 p.m. and typically took three hours. "After playing, showering and getting a bite to eat, you didn't get to sleep until 1:30 in the morning, and you had to be back on the field at 9 for a workout," Colavito said. He and another outfielder collided converging on a fly ball, resulting in Colavito's heel being spiked and the other player getting hit in the mouth. Unable to play, Colavito returned home, had his foot treated, and began to get ready for spring training. He was determined to make the parent club when the 1956 season rolled around. He normally swung a heavy bat, but switched from a 35-ounce to a 33-ounce model in a bid to check his swing better. "It only takes a split-second to be out in front or jammed by a pitch, and an ounce or two can make all the difference," Colavito said. Ted Williams later told him he wasn't as good a hitter with a bat that weighed over 34 ounces.

After Colavito hit two home runs in a March 3 game, the Cleveland *Plain Dealer* published an article about him and the promise he showed as a ballplayer.[2] Manager Al Lopez had Colavito work with Hall of Famer and batting instructor Tris Speaker, the "Gray Eagle" who compiled a sterling .345 career average over a 22-year career with the Indians, Red Sox, Athletics and Senators that ended in 1928. Speaker worked with Colavito to stand closer to the plate to better reach outside breaking pitches. "Tris Speaker broke me of this, finally," Colavito said at the time.[3] Speaker also spoke in awe of Colavito's arm strength, saying he had the "strongest arm I ever saw."[4]

That same spring, George Selkirk, who succeeded Babe Ruth in right field for the Yankees and now managed the Triple-A Wichita Braves farm club, also said Colavito had the strongest arm he had ever seen in the major or minor leagues.[5]

The instruction in spring training, Colavito said later, was an example of how much more he learned in the major leagues than in the minors.

> I've heard some people say that you learn in the minor leagues and play in the majors, and I want to tell you that nothing could be farther from the truth. I learned more baseball my first season in the big leagues than I did the whole five seasons I spent in the minors, spring training and all…. I don't mean to indicate that I didn't learn anything in the minors. But on every ball club, there were so many kids that had so much to learn that the manager couldn't handle each case individually as they do in the majors.[6]

For the first time, Colavito made the Tribe out of spring training. "Herb Score is the key to our pitching. But the boy to watch is Rocky Colavito, an

» *Membership Card* «

ROCKY COLAVITO FAN CLUB

_____

IS AN HONORED MEMBER OF THIS ORGANIZATION

ROCKO SOCKO

_____

BY AUTHORITY OF

This "Rocko Socko" membership card was sent to members of the Rocky Colavito Fan Club, formed in 1956 (Colavito's personal collection).

outfielder," Indians broadcaster Jimmy Dudley said in *Sports Illustrated*'s Hot Box column. "He is 6 feet 3, weighs 190 pounds and is 22...Rocky hit 35 home runs a year in the minors, and is hitting home runs now."[7] As a rookie, Colavito had to learn in short order how to navigate the time-honored boundaries between first-time players and veterans. "I think the pecking order teaches respect for the players who came before you, even if they were mediocre," Colavito said. "There was something good about it, even if it could be a little uncomfortable about it at times." But Colavito also believed it sometimes went too far, and when he was a veteran player, he was known for treating young ballplayers with uncommon respect.

Colavito hit his first major league home run early in the season in Kansas City against crafty southpaw Bobby Shantz. The ball bounced off a Butternut Bread sign affixed to a light tower above the left field fence, scoring Gene Woodling ahead of him. Colavito had received a useful tip before the game from outfielder Hoot Evers on what pitches to expect from Shantz. "When I hit that, I knew it was a home run. It was more of a line drive than high, and I think it hit a clock inside the sign. I was thrilled," Colavito said.

Also getting into gear that season were the 260 dues-paying members of the Rocky Colavito Fan Club. The club of mostly girls in their early teens was formed in May 1956 by Emily Fitzgibbons and Barbara O'Connor after the latter entered an Indians' bat boy contest, only to be disqualified because she was a girl. Barbara, 15, thought girls deserved equal rights, and Emily, 13, wrote her a letter of support. The two teens decided to team up to start the fan club after reading about Colavito in local newspapers. "He sounded like a nice fellow and a good ballplayer. We just liked him, that's all," Fitzgibbons, the club's "press agent," said of Colavito.[8]

O'Connor first wrote to Colavito in the summer of 1955, after she picked him out of a magazine touting Indians prospects. Colavito, seven years older, wrote her back, and they met after a September game. "He was a nice person, the kind of person you talk with and know he's your friend," Barbara Warny, her married name, recalled decades later. "It was reflected in the way he talked to you."[9] The fan club, whose slogan was "Rocco Socko," even got a mention the next year in *Sport* magazine.[10] Fan club members received a monthly newsletter, a membership card, and a bluish-green pencil imprinted with the words, "Rocky Colavito Fan Club." The club collected 50-cent dues from Ohioans and $1 from members as far away as New York, Iowa, Michigan, California and Georgia. To be near their favorite player, fan club members sat in the right field stands, which proved to be a fertile ground for attracting new recruits. "We got a lot of new club members from the kids who congregated there," O'Connor said at the time.[11] A petition drive was begun to create a Fan Club Day, on which the Indians would let members in for free. The girls set up a meeting with Harrison Dillard, who worked in the Indians' publicity department. Dillard, the first male Olympian to win a Gold Medal in both sprinting and hurdling events, and one of the first African Americans to hold a front office job with a big league ballclub, agreed to their request.

Cracking the starting lineup proved difficult for the slow-starting Colavito. On a June trip, his bat showed signs of life as his average climbed 100 points to .215. Catcher Earl Averill, Jr., who had already been sent down and brought back by the Indians, told Colavito on June 16 that he was being sent down to the minors a second time. Averill even came by the Colavitos' apartment to give them his refrigerated perishables. But when Colavito got to the ballpark later that day, he learned that the Indians had decided to send him packing instead. Upon learning he was being sent across the country to play for the San Diego Padres in the Pacific Coast League, Colavito found Greenberg and lashed out at the demotion, displaying an anger and a push-back against authority that would become a pattern when he felt wronged by managers or the front office. "I told Hank he was making a big mistake because I was just starting to feel good," Colavito said. "I told him I wasn't going and even suggested he try to trade me." Greenberg told Colavito he would bring him back in three weeks. After reconciling with the decision, Colavito was determined to return to the minors and prove he deserved to be with the Indians. "It makes an impact on you when they send you out like that," he said. "I was always worried about getting sent down until I really got established. Once I got past 1958, I didn't worry about it."

While in San Diego, Colavito participated in the kind of throwing exhibitions he had done periodically in his career. He occasionally had trouble with accuracy, but no one ever doubted how powerful his arm was. With Indianapolis in 1954, he threw a ball from home plate that sailed over an advertising sign above a 40-foot-tall scoreboard at the 385-foot marker in left field.[12] He also threw a ball more than 400 feet that landed over the center field fence at Walt Powell Park, the home field of Luke Easter and the Charleston Senators, to win a $5 bet with another player. "The bad thing is we never put the money on the table, and he never paid me, the SOB," Colavito laughed years later at the memory. In the majors, Colavito once stood behind the third-base line at Washington's Griffith Stadium and threw a ball over the beer sign atop the high right-center field wall. Standing in the outfield, he tossed balls over Yankee Stadium's right-field roof and beyond the right field grandstand roof at Municipal Stadium.

Advertisements in the *San Diego Union* promoted a throwing exhibition by Colavito on July 1, 1956, under the headline, "Colavito Eyes Record Throw." The ad read like it was hyping a carnival act. "Colavito, touted as the strongest throwing outfielder in baseball, will attempt to throw a ball 460 feet—the measured distance between the left and right-field foul poles." That was followed by another ad three days later signed by San Diego's General Manager, Ralph Kiner, the former home run slugger and briefly a teammate of Colavito's. "Great throwing arms are scarcer than Padre home runs, but I believe we have the greatest throwing arm in the history of baseball on our Padre club," Kiner wrote. "The owner of this fantastic arm is Rocco [Rocky] Colavito. Rocky can't explain why his arm is so much stronger than that of the average baseball player, and neither can anyone else in baseball. I do know that his arm is unquestionably the strongest I have ever seen, and I have had the pleasure of seeing the best in the world in recent years."[13]

Colavito made four throws in the exhibition before a Sunday doubleheader with the San Francisco Seals at San Diego's Lane Field. The first traveled 415 feet, 7 inches from the left to right field foul poles despite being heaved into a wind. The throw fell 45 feet shy of the 460-foot measured distance that would have shattered the current record. Making his last three throws from home plate, Colavito threw the first ball—believed to be the farthest of all—on top of a batting cage behind the 426-foot sign in center, which officials found too difficult to measure. The last two throws also went over the center field fence, with the longest one measured at 435 feet, 10 inches. That was slightly more than seven feet shy of the mark of 443 feet, 3 inches set by Don Grate of Chattanooga in August 1953.[14]

Baseball researcher Bill Jenkinson claims that Colavito had the most powerful throwing arm among position players in baseball history, ranking him ahead of Pirates right fielder Roberto Clemente and Yankees "Murderers'

Row" outfielder Bob Meusel.[15] Hank Greenberg, the Hall of Fame first
baseman for the Tigers and Colavito's general manager at Cleveland when
he signed with the team, claimed that Colavito had "the greatest arm I have
ever seen."[16] Indians all-time great pitcher Bob Feller also seemed to share
that view. Colavito and Feller once exchanged autographed pictures at a signing appearance in Boston. "He gave me the ultimate compliment," Colavito
said. "He wrote, 'To Rocky Colavito, my dear friend,' and then added, 'The
greatest arm ever.'" A woman who attended the church Colavito belonged to
told him of a compliment given by Mickey Mantle. She visited a restaurant
Mantle owned in Manhattan, and when he asked where she was from, she
said Reading. "Rocky Colavito's from there. Rocky Colavito had the greatest
arm I ever saw," Colavito said she told him. "I was thrilled to death to hear
that," he said. "From Mickey, Hank and Bob, those are compliments above
compliments."

Colavito wasted little time proving he belonged back with the Indians.
His locker was outside manager Bob Elliot's office, and "every time the phone
would ring my heart would drop," Colavito said. When three weeks came
around and the call from Greenberg hadn't come, Colavito reached him in a
restaurant inside a Washington, D.C., hotel, where Greenberg was eating
breakfast with Al Lopez. Colavito told him he was batting .420 and expected
Greenberg to keep his word. "'Rocky, just be patient, give me a little more
time and I'll bring you up. I have a deal brewing, and it's not completed,'"
Colavito recalled Greenberg telling him. Greenberg's agreement with Colavito
had been made unbeknownst to Lopez, and the Indians skipper was angry
when he found out. Being kept in the dark was later said to be a factor in
Lopez's resignation after the season.

When nearly two more weeks went by without any word from Greenberg, Colavito was again furious. "I thought this is it; they don't want to call
me up, I'm going home," he said. "I had a plane reservation, my bag was
packed, and I was gone. All I had to do was stop in the hotel, grab my bag
and go." Colavito was going to go home to be with Carmen, pregnant with
their first child. But there was a doubleheader to be played first. In the first
game, he went 0-for-3, but in between games the phone rang, and Elliott
called Colavito into his office to tell him he was being called up, and that outfielder Dale Mitchell, a career .312 hitter with the Indians, was being sent to
the Brooklyn Dodgers to open a spot on the roster. (Colavito would be at
Yankee Stadium that October to watch Don Larsen strike out Mitchell as a
pinch-hitter on the game's last pitch, preserving the only perfect game in
World Series history. The strikeout marked the last at-bat of Mitchell's career.)
Elliot asked Colavito if he'd play the second game, and he obliged. It was
Colavito's last minor league game. He wound up batting .368 with 12 home
runs and 32 RBIs in 35 games over five weeks. The 12 home runs gave him

an even 150 for his minor league career. "I always felt that if they had left me in the big leagues I would have hit those 12 home runs there," Colavito said.

Colavito was recalled by the Indians on July 23, and in his first game back ripped a bases-loaded triple to go with two singles and a walk. The Rocky Colavito Fan Club was elated. Fitzgibbons was asked in the *Cleveland Plain Dealer* if their favorite player's demotion had caused the fan club to have second thoughts. She said it hadn't. "We kept it going because we didn't think he should have been farmed out," Fitzgibbons said. "And then when they brought him back we were all very happy."[17] Rocky and Carmen's first child, Rocco Domenico Colavito, Jr., was born a week later, on August 1, while Colavito was playing against the Yankees. After reaching base four times with two hits and two walks, he flew home to see his wife and newborn son. Colavito was back at the team hotel a couple of days later when an elevator operator showed him a newspaper photo of mother and son at the hospital. The fan club celebrated by sending Rocco Jr., a pair of pajamas and overalls paid from club dues.

Colavito made clear with his play that he was back with the Indians for keeps. He lifted his average from .215 when he was sent down to .276 and found the confines of Municipal Stadium to his liking. The home run-friendly distances down the left and right field foul lines were 320 feet with short, five-foot-high fences. The power alleys were 365 feet, and center was 410 feet away. The dark center field bleachers also provided a good hitting backdrop for picking up the ball.

Colavito began a practice that year that he would become known for throughout his career—signing autographs after games until every kid in line received one. As a youth, Colavito had stood outside Yankee Stadium trying to get autographs, and he never forgot the disappointment of being turned down. "The biggest autograph I got was Charlie Keller. He was a gem," Colavito said of the slugger who played for the Yankees and Tigers and was nicknamed "King Kong" for his strength. "He tousled my hair, and I didn't want to wash it for a week. I always signed because I remember as a kid how disappointed I was when players wouldn't sign." Colavito, part of a swarm of autograph-seekers, once grabbed DiMaggio's arm as he came out of the Yankees clubhouse. "He pulled his arm away from me while I asked him [for an autograph], but although I was disappointed, I didn't blame him," Colavito said. "I remember trying to get Rudy York's autograph, and he kind of growled at me. I said to myself that if I ever get to the big leagues, I'm going to sign them."

After a game, Colavito would relax for a short time, sometimes with a beer, take a shower, get dressed, and go outside to sign autographs. If Carmen wasn't at the game, he'd tell her to give him two hours to get home.

When I got out there, there would be a mob of kids. I'd grab one kid and put him in front of me and tell him to give me a straight line, and for no one to cheat. I'd tell him that if they did they'd have to go to the back of the line. And I'd sign for everybody there. It got to be such a thing that when I came out the kids would see me and start lining up. One kid would say, 'Line up! Line up!' I never walked away from a line that I made, ever. It was very flattering. I was raised in that organization, and they came in hordes.

There was a measure of self-defense involved, too, in getting the kids to line up. "If you don't get some semblance of order, then they are poking you with pens and you've got to watch out because you could have an ink spot on your clothes," Colavito said. Sometimes there just wasn't time after a game to sign autographs. "If there was a bus waiting to take us to the airport, I'd come through and say something to them and explain I had to get to the bus," Colavito said. "They could see that and understand it, but I felt bad."

Warny observed Colavito around fans many times and said he was always the same. "He was totally good-natured. He just loved kids. A lot of players treated kids differently. They might sign an autograph or two and then be in a hurry and scoot off someplace. I never saw Rocky do that. He waited until the end, always."[18] In the off-season, Fitzgibbons had a letter published in *The Sporting News* to correct a mention in a column the month before that suggested the fan club's sole purpose was to supply Colavito with chewing gum. "The main function of our club is to boost Rocky in every way we can—cheering him at games, trying to familiarize everyone with his career, etc. We have given him 33 packs of gum, which he chews, and plan to make it 38 (his uniform number) by the end of the season. I hope you'll publish this letter, so no one will become misinformed about the gum."[19] O'Connor and Fitzgibbons occasionally received rides home from Colavito, with Herb Score in the front passenger seat. "He was kind of protective of us," Warny said.[20] Emily Toth, Fitzgibbons' married name, said their affection for Colavito "was not a girlish crush, or that dreamboat stuff. Sure, he was extremely good looking, but he was exceptionally kind and generous and friendly to Barbara and me. I think I was a lucky girl to have a great father and a great idol to look up to."[21]

Colavito, who grew up without fancy clothes, now made a point of dressing impeccably in public, from tailored suits to buffed shoes. "I always wanted to look nice. Every time I ever saw Joe DiMaggio come out of Yankee Stadium, he had on a suit and tie. He was always dressed sharp," Colavito said. "My father was like that, and so were my brothers. I just followed in their footsteps." Colavito was aware that he was being described in the press in glowing terms and being called flattering names like "matinee idol," but it never affected him. "I wouldn't allow myself to change," Colavito said. "You really didn't think like you were somebody. I never thought that."

The Colavitos lived in an apartment on the Gold Coast, a lakefront neighborhood of Lakewood that was about a ten-mile drive to the ballpark.

They ate at local haunts the Blue Fox, Cavoli's, and the Silver Quill, and in Little Italy, where Colavito sometimes attended the Italian-American Brotherhood Club, a social club that served food. "Little Italy was one of those places frozen in time," Colavito said. "I was very, very proud to be an Italian. I always felt that connection. I didn't think we were better than anyone else, but I was proud to be an Italian." Colavito said he never felt pressure to live up to any expectations or standards as an Italian-American icon. "I know they liked me. I couldn't help but know that, because they showed me admiration in different ways. I never felt pressure, because I wouldn't know what standards they held me up to. I was just being me, and tried to be a gentleman, and tried to do things right. That was always taught to me as a kid at home."

Colavito had one of his biggest thrills in Yankee Stadium on June 9, 1956. After fouling off a ball Yogi Berra couldn't hold

Colavito waits his turn in the on-deck circle in 1957 (Barcroft Media).

onto, he drove the next pitch against Don Larsen deep into the left field seats for his first home run in the Bronx. Colavito's father, brother Dom, and other relatives were on hand to see it. "I always dreamed of hitting one there," he said. The home run came when the Indians trailed, 6–0, sparking the team's comeback in a 15–8 win. Colavito hit his first grand slam home run at home on August 16 off the Tigers' Billy Hoeft in a 5–4 victory. Another highlight was clouting a tenth-inning, three-run homer into Cleveland's lower deck on September 25 to break a 1–1 tie and give Early Wynn his 20th victory of the season.

Cleveland fans took a shine to their emerging right fielder. They liked his unbridled enthusiasm, his hustle, and the appreciation and respect he showed them. The home run-hitting outfielder, with a cannon of an arm, had quickly become a crowd favorite of adults and kids alike. "Rocky remains a starry-eyed rookie through all this display of power. He never refuses an autograph and will stand in front of the stadium, pencil in hand, as long as there are those seeking his signature," a local scribe wrote. "That someone should want his signature still seems unbelievable to this unusual, friendly young man."[22]

After Lopez penciled Colavito's name in the starting lineup for the rest of the season, he batted .305 and hit 16 home runs over the remaining 64 games. In all, Colavito batted 322 times in 101 games. His .276 average was tops among the Indians' starters, his 21 home runs were second-best, and his 65 runs batted in were the third-most on the team. The Indians finished the 1956 season in second place, a distant nine games behind the Yankees. The team's brightest spot was its pitching, with the staff leading the American league in ERA and shutouts. The Indians' team batting average, however, tied for lowest in the league.

Colavito's strong finish was good enough for him to get a vote for the Rookie of the Year Award from the Baseball Writers Association. He tied Orioles outfielder and future teammate Tito Francona for second place, far behind the White Sox's Luis Aparicio. The speedy Venezuelan shortstop played the entire season, led the league in stolen bases and racked up 211 more at-bats than Colavito. He received 22 votes, though Colavito outhit the defensive whiz by ten points and out-homered him, 21 to 3. After six years of playing pro ball, Colavito was now a certified major leaguer.

In the off-season, Colavito played in a dozen games for a team that barnstormed through New York and the New England states. His teammates included Walt Dropo of the White Sox, Moe Drabowsky of the Cubs, Art Ditmar of the Athletics, Frank Thomas of the Pirates, and Sammy White of the Red Sox. For the

Kerby Farrell, right, was Colavito's manager at minor league stops in Reading and Indianapolis, and with the Cleveland Indians in 1957 (Colavito's personal collection).

1957 season, Colavito sought a $9,000 raise to $12,000. GM Hank Greenberg offered only $1,500 more but told the ballplayer he'd get the additional amount if he played in 100 games that season. When Colavito reached his 98th game, a check was drawn for him. When he reported to spring training for the 1957 season, he was ready to cement his place in Cleveland's outfield. Waiting to greet him was the team's new manager, Kerby Farrell, Colavito's skipper at Reading and Indianapolis.

Farrell was named in the off-season to replace Lopez after six years at the helm. Farrell won *The Sporting News'* Minor League Manager of the Year Award both years with Colavito on his team, and would win the honor again in 1961, becoming the only three-time winner of the award. After toiling in the minors as a manager since 1941, this was Farrell's first shot at the big time, and he was counting on the young slugger to help the team improve. Colavito was pleased to see his old skipper, recalling his batting assistance in 1953. "Kerby closed my stance and told me to forget about DiMaggio," he recalled. "I wasn't aware of copying DiMaggio, but Kerby told me to think more about being Colavito."[23] Colavito got ready for the season opener by walloping three home runs in a spring training game against the Giants on April 7, including his second go-ahead homer in the ninth inning in successive games.

The Tribe's starting lineup for the April 16 opening game had Al Smith leading off in center, Bobby Avila at third base, Vic Wertz at first base, and Colavito in right field and batting cleanup. Roger Maris, a rookie up from Indianapolis and the only newcomer in the lineup, was hitting fifth, followed by Chico Carrasquel at shortstop. The bottom third of the batting order had Jim Hegan, the team's catcher, second baseman George Strickland, and pitcher Herb Score. *Cleveland News* beat writer Hal Lebovitz wrote in *The Sporting News* that the Indians were a "strong contender" because the team's pitching staff was "still the best in baseball, with a couple of talented rookies likely to make it even better."[24] Score was expected to pick up from his 20-win, 263-strikeout season, though Early Wynn, 37, and Bob Lemon, 36, were question marks due to their advancing age despite 20-win seasons the year before.

Colavito had a tough opening game, failing to get the ball out of the infield in five at-bats and making an error as the Indians lost to the White Sox, 3–2, in 11 innings. The first week of the season saw Colavito throw the Tigers' Bill Tuttle out at the plate with a 325-foot bullet from the right field corner. But the Indians right fielder, stuck in one of his frequent slow starts, was "overstriding or lunging" at the plate and couldn't get untracked.[25] Nearly a month into the season, he was hitting just .189 with two home runs and four RBI. Worse, Score, the Indians' star pitcher and Colavito's roommate, was hit in the right eye by a line drive on May 7, tearing the retina and causing him to miss the remainder of the season. It was a devastating blow to the pitcher and to the team's young season.

Colavito's bat woke from its slumber on May 12 with two singles and a home run while knocking in four runs as the Indians beat the Kansas City Athletics, 7–4. He kept up the hot streak and raised his average to .317 after collecting four hits on May 19. In June, Colavito threw out six baserunners in nine games, and in a June 25 game at Yankee Stadium, he made manager Casey Stengel pay for intentionally walking Maris ahead of him by hitting a grand slam. In the same game, Colavito flied out to the center field fence, some 457 feet away. In another game against the Yankees, Colavito was trying to concentrate on the pitcher as Yogi Berra was bantering back and forth, trying to distract him. "I stepped back and said to Yogi, 'You're Italian, and I'm Italian. Give me a break. I'm trying to hit here,'" Colavito said. "And you know what, he never bothered me again."

Hank Greenberg, the Hall of Fame slugger, sometimes offered Colavito batting advice from behind the batting cage.

> Hank was not only my boss, but he had also been a great hitter when he was a player. You listen when you have respect for a man's ability. He was never a critical kind of instructor. He would never say, don't do this or don't do that, or why don't you try this? Instead he'd say, "That was a good swing, Rocky. You were in the groove that time." I'd try to get the bat around the same way the next time, and pretty soon I found myself swinging the way I should.

The 1957 season proved to be a disappointment. At the All-Star break, the team was 39–38, a half-game above the fifth-place Tigers. Colavito had recovered from his slow start to hit 15 home runs, but he was being moved in and out of the lineup. In July, he accepted an invitation to attend a meeting of the Rocky Colavito Fan Club at O'Connor's house. News of his appearance spread quickly, and more than 100 kids were on hand, many of them not even members. "Rocky stayed a long time and was very gracious," O'Connor said. "He had all the kids line up and signed autographs for everyone."[26]

Late in the season, Colavito looked at the lineup card and was shocked to find that Farrell had recalled minor league first baseman Joe Altobelli and put him in his place in right field. Colavito exploded at Farrell, who told him he could call Greenberg if he didn't like it and pointed to the phone. Colavito did just that, unleashing his hair-trigger temper and demanding for the second year in a row that Greenberg trade or release him. Greenberg responded by telling Colavito to see him after the game. Colavito was inserted into the game as a defensive replacement, and in the ninth inning drove a pitch into the upper deck in the winning effort. After the game, Colavito sat down with Greenberg. "He said to me, 'Calm down, Rocky, he won't be here next year,'" Colavito recalled. "That really took the wind out of my sails."

With Score out for the year and Lemon suffering an arm injury, the Indians tumbled out of the first division for the first time in ten years, landing in sixth place. In the final home game of the season, Colavito and Maris each hit home runs to prevent the Tigers' Jim Bunning from reaching 20 wins. Only 3,021 fans came out to the cavernous, 73,811-seat Municipal Stadium to see the game, bringing the season attendance to 722,256, the team's lowest total since 1945. Colavito hit 25 home runs to go with 84 runs batted in. That was four home runs and 21 RBI above the previous season's total, but in 31 more games. His .252 batting average was 24 points lower. Colavito also had the dubious distinction of tying Jackie Jensen of the Red Sox and Gus Zernial of the Athletics with a league-leading 11 outfield errors.

Farrell's first season managing in the major leagues would be his last. He was fired after the team's disappointing season and replaced by Bobby Bragan, who had formerly managed the Pirates. Farrell, who played an important role in Colavito's career, would go on to coach several years with the White Sox and the Indians, and to manage farm clubs for the Phillies, Twins and Mets, capping a 21-year minor league managing career. Greenberg wouldn't be around to see the results of his decision. The Indians' brass, disappointed by the play on the field, decided it was time for a wholesale change. Indians owner William R. Daley replaced Greenberg with Frank Lane, who had held a similar position with two previous teams. Greenberg, the Indians GM since 1949, would reunite the following year with former boss Bill Veeck as general manager of the Chicago White Sox.

Lane's first official move was to dismiss popular Indians legend Lou Boudreau, the team's batting coach. He had been an all-star shortstop who, as player-manager, led the Indians to its last World Series victory in 1948. Lane notified the league's other general managers that virtually all the Indians' ballplayers were available. The new GM also revealed that he had rejected a trade proposed by Arnold Johnson, owner of the Kansas City Athletics, that would have sent Colavito and Vic Wertz to the A's for first baseman Vic Power and second baseman Billy Martin. Lane said he was reluctant to part with the Indians' right fielder.[27] The following month, it was reported that the Indians' mailbag was heavy with letters from fans urging that Colavito not be traded. Lane was noncommittal. "Only Herb Score and Roger Maris aren't available," he said. "But that doesn't mean I'll trade Rocky. It merely means: Don't worry."[28]

6

"Those Guys Were the Future"

At first glance, Rocco Domenico Colavito, an Italian who grew up in the hustle-and-bustle of the Bronx in New York, and Roger Eugene Maris, a Croatian born in Hibbing, MN, and raised on the wide-open plains of Fargo, ND, appeared to have little in common. Yet the two power-hitting right fielders signed to contracts by the Indians one year apart were in many ways cut from the same cloth. Colavito and Maris shared a blue-collar work ethic, were devoted family men and consummate team players, and commanded the respect and admiration of teammates and opposing players alike.[1] They were also proud, confident, and stubborn, had short fuses, and could carry a grudge. They expected to be treated fairly and weren't shy about demanding respect if it wasn't forthcoming.

Maris, exactly 11 months younger than Colavito, began his professional career in 1953 at age 18 in the Indians' minor league camp in Daytona Beach. The two ballplayers probably met shagging fly balls, Colavito recalled, and spent a lot of time together that spring. On several occasions, they rode the municipal bus across town to a local pool hall, where they took turns racking them up. Maris called Colavito "Rocco Socco." "I just liked him," Colavito said. "I liked his honesty. I think it was mutual admiration. Roger was a great guy and easy to be around. He was a no-bullshit guy; there was no phoniness about him. He either liked you or he didn't." Those attributes were also often affixed to Colavito. In many ways, Maris was just a more extreme version of Colavito. It's little wonder they became close friends.

After spring training, Maris was assigned to stay in Daytona Beach and play on the Indians' Class D minor league ball club. But he insisted instead on joining the Fargo-Moorhead Twins in the Northern League, in his hometown. It was Class C ball, one up from D Ball, and Maris wasn't taking no for an answer. "I'm going to Fargo. Either I go there to play ball and live, or else I'll go there just to live and find another job. It's up to you," Maris said in an ultimatum to the Indians' brass.[2] "If Roger said that, you could bet your potatoes he meant it," Colavito said. "Roger made up his mind he wanted to play in C ball, and you know that there was no real difference between C and D from what I saw, because it was basically the same caliber of players. He wanted to play in his hometown and I don't blame him. He could save some money living at home." Maris got his way and justified his ultimatum by batting .325 with nine home runs and 80 RBIs and winning the league's Rookie of the Year Award. Colavito, in his third minor-league season, hit .271 with 28 home runs and 121 RBIs for the Double A Reading Indians in the Eastern League.

Former Indians pitcher Jim "Mudcat" Grant remembers quite a buzz about Maris when he joined Fargo-Moorhead the following season. "He was the Northern League Rookie of the Year in 1953, and I won the award in 1954," Grant said. "I heard from everyone that Roger would be a great player. Throughout the Indians' farm system, you heard 'Roger Maris and Rocky Colavito, Roger Maris and Rocky Colavito.' Those guys were the future. There was no way I ever thought either one of them would be traded."[3]

The Indians wanted Maris to remain at Fargo-Moorhead for the 1954 season, but the ballplayer, believing he had nothing left to prove at that level, insisted on being promoted. With the Class B Keokuk Kernels in Iowa, Maris hit .315, slugged 32 home runs, knocked in 111 runs, and stole 25 bases. In 1955, playing with the Tulsa Oilers in Class AA, Maris made a costly error by overthrowing third base. Dutch Meyer, Tulsa's manager, made Maris practice his throws to

Indians outfielders Colavito, Roger Maris, and Gene Woodling chat around the batting cage at spring training in 1957. Colavito and Maris roomed together that spring (Everett Collection Inc./Alamy Stock Photo).

third for a half-hour after the game. Finally, Maris—believing the extra throwing was simply vindictive—walked off the field. "I'm not blowing my arm out for you or anybody else," he told Meyer, despite the manager's threat to retaliate.[4] After the incident, General Manager Hank Greenberg sent Maris to the Reading Indians, where he put together a solid season with 19 home runs in a pitcher's park and stole 24 bases. Meyer was fired a short time later, though it wasn't clear that this incident was a factor. Maris shared a 1956 Indians Rookie Stars baseball card with Colavito, but he wound up playing the whole season in Indianapolis, hitting .293 with 17 home runs and 75 RBIs. In Maris's four minor league seasons, he hit .303 with 78 home runs. All five minor league teams he played for saw their won-lost records improve over the previous season.

Maris and Colavito were roommates in 1957 at the Indians' spring training camp in Tucson, Arizona. One night at the Santa Rita Hotel, where the team was staying, Maris became ill. "He was shivering like you wouldn't believe," Colavito said. "I ran around and got seven or eight blankets to keep him warm. He let me know for a long time after that how much he appreciated it." Maris made the Indians that spring, and many were predicting big things for the newly-minted major leaguer. That included Kerby Farrell, Maris's manager with the Indianapolis Indians, who won the pennant and the Junior World Series in 1956, earning the skipper a chance to manage the parent club. "The kid's going to be great someday," Farrell said. "Wait until you see him. He can run, he's got a fine arm, and he came along great last year after a slow start. If determination and desire count, he'll be somewhere with us."[5] Pitcher Herb Score was also impressed by Maris's potential. "I saw Roger when he first signed, at spring training and through the minor leagues. Roger was just one of those fellows that you … knew was going to be a big leaguer."[6] The baseball press took notice, too. "Maris has the tools to become another Mantle, lacking only the powerful arm Mickey owns," the March 1957 issue of *The Sporting News* declared.[7] *Sports Illustrated* proclaimed Maris one of baseball's top rookies. "Here is the youth who could add needed speed to a lead-footed Cleveland offense," the story said. "Extremely fast, he can bunt or pull the long ball to right."[8]

Maris played his first major league game on April 17, 1957, going 3-for-5. In the next game, he hit his first major league home run, an 11th-inning grand slam against the home team Detroit Tigers in a winning effort. Colavito, starting his second full season with the team, and Maris, with wives in tow, would alternate driving to Municipal Stadium from their homes two blocks from one another in Parma, south of Cleveland. "We rode to the ballpark together every day at home in 1957, and we never talked even once about being in competition," Colavito said. "I think it was mutual respect." Sometimes they would stop at St. Francis de Sales Church to attend Mass. Maris

Roger Maris played for the Cleveland Indians in 1957 and was sent to Kansas City the following year in a mid-season blockbuster trade (Everett Collection Inc./Alamy Stock Photo).

played all outfield positions that year. "Roger had speed, something I did not have," Colavito said. "I got a good jump on the ball, but Roger had out-and-out speed. He didn't have Mickey Mantle or Willie Mays speed, but he had damn good speed."

Maris was hitting .315 early in the season when he tried to break up a double play. Kansas City's rookie second baseman, Milt Graff, landed on him with both knees, breaking two of Maris's ribs and knocking him out of the lineup for a couple of weeks. Maris struggled to get back on track after being rushed back onto the field, sore ribs and all, and his confidence waned as he pressed to regain his batting stroke. Maris also pulled a hamstring chasing a fly ball and injured a wrist. He ended his rookie season with a .235 batting average, 14 homers and 51 RBI in 116 games. Colavito hit 25 homers, knocked in 84 runs, and batted .252. The Indians finished one game under .500 in sixth place, their worst season since 1946. In the off-season, a new general manager was hired to replace Greenberg, and Colavito and Maris would soon come to share in their loathing of Frank Lane.

After accepting the job, Lane said Maris and Score were not on the trading block, but that proved to be short-lived.[9] Lane notified Maris that he expected him to play winter ball in the Dominican Republic. Maris told Lane he had a job in the sports department of a radio station in Fargo and was going to stay home with his family, including a newborn daughter. Lane didn't like that, and he liked it less when Maris returned a torn, unsigned contract in the mail as a commentary on the general manager's proposed raise.[10] "Roger was honest to a fault, and that got him into trouble sometimes, but I loved him for it," Colavito said. "I didn't take too much shit, but Roger didn't take any." Carmen Colavito appreciated how much Maris cared about children. "I loved Roger Maris," she said. "He loved babies more than baseball." Colavito had problems with Lane that off-season, too, also sending back an unsigned contract although his was intact. Colavito had boosted his home runs in his second full season from 21 to 25, upped his RBIs from 65 to 84 and doubled his outfield assists to a dozen. He thought he deserved a modest $3,000 raise, from $12,000 to $15,000, but despite heated negotiations Lane refused to budge from his final offer of $13,500.

Maris began the 1958 season as the starting right fielder and got off to a fast start, only to cool off after a back injury. He wanted to avoid the mistake he made the previous season of returning too soon with an injury, but it didn't help when manager Bobby Bragan questioned whether the injury was serious enough to keep him out of the lineup. After Lane turned down the Yankees' offer to trade Bobby Richardson for Maris, the Indians outfielder was shipped to Kansas City in June 1958 in a multi-player deal for first baseman Vic Power and shortstop Woodie Held.[11] That came after the Athletics first inquired about Colavito and were told trading him would cause an uproar with Cleveland fans.[12] Lane made the A's promise that if they intended to trade Maris to the Yankees, where so many A's players wound up, they would have to wait to do so. Many thought Lane was hasty in giving up on Maris. "That was a bad deal for us because Roger was better than both players we got for him," Mudcat Grant said. "The guy was a star."[13] The trade of Maris left Colavito wondering about what might have been. "You expected anything in those days, especially when you had an asshole like Frank Lane," Colavito said. "I know this: I did not like it. It was apparent Roger would have been the center fielder, I would have been the right fielder and Tito Francona would have been the left fielder. And Lane blew the cork off that. I can't emphasize enough that he was a bad baseball man."

Getting the chance to play every day for the A's in 1958, Maris hit .247 but cracked 19 home runs in 99 games, giving him a combined 28 for the year. The next year, he started in right field for the American League in the second All-Star Game, entering the August 3 game with a .326 average. It was the first of four consecutive years in which two All-Star games were staged to benefit the players' pension. Maris was replaced in the sixth inning by Colavito, who homered two innings later in a winning effort. Missing a month of the season with an appendectomy, Maris saw his batting average plummet the last two months to .273 as the A's finished seventh in the eight-team league.

In the off-season, Maris was sent to the New York Yankees in a seven-player blockbuster trade. The Yankees treated the Kansas City Athletics, owned by Arnold Johnson, like their own farm team from 1954 to 1959, making 16 trades involving 59 players.[14] It was another case of the Athletics sending up-and-coming players to New York for ballplayers past their prime. The Yankees got Maris, shortstop Joe DeMaestri, and first baseman Kent Hadley in exchange for pitcher Don Larsen, outfielder Hank Bauer, outfielder-first baseman Norm Siebern, and first baseman Marv Throneberry. Lane couldn't resist telling reporters that Maris was the weak link in the trade. "Norm Siebern will outhit Roger Maris. Kansas City may have the better of that trade," Lane said.[15]

Maris won back-to-back American League Most Valuable Player awards in 1960 and 1961 and played an integral role on five consecutive pennant-winning teams in New York and two world championships. In 1960, Siebern hit 20 fewer homers, knocked in 43 fewer runs, and had a lower batting average than the slugging right fielder. In 1961, Maris hit 61 home runs to break what was arguably baseball's most cherished record—Babe Ruth's single-season mark of 60, set 34 years earlier. Maris's record would stand for 37 years. Many, Colavito included, consider Maris still the rightful all-time single-season home run champ, since the three who eclipsed him—Barry Bonds, Mark McGwire and Sammy Sosa—cheated by using steroids.

"One can only imagine an outfield that had both Rocky and Roger, two of the premier home run hitters of that era," said Bob DiBiasio, the Indians' vice president of public affairs. "As Tribe fans, we can only dream of the chase to 60 being Rocky and Roger, instead of Mickey and Roger."[16] Lane, whose judgment of baseball talent was harshly condemned by many during his tenure as a general manager with five teams, never let on that letting Maris go was a loss for the Indians. "The best deal I made for Cleveland was Roger Maris for Woodie Held and Vic Power," Lane said, after Maris won the MVP Award in 1960.[17]

Maris teamed with Mickey Mantle for seven years as the "M&M boys" to create the most feared one-two punch for the Yankees since Babe Ruth and Lou Gehrig, and one of the greatest duos of all-time. He hit 33 home runs and knocked in 100 runs in 1962, but injuries in 1963 limited his playing time to 312 at-bats in 90 games, though he still hit 23 home runs and added 26 more in 1964. But in June 1965, Maris suffered a hand injury that permanently robbed him of his power. Maris believed the Yankees compounded the problem by keeping him in the dark about the extent of the damage.. His 1965 season had been initially slowed by a pulled hamstring muscle in his right leg suffered on April 28, causing him to miss 26 games. On June 28,

Maris hit his 61st home run record on October 1, 1961, to set the new major league record (Baseball Hall of Fame).

after hitting a home run earlier in the game, Maris hurt the ring finger and pinky on his right hand sliding home after being stepped on by home umpire Bill Haller's spiked shoes. Maris was in excruciating pain, and further damage was done eight days later. "There was a real sharp pop in my hand, loud enough that I could hear it," Maris said. "It was just like you snap a pencil. The hand swelled up right away, double its size."[18] Maris's hand was broken, but despite x-rays taken by the ball club in New York and later Washington and Minneapolis, he claimed the team kept him in the dark about the full extent of his injury. It wasn't until September that he learned from a doctor independent from the Yankees, and without their permission, that the hamate bone at the base of his hand had been fractured.[19]

"All the Yankees management cared about was Roger playing, not whether he had a broken bone in his hand," veteran New York sportswriter Maury Allen said. Allen thought fault rested with Sidney Gaynor, the Yankees' doctor, for concealing the true extent of Maris's injury. "He was a very nasty man whose job was to get hurt players on the field," Allen said. "His attitude was that they were a bunch of crybabies."[20] Maris, who had eight home runs and a team-leading 27 RBIs at that point in 155 at-bats, made just four pinch-hit appearances the rest of the season. Still, he continued to be asked to take batting and fielding practice on occasion, with his playing status listed as day to day. The team, under manager Johnny Keane, insinuated that he was healthy enough to play, just as Bobby Bragan had done in Cleveland, leading sportswriters to raise doubts and fans to turn on him as the team stumbled to a sixth-place finish, its lowest position in the standings since 1925.[21] When Maris presented evidence of his broken hand at the end of the season to Ralph Houk, the team's general manager, he was told, "Rog, I might as well level with you. You need an operation on that hand." That confirmed to Maris that the Yankees brass had known the seriousness of his injury all along.[22] The delay in getting appropriate treatment for Maris's hand injury resulted in it never healing correctly. "Once I broke the hand in '65, really, it was all over for me, because even today I don't have the gripping strength in two fingers of my right hand. I would swing the bat and have that hand slip right out of there," Maris told author Peter Golenbock in 1975.[23]

Because of the injury and perhaps because of the way he had been treated by Yankees' management, Maris planned to retire after the 1966 season. He was persuaded by Houk to hold back on a public announcement until spring training in case he changed his mind.[24] In the off-season, General Manager Larry MacPhail checked in with Maris, who told him he still planned to hang 'em up. Ignoring Maris's wishes, MacPhail dealt him to the St. Louis Cardinals anyway, for unheralded third baseman Charley Smith.[25] Maris decided to go only after Cardinals owner August Busch offered him a beer distributorship in Gainesville, FL, when his playing days were over. Maris helped the Cardinals win two consecutive pennants and a World Series before retiring following the 1968 season, bidding goodbye to baseball at the same time as Colavito, Mantle, and Eddie Mathews. Maris's total of seven pennants with the Yankees and Cardinals and three World Series championships were the most of any player in the 1960s.

After Maris's career was over, he stayed away from Yankee Stadium for years despite overtures from ownership, concerned that he might get a negative reception from fans. He finally agreed to make an on-field appearance with Mantle on Opening Day in April 1978 and drew a warm ovation, telling a reporter afterward he was glad "to be home."[26] Maris's No. 9 was officially retired in 1984 by the Yankees, and a plaque commemorating his career was placed in the stadium's Monument Park, alongside teammate Elston Howard, whose No. 32 was also retired that day. Maris, dressed in his New York Yankees uniform, was especially proud of the words on the plaque:

> Roger Eugene Maris. Against all adds in 1961 he became the only player to hit more than 60 home runs in a single season. In belated recognition of one of baseball's greatest achievements ever, his 61 in '61, the Yankees salute him as a great player and author of one of the most remarkable chapters in the history of Major League Baseball. Erected by New York Yankees July 21, 1984.

Maris appreciated the recognition and the Yankees' unambiguous acknowl-edgment of the 61 home runs. "He walked away saying, 'Wonderful,'" said Dick Savageau, a lifelong friend of Maris's from Fargo. "This is what it should have been like. This was what I was waiting for."[27] Maris died less than 17 months later from Hodgkin's lymphoma. He was 51. Colavito admired Maris for the courage he showed at the end of his life. "Roger showed so much class in the way he dealt with his illness," he said. "He was really something."

Maris's injury-curtailed career bears some similarity to that of Hall of Famer Sandy Koufax, who strung together six incredible seasons on the mound during his ten full seasons and parts of two others before he was forced to call it quits due to an arthritic elbow. Only Dizzy Dean and Addie Joss won fewer than Koufax's 165 among starting pitchers enshrined in Cooperstown. Maris played for 12 seasons but averaged just 341 at-bats his last six years due to injuries. His 275 career home runs, along with six he hit in the seven World Series he participated in, are low for home-run hitters by contemporary stan-dards. But at the time of his retirement, Maris had compiled the fifth-most career home runs for an American League left-handed hitter ever, trailing only Hall of Famers Babe Ruth, Ted Williams, Lou Gehrig, and Yogi Berra.

Ralph Terry was Maris's teammate in 1958 and 1959 with the Athletics. He came over to the Yankees in the trade prior to the 1960 season, and they remained teammates through 1964. In 1962, Terry won 23 games and pitched a 1–0, complete-game shutout in the seventh game of the World Series. "Roger was a great player who was twice MVP, broke the all-time home run record, was flawless in the field, had an accurate throwing arm, and was a good base run-ner. He's not in the Hall of Fame. Why even have a museum?" Terry said.[28] Terry was also an admirer of Colavito, to whom he surren-dered 13 home runs, more than any other hurler.

Roger Maris holds the ball he hit for his 61st home run, caught by Sal Durante (at right) in the right field stands at Yankee Stadium (Baseball Hall of Fame).

I loved Rocky. When I played against him, he was one of the toughest hit-ters I ever faced. He stood on top of the plate and you couldn't throw your fastball by him on the inside. We played together in '65 with

Cleveland. He had a good year, and I really enjoyed playing with him. I played against him in the minor leagues in '55 with Denver when he was with Indianapolis, and you could see without any question he was a big-league ballplayer then. Rocky is a Hall of Famer in my book. He batted cleanup, was a stud during his era and had a strong arm.

Colavito and Maris shared a lot in common, Terry said. "Rocky and Roger weren't party animals. They were serious ballplayers, serious professionals, and great competitors as well as power hitters who played hard and played fair. They were special people." Terry added, "Roger, you crossed him once, and you wouldn't cross him again."[29] Herb Score made a similar observation about Colavito: "With Rocky, his word is his bond. If he says he will be there at 5 o'clock, he is there at 5 o'clock. He is the most honorable man I know. But if you promise to do something for him and you don't, you're off his list. He never forgets anything."[30]

Colavito considered Maris and Minnesota Twins outfielder Tony Oliva the two most underrated players he played with or against throughout his career. Both, he said, should be in the Hall of Fame. "Roger could do everything. He could run, throw, field, hit, and hit with power. He wasn't one of those guys who could hit them 500 feet, but he had consistent power. And I never saw him make a bad throw in my life. He was as good in right field as you were going to get. He was also as good as there was on the base paths. Roger could do it all," he said.

While Colavito was on his way in 1961 to hitting 45 home runs and knocking in 140 runs, he kept track of Maris's pursuit of the Babe's home-run record.

I felt bad for him in one way because I knew there was a lot of pressure, especially from those New York writers. The writers would call in the morning, and it was hard for him to get rest. Early in the season we played in Detroit, and after the game we talked in the walkway outside the clubhouse. I said, "Rog, how're you doing?" and he said, 'I went 1-for-5.' He had hit a home run that day. I said, "It isn't so bad when you hit a home run," and I remember trying to comfort him. He wasn't happy with it. I think he was feeling pressure to get his batting average up. But I also thought what he was doing was historic. He was doing something not many guys ever did.

No one could have predicted that the two friends and former 1957 spring training roommates would retire the same year, with Colavito ranked third in the American League for career right-handed home runs and Maris ranked fifth for left-handed home runs. Colavito still chuckles at the memory of the left-handed Maris needling him when he was a batting coach with the Royals in the early 1980s. "Roger said, 'What do you know about left-handed hitting?' I said, 'Not much, but when I need help I'll call you.'"

7

Stardom

Hank Greenberg had been the only general manager Rocky Colavito knew. The Hall of Fame ballplayer and fellow Bronx native was there when Colavito signed with the club in 1951 at age 17. He overruled the farm director who thought the teenage Colavito, due to his lack of speed, could only be successful as a pitcher. Greenberg gave Colavito informal batting instruction over the years and had an open-door policy with the young slugger. Colavito trusted him. "He was a prince. When Hank gave you his word, it was as good as gold," he said. Frank Lane? He was a different matter altogether.

Lane had a reputation for coming into a town like a tornado, sweeping up most of the ballplayers he inherited, and scattering them in all directions as fans braced for the departure of their favorite players. Lane's first job as general manager was with the Chicago White Sox in 1949, when the club finished in last place with a 51–101 record. He traded, released, waived, or sent down 38 players on the team's 40-man roster in his first year.[1] After Lane resigned in 1955, he was hired by the St. Louis Cardinals and promptly announced that six Cardinals wouldn't be put on the trading block. He then proceeded to trade four of them and considered unloading Cardinals all-time great Stan Musial until owner August Busch intervened.[2] "They used to say that the toughest job on any club Frank Lane was running belonged to the guy who had to take the team picture," said Joe Garagiola, who began his career as a Cardinal and went on to a long career in broadcasting.[3]

Lane inherited an Indians team that finished the 1957 season mired in sixth place, 21½ games behind the Yankees. The record of 76–77 was a far cry from the 1954 club three seasons earlier that set an American League record for wins in a season with 111 that stood until 1998. Gene Woodling led the team with a .321 average, 39 points higher than anyone else, and was voted the Indians' Man of the Year by local baseball writers. But Lane wasted little time shipping Woodling off to the Orioles for former Indians outfielder Larry Doby and pitcher Don Ferrarese. Doby was the American League's first black ballplayer and a future Hall of Famer but was on the down side of his career.

Lane quickly demonstrated that he couldn't have been more different from Greenberg when contract negotiations for the 1958 season opened. "We didn't hit it off from the beginning," Colavito said. "He tried to chisel you. I was trying to be fair, but I learned you couldn't be fair with him." Lane convinced Colavito to take a $1,500 raise with the promise that he'd get an additional $1,500 if he played well that season. But when Colavito, who would enjoy one of his two greatest seasons in 1958, reminded Lane of the deal they had struck later in the season, Lane acted like he had made it up, and Colavito didn't get the money. "I called him a fucking liar," Colavito said.

Frank Lane replaced Hank Greenberg as Indians general manager in November 1957 (Baseball Hall of Fame).

Colavito's already frosty relations grew worse. Lane was the first of several general managers and owners Colavito felt were not very knowledgeable about baseball and treated players poorly.

> Loyalty was a one-way street in baseball, and it always bothered me. They always put you down when you were renegotiating your contract. They wouldn't compliment you because they were afraid you would want more money. They could have been a lot kinder or a lot nicer and encouraged you to do better, so you could do more to help the team. But instead they made you feel like shit, like you were nothing. And if they thought you were used up, so to speak, they'd drop you in a minute.

Colavito recalled a spring training conversation in 1957 about Greenberg with teammates Bobby Avila, Ray Narleski, and Don Mossi. "They were talking about how tough he was in contract talks. I looked at them and said, 'You guys are going to be sorry. Greenberg is one of the most honest people you're ever going to meet. Wait until we get someone else in here, and you are going to see things differently and regret what you thought of this guy because he's a good man.' Who did we get but, lo and behold, Frank Lane. A couple of them came up to me later and said, 'You know what, Rocky, you were right.'"[4]

With two years of major league ball under his belt, Colavito was poised for a breakout year in 1958. In the off-season, he ran sprints, did push-ups, and swung a heavy lead bat to stay in shape. He also worked again loading baskets of mushrooms off a truck and into coolers. "I'm really looking forward to this season," Colavito told the *Cleveland Plain Dealer*. "In fact, I intend to go out to Tucson a couple days early. It can't start soon enough for me."[5] The article referred to him as "the 24-year-old favorite of the Cleveland fans." But as Colavito soon discovered, there was no guarantee he would be in the starting lineup when the regular season began.

That became clear when spring training games got underway and Colavito's bat was slow to get going. "Certainly, neither Roger Maris or Rocky Colavito, last year's regulars in center and right, has a job locked up," an Indians beat writer wrote. "Maris has performed satisfactorily in exhibition games, but Colavito has been unbelievably bad."[6] Bobby Bragan, the team's new manager, agreed about Colavito. "If he were a rookie without a major league track record, he'd be back in Daytona Beach now," he said.[7] The criticism continued a couple of days later, when Bragan said, "If Rocky doesn't snap out of it, he won't play at all."[8]

Bragan had Colavito work on his fielding and throwing with Bob Kennedy, a recently retired player now coaching in the Indians' system. Kennedy taught Colavito to back off a step when fielding a fly ball with men on base and to move into the catch at the last moment to be better positioned to let the throw go. He also encouraged Colavito to field the ball off his right shoulder and lower his throws to the cutoff man. That broke a habit of lofting his throws that Colavito had developed as a youth throwing stones over the elevated subway tracks in the Bronx. "Kennedy cut down my exaggerated throwing motion," Colavito said. "He made it a short firing delivery, and it increased my accuracy. Kennedy made it a pleasure for me to use my arm. I loved to throw, and I found less guys running on me than before."

Concern about Colavito's lack of speed in the field and on the base paths led Bragan to have former track and field star and Indians executive Harrison Dillard coach him. Dillard tried getting Colavito to take shorter strides. "He tried to help me," Colavito recalled. "If you have God-given speed you're going to be able to run, but if you don't, no matter who helps you, you might improve a little but not a whole lot. I think he helped me a little." To help Colavito with his flat arches, the team bought him a black and a brown pair of street shoes with special arches for the lofty price of $90 a pair. "They weren't very good looking—they looked like Frankenstein shoes—but they were very comfortable," Colavito said. Convinced that Colavito's lack of speed made him more suited as an infielder, Bragan had Colavito practice fielding at third base before settling on first base. By the end of spring training, he was proclaiming Colavito "the Indians' future first baseman."[9] Colavito that spring exchanged the No. 38 he wore for a lower uniform number, since he felt higher numbers indicated a rookie. He was assigned No. 6, which led pitcher Stan Pitula to kid him by saying, "You're getting closer to DiMaggio," who had worn No. 5.[10]

The Tribe had a lot of question marks going into the 1958 season, beginning with its starting pitching. The biggest question was whether Herb Score would rediscover his past pitching form after being hit in the eye the previous May, curtailing his season and nearly ending his career. The team was expecting additional punch in the lineup from left fielder Minnie Minoso, reacquired in a trade that sent Al Smith and Early Wynn to the White Sox; and aging ballplayers Larry Doby, who also returned to the Indians a second time after being acquired in the Woodling trade, and two-time batting champion Mickey Vernon, claimed on waivers from the Red Sox. Vernon, 40, was expected to back up Vic Wertz at first base but saw more playing time after Wertz broke his ankle before the season began. Vernon broke Lou Gehrig's American League record for most games played at first base 20 games into the season.

Outfielders Colavito, Maris, and Gary Geiger were still considered question marks by Bragan when the 1958 season opened at home on April 15. Colavito sat on the bench as Maris started in right field, and Score, who would finish the year 2–3 after suffering another early-season injury, lasted just three innings in a losing effort. Colavito started the next seven games at first base, making two errors while otherwise adequately covering the position. His first home run of the year, along with homers by Maris, Minoso and catcher Dick Brown, came at the end of the week in a win over the Tigers. Colavito then sat out three games in a row, only to return to the lineup and make two more errors at first base in a 9–5 loss. Alarmed, Bragan had Vernon and Colavito room together for a while to help him learn the position.[11] But Colavito made only three more appearances at first.

The Indians' outfield had Minoso in left field, with Maris in right and occasionally center, along with Geiger and Carroll Hardy. But when an injury forced Maris out of the lineup for several games, Colavito was back in right field. He began the season hitting well over .300, but his average steadily plummeted. Carmen's pregnancy was also on his mind. On May 19, she gave birth at Lakewood Hospital, outside of Cleveland, to the couple's second child, Marisa Ann Colavito. She was born 21 months after Rocco Jr. Unbeknownst to Rocky, Lane tried to trade him the following week. Senators owner Calvin Griffith nixed a trade offer from Lane on May 24 while watching a ballgame from the right field bleachers. The trade would have sent Colavito, Doby, and pitcher Cal McLish to the nation's capital in exchange for third baseman Eddie Yost, slugger Jim Lemon and pitcher Pedro Ramos.[12]

As the June 15 trade deadline neared, Lane also discussed sending Colavito to the Kansas City Athletics for six players: first baseman Vic Power, outfielders Bill Tuttle and Hector Lopez, shortstop Woodie Held, pitcher Duke Maas and rookie outfielder Dave Melton.[13] That helped lay the groundwork for a June 15 trade that would send the highly-touted Maris, along with Preston

Ward, who was batting third in the league with a surprising .338 average, and pitcher Dick Tomanek to Kansas City in exchange for Power and Held. When trade talk around Colavito reached the news, *Cleveland News* columnist Hal Lebovitz coined the phrase "Don't Knock the Rock," which would soon echo as a term of endearment from the stands of Municipal Stadium to Cleveland's Little Italy. Colavito admitted getting a kick out of the phrase, which stayed with him throughout his career. "I liked it. I thought it was kind of cute, and it stuck, too," he said.

The uncertainty Colavito experienced over whether he would be platooning in right field, at first base, or riding the bench and pinch-hitting was something he had never gone through before. After sitting out the second game of a May 25 doubleheader, he decided to do something about it. Colavito went to Bragan and guaranteed he would hit 35 home runs if given the chance to play every day, only to quickly lower the number to 30. It was a heady prediction, given that Colavito was hitting .241 with two home runs and the season was seven weeks old. Impressed by Colavito's confidence, Bragan agreed to write his name in the lineup card every day. But to Colavito's dismay, the manager told the press he had promised to hit 35 home runs and not the revised number of 30 round-trippers. "I was steaming when I saw that," Colavito said. "I took that paper and went right to his office and said, 'Bobby, I told you I changed it from 35 home runs to 30.' He said, 'Now, son'— in that Southern accent of his—'just take it easy. You're going to get your chance.'"

Colavito played right field in the next game, homered in the next three games and soon embarked on a 13-game hitting streak. In a doubleheader at Yankee Stadium in front of family and friends, he slugged two home runs, including one into the left-field upper deck, a 450-foot triple, a double and a 425-foot fly ball caught by left fielder Norm Siebern against the scoreboard. "That day, Rocky would have had five homers in any other park," *The Sporting News* said. "In the expanses of Yankee Stadium, he had to settle for two."[14]

Ted Williams was one reason why Colavito's bat was booming again. Kerby Farrell, Hank Greenberg, Tris Speaker, and Rocky's brother Dom had been instrumental at different times in helping Colavito with his hitting. But there was no hitter alive that he held in higher esteem than Williams.

> Ted Williams was without a doubt the best hitter I ever saw. I didn't compare anyone to him. When I came up, we played 154 games, and 22 of them would be against each team. I never saw him look bad. I never saw him fooled and get out in front of a pitch. The worst I ever saw was when he had a 3–2 count with Gary Bell and took a breaking ball right over the plate for the third strike. Teddy just flipped the bat away and went out to his position like nothing ever happened. The next time up, in the ninth inning, he hit a ball into the upper deck in Cleveland, and you didn't see too many hit there.

Colavito approached Williams for help early in the season, when Boston was playing in Cleveland. He was aware of the Red Sox slugger's penchant for doling out advice to players who sought it. "I asked Ted to look at me and tell me what was wrong," Colavito said. "He watched me a few minutes in batting practice and then suggested that I close my stance, move away from the plate and try to hit the ball up the middle or to right center. 'Try it for a few days, and I think you'll find yourself back in the groove again,' he said, and I did." Colavito continued to turn to Williams when he felt it would help. "Anytime I was in a slump, I would go right up to Teddy. I would tell him what my problem was, and he was always helpful. Talking to him was a confidence builder. He'd tell me an adjustment to make. I had such a good day one time after talking to him, hitting a bullet to right-center and a homer to left-center." Williams also praised Colavito's work ethic and spoke highly of him to the press. "I can't think of any player who is striving more to improve," the "Splendid Splinter" said. "He's always trying. He eliminates the bad and keeps the good. A good young hitter."[15]

Bobby Bragan, Greenberg's hire shortly before his firing, was axed by Lane after only 67 games with the team languishing five games below .500. "All Lane wanted to do was blow his own horn and denigrate everything and everybody else," Bragan later said.[16] Joe Gordon, who had played second base for the Indians and Yankees, was brought in to replace him. In Gordon's first game on the bench, he installed Colavito in the cleanup slot, and his right fielder responded with a home run and two doubles in a winning effort. Gordon took Colavito under his wing, determined to help the young slugger cut down on his swing. To get him away from pulling everything, Gordon wanted Colavito to hit down on the ball and to hit it where it was pitched. In a game in Kansas City, Gordon told Colavito before walking up to the plate to hit the ball the opposite way. To Colavito's surprise, the ball carried 440 feet over the left-center field fence. Gordon began flashing a finger in the air when Colavito came to bat, reminding him to try for a single with the knowledge that the ball could still leave the park.

Colavito's bat picked up steam. He slammed nine home runs in July and 13 in August. Two late-July home runs, including a grand slam, came in a doubleheader against the Yankees in Cleveland, two of the seven he hit that season against them. Colavito began August the same way, blasting two home runs on the first day of the month at home against the Red Sox. Meanwhile, his throwing arm drew oohs and ahhs. In a game against the Red Sox, Colavito threw a ball 380 feet on the fly from deep right field to third base to nail a runner.[17] Later in the season, Gordon would remark, "Fundamentally, he doesn't have a weakness except for his own intensity. He can hit any kind of pitch to any part of the field."[18] But Colavito could also mess up, such as when the Athletics' Harry Chiti's catchable fly ball dropped untouched behind him in the right field corner with the bases loaded in an 8–7 loss, prompting a reporter to call the play a "colossal fluff."[19]

The *Cleveland Plain Dealer's* Harry Jones marveled over Colavito's earnestness and unfettered love of the game. "That must be part of Rocky's tremendous popularity in Cleveland—and no player has ever been more popular with the fans there," Jones wrote. "They must sense his rugged determination and self-confidence. Of course, he is popular also because he plays hard every minute of every game. To the spectator, Rocky looks as though he plays baseball for the sheer enjoyment of the game."[20] Colavito visited children in area hospitals during the season to boost their spirits. One visit was particularly hard. "A boy's last request was to meet me," Colavito said of a frail child who had barely reached his teens and had lost 50 pounds. "I never minded the time to do that type of thing, but it broke my heart to see him, knowing he was going to die," an emotional Colavito recalled 60 years later.

Colavito reached the 30-home run mark he had predicted to Bragan and hit his 35th on September 12 with a flourish, smashing a grand slam into Municipal Stadium's upper deck in left field, one of the longest home runs Colavito hit there. The four-bagger gave him 102 runs batted in for the year, the first time he reached the 100-RBI mark. Colavito received a congratulatory telegram from Bragan the following day. The accomplishment meant a lot to Colavito, who had been burdened by Bragan's announcement to the press that he had promised 35 home runs instead of 30. Colavito hit his 40th home run of the year in Cleveland on September 26 off the Tigers' Billy Hoeft, but Gordon was more impressed with a ball the slugger pushed into right field with the bases loaded to knock in the winning run. "He's just coming into his own as a great hitter," Gordon said.[21]

Colavito had a brief scare at home in September, when two-year-old Rocco Jr., was hospitalized in an oxygen tent with suspected bronchitis. He rushed home to be with his son. When little Rocco improved, he returned to the team and concluded the season with his 41st home run off Jim Bunning as the Indians squeezed past the Tigers to finish in fourth place. The victory earned the players, most of whom worked off-season jobs, an extra $500 each. The home run also forced Mickey Mantle, who held a slim, 42–41 lead in home runs over Colavito, to stay with the Yankees for the team's final game, Colavito recalled with some amusement. "Mickey said I made him miss his plane. They were going to let him take an early flight and skip the last game, but made him stay just in case I homered," Colavito said. Mantle's lead held up when Colavito was unable to connect in his last game.

Colavito excelled in another way in 1958—as a pitcher. He often warmed up before the game with a catcher since they had padded mitts to catch his fast throws. "How fast is he?" Gordon asked catcher J. W. Porter one day, curious about how hard Colavito threw. "Faster than anybody," Porter replied.

"Faster than Score or Duren?" Gordon asked, referring to Herb Score and fireballing reliever Ryne Duren. "Faster than anybody," Porter repeated.[22] The Indians and the Cincinnati Reds played an annual home-and-home exhibition series for charity, and Gordon asked Colavito to pitch in both games. Colavito proceeded to record an eyebrow-raising five strikeouts in two innings to go with no walks and two singles. "Displaying amazing control, considerable poise, and a blazing fast ball, the Rock was an instant success in his debut on the mound here tonight," the *Cleveland Plain Dealer* reported.[23] He pitched four days later in the return match in Cleveland, tossing another scoreless inning despite loading the bases.

The results convinced Gordon he'd try Colavito in a regular-season game. "I know that if I ever was going to use him it would be with first base open, runners in scoring position and needing a strikeout," Gordon said.[24] That turned out to be in the second game of an August 13 doubleheader at home against Detroit. The Tigers were ahead, 2–1, with runners on second and third and no outs in the seventh inning when Gordon came out to the mound, took the ball from Hoyt Wilhelm—who had a Hall of Fame career as a reliever—and motioned to Colavito in right field. "I thought he was bringing in either Ray Narleski, whose sign was one index finger straight down because he could throw hard, or Don Mossi, for whom Gordon would put his two hands behind his ears and stick them out, because he had big ears," Colavito said. "This was before there were phones in the bullpen. I turned around to see which one he wanted, and then I realized he wanted me. I pointed at my chest and he shook his head up and down, so I trotted in." The crowd couldn't believe it, either. "In all my years I have never experienced the sense of sheer electric excitement that filled the park at that moment," a veteran Cleveland sportswriter said.[25]

The 14,351 in attendance watched Colavito run in to the mound and take his eight warmup pitches. Then they waited on the edge of their seats to see how the power-hitting outfielder would do from the pitching rubber. Colavito inherited a one-ball, one-strike count on light-hitting shortstop Coot Veal, and the first pitch was in for a strike. Colavito thought he struck Veal out on the next pitch with a high fastball right down the middle, but home plate umpire Ed Runge called it a ball. Coach Jo Jo White was ejected when he protested the call from the bench. Russ Nixon, Colavito's catcher, also expressed his disagreement with the call, later telling the press, "the ball got a good piece of the plate."[26] On the next pitch, Veal lifted a fly to left field deep enough to score the runner from third for what proved to be the winning run. After Colavito walked pitcher Herb Moford, Nixon said something Runge didn't like and he, too, was tossed out of the game, with Gordon ejected right after him. With Porter now behind the plate, Colavito induced Harvey Kuenn to pop up to the outfield and retired Rene Bertoia on an infield pop to close out the inning. "It was a novelty, and the crowd went bananas," Colavito said. "They were clapping, and when I went off the field, Carmen and my mother-in-law went bananas too."

Colavito went on to pitch scoreless eighth and ninth innings, allowing three walks, no hits, and striking out one in three innings of work. He also contributed with his bat, hitting a double and triple in the 3–2 loss. It was quite a showing for the right fielder-turned-pitcher who had never worked with a pitching coach. "I had an idea what pitching was about, and I never felt awkward as a pitcher," Colavito said. "I would have loved to pitch if they would have let me play the other three days." It was the only time he would pitch for the Indians. "He's my right fielder, period," Gordon said in 1959. "But I'll tell you this. As a pitcher, he'd be a 20-game winner. He has the greatest arm I ever saw."[27]

Colavito said previous history affected the home plate calls that resulted in the three ejections. He claimed Runge had it in for him for a past incident in Kansas City, in which they clashed over a call at second base after Colavito was called out. Colavito insisted his foot was on the bag and he should have been safe, and Runge countered by saying, "You're a fucking liar," Colavito said. That led the ballplayer to lose control and fire a few choice words of his own at the umpire before being restrained by teammates. The next day, Colavito said a pitcher told him that Runge had said he would call Colavito out if he threw a pitch anywhere close to the plate.

> I never got fined, suspended or thrown out for what happened, but from that day on, he stuck it to me royal. We're in Scottsdale at spring training a couple of years later, and twice with the bases loaded Runge called me out on pitches high and outside that you couldn't reach. We played the Cubs in Mesa the next day, and while we're sitting around the batting cage, Runge called me over. He said, "Hey Rock, everything all right?" I said, "Yeah, why?" and he said, "OK."

Colavito felt Runge was testing him to see if he would complain about his treatment. "From then on, he gave me a fair shake," Colavito said. "He was a good balls-and-strikes umpire when he wanted to be."

The fourth-place Indians finished the 1958 season with a 77–76 record, 14½ games behind the Yankees, a one-game improvement over the previous year. Russ Nixon, in his second season, had a career year with a .301 average in 301 at-bats. Vic Wertz slugged 28 home runs, and Vic Power, a defensive whiz, hit .317. Colavito was enamored of Power's glove work. "Vic Power was the best first baseman I ever saw, without a doubt," he said. Cal McLish anchored the pitching staff with a 16–8 record and 2.99 ERA. But the team's most productive player was Colavito, who had a career-best .303 batting average with 41 home runs and 113 RBI. His home run total was one shy of Mantle's despite 52 fewer at-bats. Colavito was just two home runs shy of Al Rosen's all-time Indians record. His 113 runs batted in was also runner-up to Red Sox outfielder Jackie Jensen's 122. Colavito led the league in extra base hits and home runs per at-bat, and he had a major league-high .620 slugging percentage, besting the .616 mark of Cubs shortstop Ernie Banks. Colavito also led the league in a defensive category, throwing out six runners on the tail end of double plays. Colavito said he wasn't that disappointed for falling one home run short of tying for the American League home-run crown because he hit over .300, the only time in his career he did so. "I thought hitting .303 was a helluva accomplishment because I didn't run exceptionally well, and infielders could play deep and still throw me out by half a step," he said.

Without Colavito, the Indians might easily have sunk into the second division, and the post-war attendance low of 663,805 might have been even lower at a time when William R. Daley, the Indians' chairman of the board, was considering moving the team. Still, attendance was in a free-fall. There were half as many people at Indians games as there were four years ago, and only about a quarter of the 2.6 million who flocked to the stadium ten years earlier in 1948. Only the Washington Senators had a lower attendance in the American League.

Colavito's break-out year placed him third in voting for the 1958 Most Valuable Player Award. He received 181 votes, behind Jensen, who received

Colavito listens to Cleveland Indians President William R. Daley after being presented the Indians' Man of the Year Award at a 1958 banquet (Colavito's personal collection).

233, and Yankees 20-game winner Bob Turley, with 191. There were Colavito boosters who felt he was more deserving than Jensen, who hit .286 with 35 home runs to go with his 122 RBI. "The selection of Jackie Jensen by the baseball writers as the Most Valuable Player in the American League is a travesty of justice," one fan wrote. "The Rock led Jensen in batting and home runs as well as in slugging percentage. Although having fewer times at bat, Rocky was a close runner-up in the runs batted in department."[28]

Colavito was voted Indians' Man of the Year by the Cleveland chapter of the Baseball Writers' Association of America. "Colavito would be the popular choice if the fans in Cleveland were allowed to vote. He has become the town's top baseball hero, and every move he makes on the field is applauded," *The Sporting News* reported after the young slugger edged out McLish for the honor.[29] The award was presented to Colavito at the annual Ribs and Roast show held in Hotel Hollenden in front of 600 people. He spoke along with Daley and Will Harridge, the retiring president of the American League. Colavito was also spoofed in a "This is Your Life" skit, with *Cleveland Plain Dealer* sportswriter Tom Riley portraying him.

Colavito was also a frequent guest on the banquet circuit after the season ended. At the annual Arco Club Baseball Night in Youngstown, Ohio, he signed autographs and spoke in front of 600 people. "He even passed up the hospitality room, where newsmen, sportscasters and other major leaguers were partaking of refreshments, to mingle with the crowd and to shake hands with all the zest of a veteran politician," a writer said.[30] Colavito attended Pittsburgh's annual Dapper Dan banquet and was honored along with other athletes, including Cleveland Browns running back Jim Brown and Pittsburgh Pirates outfielder Roberto Clemente, on leave from the Marines.[31] Colavito, Mantle, and Ernie Banks, the NL MVP, were honored by the Maryland Professional Baseball Players' Association in Baltimore, and Colavito and Jensen were among those feted at the Columbus Touchdown Club in Columbus, Ohio.[32] In Ashtabula, Ohio, Colavito spoke to a packed crowd of over 550 at the Hotel Ashtabula, discussing the Tribe's chances for the upcoming season. He also appeared at a smaller event that day in the Sons of Italy Hall.

"I did 35 banquets that year," Colavito said. "I didn't want to look at chicken again." Colavito was also named to an all-time team of Italian extraction that winter by the Lt. Milton Kelkey Post No. 575, Jewish War Veterans in Philadelphia. Dolph Camilli was chosen at first base, Tony Lazzeri at second, Phil Rizzuto at short, Frank Malzone at third, and Colavito, Joe DiMaggio, and Carl Furillo were the choices for the outfield. Yogi Berra was picked behind the plate, with Johnny Antonelli on the mound and Dom DiMaggio, Ernie Lombardi and Cookie Lavagetto on the bench.[33]

Colavito also played in several barnstorming games that off-season. The games were a way for cities and towns without baseball teams to see major leaguers up close. That would change with the spread of television and team expansions into more cities. Colavito participated in a four-game set billed as the Mickey Mantle All-Stars versus the Willie Mays All-Stars. Mantle's team included Colavito, Elston Howard, Mickey Vernon, Nellie Fox, Billy Martin, Whitey Ford, and Harvey Kuenn. Mays's roster included Banks, Gil Hodges, Richie Ashburn, and Junior Gilliam. They played their first game in Yankee Stadium, followed by games in Philadelphia, Rochester, and Syracuse. For the final game, the name of the Mantle team was changed to the Rocky Colavito All-Stars to appeal to that city's Italian population. The name change used in advertisements also meant an additional $500 in his pocket. Colavito also played three games in Baltimore that off-season for the Bob Nieman All-Stars, in which major league ballplayers went up against semi-pro players. Colavito hit a pair of round-trippers, and Hal Smith of the Athletics added another in one of the games, played before a crowd of only 700.[34]

Colavito's big year landed him on the cover of *Sport* and other baseball magazines during the season, where he would be featured often over the next several years. His stardom also brought commercial endorsements that boosted his name recognition and bank account. Colavito had lent his name to Carling Black Label Beer in 1957, one of the radio sponsors for Indians games, but the offers started to roll in as he moved into the upper echelon of baseball stars. His endorsements, and often his likeness, began appearing in newspapers, magazines, and other periodicals, promoting a variety of goods that included baseball gloves and bats, hair tonic, hot dogs, chewing gum, scotch whiskey, gasoline, cereal, tea, jello, tires, and a dart game. The companies Colavito pitched products for included Spalding, Louisville Slugger, Armour Meats, Kahn's, Republic Steel, Vitalis, Cooper Tires, General Foods, and Bazooka.[35] Colavito later regretted appearing in an ad for Chesterfield cigarettes, a product Joe DiMaggio, Ted Williams, Willie Mays, Jackie Robinson, and Stan Musial also endorsed. "I was paid $500, which at that time was pretty good, but I wish I never did that because of the kids," he said. "I had to smoke 18 cigarettes to get it right. My wife said it looked awful because anyone could tell I wasn't a smoker."

His involvement with the Spalding company began in the minor leagues when Duke Zilber, a promotions manager and former general manager of the Reading Indians, began signing budding minor leaguers for future endorsements. Zilber made Colavito and Roger Maris his first two signings. They were given a glove and two pairs of baseball shoes each season, regardless of whether they made the majors. Later, royalties were negotiated. Personalized gloves bearing Colavito's signature began appearing in stores in 1959, one year before Maris.[36] "For years, my father would drive up to the ballpark with a trunk full of shoes and gloves," recalled Cindy Yost, who accompanied her late father on summer trips in Pennsylvania and Upstate

THE ROCK PASSES WHITE GLOVE TEST

(HE USES GREASELESS VITALIS)

Rocky Colavito, sensational Cleveland slugger, uses Vitalis for his dry, stubborn hair. Creams and cream-oil hair tonics? He took a cut at 'em but didn't like 'em. They gave his hair that greased-down look, left messy stains. That's why the Rock goes for Vitalis. Vitalis® took the grease *out* of hair tonic ... put in V-7®, the *greaseless* grooming discovery. It keeps hair neat all day, leaves no greasy stains as leading creams and cream-oils do. And Vitalis protects against dry hair and scalp, fights embarrassing dandruff. Try Vitalis yourself ... today!

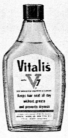

VITALIS KEEPS HAIR NEAT ALL DAY WITHOUT GREASE

...prevents dryness, too.

ANOTHER FINE PRODUCT OF BRISTOL-MYERS

Colavito did numerous commercial endorsements beginning in 1958. This one is for Vitalis hair tonic (Colavito's personal collection).

A baseball dart game was among Colavito's commercial endorsements (Harvey Weber's personal collection).

and Western New York. "We'd go super early, and the guys would all come out and gather around the trunk. These guys were starting out and had nothing, and they never forgot him for that when they made it. He was so beloved. He was way ahead of his time in marketing and building relationships," Yost said.[37] Zilber had also been a minor-league umpire for ten years, including at the Brooklyn Dodgers' Vero Beach, FL, spring training site in 1946, where newly-signed Jackie Robinson was trying to make the Montreal Royals, the team's top minor league club. Because of segregation, Robinson wasn't allowed to change his clothes with the white players, so Zilber, a Jew and no stranger to discrimination, brought Robinson into the umpires' dressing quarters to change, Yost said.

As the 1959 season began to take shape in the off-season, Colavito found himself the only outfielder still on the team from the eight on the roster one year earlier.[38] He expressed confidence to a reporter that the 1958 season wasn't a fluke. "I always had complete confidence in myself because I always knew I wanted to be a big-leaguer more than anything else in the world, and no matter what happened I was going to bear down and be one," he said. "I'm just as confident that my strong finish wasn't luck."[39] Before the season began, Colavito had another contentious contract negotiation with Lane. It was still nearly two decades before the start of free agency, which would offer a pathway for players to make more money by signing with other clubs. Salaries were still minuscule compared to the multi-million-dollar contracts that would become commonplace. Mantle had earned $75,000 in 1958 and was seeking $90,000, which baseball scribes noted was closing in on the still unattainable $100,000 contract as team salaries approached a milestone. "The Yankees' team budget was nearing $700,000. Are the majors going to see the million-dollar payroll? The players think so," a columnist in *The Sporting News* said.[40] As Lane and Colavito disagreed over salary in what was officially a holdout, Lane blasted him in the press in an effort, Colavito thought, to turn the public against him. Colavito was seeking $35,000, but ultimately settled for $28,000. Bob Kennedy, now working as an aide to Lane, said the GM was furious at Colavito. "Frank would be hollering and swearing on the phone … hollering like blue blazes, and you could hear him out in the office. And I know that all Rocky was saying on the other end was, 'No.' He wouldn't argue with Frank. He'd just say no, and I think that made Frank ten times madder."[41]

The accolades for Colavito were rolling in as the 1959 season approached. "The kid next door, all dressed up in an Indians suit, is about to take over as baseball's foremost gate attraction," the *Cleveland Plain Dealer's* Gordon Cobbledick wrote. "The name—mark it well—is Rocco Domenico Colavito. He's a handsome, boyish, 25-year-old outfielder who doesn't smoke, drink or use violent language. He says 'Please, sir' and 'Thank you, sir,' and likes practically everybody, including the pitchers who knock him down, in retaliation for what he does to them." Cobbledick went on to say that Colavito had "won the tag of 'the new Babe Ruth.'"[42] Colavito was also compared to the popular "The Rifleman" series starring Chuck Connors in a letter from a New Jersey fan to *The Sporting News*. "I think the fans will agree with me on this count:

Although Rocky Colavito is not six feet, six inches tall, doesn't have blond hair, never played for the Dodgers and doesn't appear on a weekly TV show, when the Rock fires that ball from his right-field post, he certainly looks like 'The Rifleman' featured on TV."[43] (Colavito met Connors, who also played for the Chicago Cubs and the NBA Boston Celtics before turning to acting, in 1966.)

Going into the 1959 season, the Tribe's pitching staff was headed by Cal McLish, Gary Bell and Mudcat Grant, with Herb Score still on the comeback trail. The outfield was set with Minoso and Colavito at the corners and Gold Glove center fielder Jimmy Piersall in center, after being acquired from the Red Sox for Wertz and Geiger. Carroll Hardy and newly-acquired Tito Francona were slated for outfield reserve roles. Russ Nixon and Dick Brown were handling the catching chores, with Vic Power at first base, Billy Martin at second, Woodie Held a shortstop, and George Strickland at third. Getting ready for the season, Colavito hit three home runs in an exhibition game against the Giants in an 11–8 loss on March 19, but one was taken away for batting out of turn.

Colavito hit his first homer of the season as the Indians won their sixth game in a row out of the starting gate. The blast off relief pitcher George Brunet, which just cleared the left field fence, came in a 13–4 rout of the Athletics, along with round-trippers by Power, Held, and Martin. Colavito's seventh homer, on May 8 against the White Sox, put him 30 games ahead of his 1958 pace. The team's record after that game stood at 15–6. White Sox manager Al Lopez acknowledged following the game that he had sold Colavito short. "There was a doubt in my mind about Rocky," his former skipper said. "Because he is slow, I thought he'd have to hit a ton to overcome his weaknesses. Because he could be pitched to, I questioned whether he'd ever hit enough. He's come a long way. He's an improved hitter, and Joe Gordon deserves credit for making him better. Rocky deserves credit, too, for his determination."[44]

On May 28, Colavito hit his 100th career home run off the Athletics' 16-game winner, Bud Daley. It came in his 1,432nd at-bat, making him the fastest American League player and the second-fastest player in history to reach 100 home runs. Only Ralph Kiner, with 1,351 at-bats, reached the milestone faster. It was quite an accomplishment for the 25-year-old. But Colavito's greatest individual game was less than two weeks away.

8

The Fantastic Four

Rocky Colavito was stuck in a slump even if he pretended they didn't exist. After getting off to an uncharacteristically fast start, the Tribe's cleanup hitter was 5-for-41 since May 28, a stretch of 11 games, as the Indians prepared to play the Orioles on June 10, 1959. His dormant bat had dropped his batting average 41 points, from .318 to .277. Colavito wasn't batting at home in the friendly confines of Municipal Stadium, or home run-friendly Fenway Park with its beckoning Green Monster. The Indians were at Baltimore's Memorial Stadium, the most difficult ballpark in the league to homer in since the St. Louis Browns relocated there in 1954.

The foul poles down each line were 309 feet away, but the power alleys in left- and right-center fanned out to 380 feet from home plate, with the center field fence 410 feet away. The ballpark fences were farther away in the team's first few years, when the power alleys were 446 feet from home plate, before the distance was reduced to 405 feet in 1956 and 380 feet in 1958. The center field fence began 445 feet away, went to 450 the next year and 424 the third before being brought in to 410 feet in 1958. In the five-plus seasons the Orioles had played there, only seven players had hit two home runs in one game, and no team had slugged more than three.[1] It was probably no accident that the 1958 All-Star Game in Baltimore is the only Midsummer Classic played from 1933 to 2018—including the four years in which two games were played—where there were no extra-base hits. That happened despite the likes of Willie Mays, Stan Musial, and Ernie Banks batting for the National League, and Mickey Mantle, Ted Williams, and Jackie Jensen swinging for the Junior Circuit.

Before the Baltimore game, *Cleveland Plain Dealer* sportswriter Harry Jones asked Colavito, as he waited his turn at the batting cage, whether he expected to get untracked that night. "Hey Rock, when are you going to come out of the slump?" Colavito responded as he often did when the notion of a slump was suggested. "I turned around slowly and said, 'Harry, what slump?' and he said, 'Come on, you know what I mean.' And I played stupid and said,

'I don't know what you're talking about. If you're saying I'm having a little tough time, that's true, but a slump? I don't believe in them.' I added, 'You never know, Harry, it just might be tonight.'"[2] Colavito's confidence at the plate extended beyond how he was hitting at any given time. "I always thought I could do it," he said. "I could go 0-for-30, and thought I was getting a hit in my 31st at-bat," he said. An article that came out that day in *The Sporting News*, "Best Bet to Beat Bambino's 60?" put added attention on Colavito and his suddenly quiet bat. He was named the American League player most likely to break Babe Ruth's single-season home run mark.[3]

There was no indication anything unusual was in store during Colavito's first at-bat. He drew a walk from pitcher Jerry Walker and scored on a three-run homer by left fielder Minnie Minoso, staking Indians starter Gary Bell to an early lead. Colavito's bat became unglued in the third inning when he lofted a slider down the left field line, watching at home plate to see which side of the foul pole it would pass. "I knew it would go far enough, but I was worried about staying fair because it was close to the line," Colavito said. "It was only 309 down the line, but there was a wall close to 15 feet high. It was like a wall and then a small fence on top of the wall. I stayed right at home plate, which you don't do if it's a line drive." When the umpire signaled the 360-foot drive fair, Colavito trotted around the bases with his team now up, 6–3. Colavito was challenged defensively in the bottom of the inning, when Orioles leadoff hitter Albie Pearson pulled a line drive down the right field line. Colavito got a good jump and made the catch near the wall. But as he caught the ball with his glove hand out, a spectator threw a cup of beer into Colavito's face. "You talk about angry or livid, that was me," Colavito said. "That was really unsportsmanlike. I was so mad and upset. I said, 'You son of a bitch. I'll meet you after the game and see how tough you are. I'll kick your ass all over the park.' "He said, 'I'll be there.' I said, 'I'll meet you right outside the clubhouse.'"

When Colavito came up for a third time in the fifth inning, Walker had been replaced by reliever Arnold Portocarrero. The pitcher threw a low fastball on the outside corner, knee-high, and Colavito crushed a line drive 425 feet, landing nearly 50 feet past the fence in left-center.[4] Portocarrero was still on the mound when Colavito came up in the sixth inning with a runner on base. This time, he tagged a low fastball 420 feet over the fence in left-center, marking the second time he had hit three home runs in a game as a professional. The other time had come in an Eastern League Class A game in 1953. As Colavito trotted out to right field in the bottom of the sixth, he was greeted by a standing ovation from the bleachers, including the man who had doused him with beer three innings earlier.

I was standing in the outfield after my third homer and I heard somebody yell, "Break the record. Hit another the next time up." Subconsciously, I was thinking of that, too. But I forced the thought out of my mind. I looked up toward heaven and said, "Dear God, I'm not greedy. I'll be happy if I can get a single next time. I always talk to God. He's been good to me. He gave me whatever talent I have. The rest is up to me to use it."[5]

Colavito came up for one more at-bat in the ninth inning against Ernie Johnson, a veteran relief pitcher in his last season. Johnson bragged to some of his fellow pitchers, Colavito was told later, that he'd show them how to get the Indians' slugger out. Herb Score, sitting at the edge of the dugout, offered words of encouragement. "OK, roomie, don't fool around. Go hit that fourth home run," Colavito recalled. "I turned around, and as I'm walking up I said something like, 'Yeah, right, roomie. I'll be glad if I get a single.' And Herbie said, 'Bullshit! Go out and do it,' and I looked at him over my shoulder as I walked toward the plate." Score wasn't alone in thinking about a fourth home run. So were the players on the field and in the dugouts, the 15,883 fans in attendance, and those glued to their radios and televisions as broadcasters Jimmy Dudley and Bob Neal called the game on WERE-AM, with Ken Coleman behind the mic for TV station WEWS, a rarity since games weren't usually televised on weekdays. But Colavito didn't go up to the plate trying to hit a home run. "No way," he said. "I really didn't go up there thinking about it. I wasn't putting pressure on myself, and I hadn't had a 4-for-4 night maybe all season. I was only interested in hitting the ball hard. I always tried to hit the ball hard somewhere."

Colavito settled in at home plate for that eventful at-bat. "The first pitch Ernie Johnson throws me is under my chin. I took it and let it go past. He throws me another fast ball up and in, only this one is in the strike zone, and the high fastball is the ball I like to hit, and I hit that one as good as any of them." Left fielder Gene Woodling could only watch as the ball landed in an exit halfway up the bleachers, 420 feet away. Colavito circled the bases, jumped on home plate with both feet, and tipped his cap to the roaring crowd. When he ran out to right field for the bottom of the ninth, he was greeted once more by a standing ovation, including his antagonist. "I didn't completely forget he threw the beer in my face, although I looked right at him, and the look on his face was respectful," Colavito said. (He still went to the clubhouse door after the game in the event the guy showed up. "I made sure I wasn't backing down from nobody," he said.)

Bell, the starting pitcher, returned from the clubhouse to the dugout in case Colavito hit the historic homer. "I was standing in my shorts when he hit the last one because I had come running out to watch the last at-bat," Bell told a reporter after the game. "I just wanted to see it."[6] The fourth home run gave the team an added cushion in the Indians' 11–8 victory. In attendance that night was one of Colavito's favorite people in baseball, former Indians general manager Hank Greenberg. He had planned to leave early but stayed after the third home run to see if Colavito could hit a fourth. "It really hit home when the game was over, and people congratulated me," Colavito said. "There were no flukes," marveled Indians center fielder Jim Piersall after the game. "He deserved every one. The Rock hit them in the toughest park in baseball."[7] Indians GM Frank Lane remarked, "I think the only park harder to hit it out of was Yosemite."[8] Back in Reading, Carmen was at home listening to the game with her parents and neighbors. "I understand they went bananas when I did it," said Colavito, who called her after the game to share his excitement.

Twelve-year-old Basil Russo watched the game on TV with his Sicilian grandfather inside a two-family home in an Italian neighborhood off Woodlawn Avenue in Cleveland. He sat on a couch in the den next to the easy chair reserved for his grandfather. "My grandfather loved Rocky Colavito, and with each home run he hit, he became more and more excited," Russo recalled a half-century later, choking up at the memory. "He was a tough, crusty old immigrant who did not show a lot of emotion. But when Colavito hit that fourth home run, my grandfather actually had tears of joy running down his face. That was the only time in my life I ever saw my grandfather shed a tear. He grabbed my hand, and I hugged him. It is the most precious memory I have of him."

Ten-year-old Thomas Rudar, Jr., watched Colavito's feat on a 12-inch RCA television screen with his father in their home in Cleveland's Little Italy. It was hot, and a fan was whirring in the center window. When Colavito hit the fourth home run, Rudar's father shouted, "There she goes. When Rocky hits them, they stay hit," his son recalled. The sounds of neighbors excited by what had just

Colavito's four-home-run game was big news on the *Cleveland Plain Dealer*'s front page (Barcroft Media).

happened also filled the air. "We lived next to Lakeview Cemetery, and the next day about a half-dozen of my friends and I took turns trying to imitate Rocky by hitting four in a row over the cemetery wall," Rudar said. "Rocky's four home-run night was all we talked about that summer."

The ball Colavito drove into the left-field bleachers for his last home run was retrieved by Indians traveling secretary Harold "Spud" Goldstein. He gave the fan who caught it an autographed ball from Colavito, a second autographed ball from Score, and $25. "Place the name Rocky Colavito next to those of baseball's immortal sluggers," the *Cleveland Plain Dealer* said the next day under the six-column headline, "Colavito Slams 4 Homers: Tribe Wins."[9] The *Associated Press*'s headline read, "Tribe's Rocky Colavito Ties Record in Major's Toughest Home Run Park." The photograph showed a smiling Colavito in the clubhouse, flanked by Minnie Minoso and second baseman Billy Martin, who also homered in the game to double the Baltimore ballpark's record for home runs by a team. Both pretended to be admiring Colavito's arm muscles.[10] Another AP photo that went out across the country showed Colavito kissing his "power-laden bat." "I felt no pressure whatsoever," a grinning Colavito said after the game. "I wasn't trying to hit the ball out of the park on any of them. I was only trying to get base hits."[11] Asked by a reporter if he would try for a record fifth consecutive homer in the next game, he joked, "No, I think I'll bunt," as he headed for the showers.[12] "The Cleveland clouter's four circuits in successive times at bat in Baltimore Wednesday night stands as one of the great batting feats in baseball history," the *New York Daily News* proclaimed. "He looks like DiMaggio, and he's hitting homers at a Ruthian clip."[13] The *Baltimore News-Post* ran a photo a couple of months later that superimposed Gene Woodling in the left field stands when Colavito was at-bat with the headline, "The Colavito Shift."[14]

Colavito scored five runs, drove in six and had 16 total bases in the game. The home runs were also his 15th, 16th, 17th and 18th of the season, one behind the Senators' Harmon Killebrew for the league lead. Fifteen had come off right-handed pitchers, despite the disadvantage right-handed batters face compared to batting against left-handers. The four-home run game drew an invitation to appear on "The Ed Sullivan Show" that coming Sunday, along with a check for $500 from CBS contingent on his appearance. But the game against the Bronx Bombers in Yankee Stadium ended at 9:40 p.m., too late for the waiting limousine to get him to the theater for the one-hour show that aired at 8. "All I had to do was stand up and wave—for $500!" Colavito said later in almost disbelief.[15] "Good night, Rocky, wherever you are," Sullivan said at the end of the show.[16] The slugger was presented with a plaque in recognition of his feat by Lawrence Gerosa, New York City comptroller, before the Indians-Yankees game on June 20. That evening, Colavito was celebrated at a block party in his old Bronx neighborhood, with

Colavito was honored in his hometown Bronx neighborhood on June 20, 1959, ten days after tying a major league record by hitting four home runs in a game (Colavito's personal collection).

his father and other family members present. Several teammates, including Score, also attended.

Hitting four home runs in a game remains one of baseball's rarest and most difficult feats. When Reds second baseman Scooter Gennett launched four home runs in a row into the seats at Cincinnati's Great American Ballpark in June 2017, and Diamondbacks right fielder J. D. Martinez hit four out in Dodger Stadium three months later, that marked just the 15th and 16th times since the live-ball era began in 1920. Colavito was the fifth to do so, and only the second after Lou Gehrig, one of Colavito's favorite players as a kid, to hit all four in a row. Joe Adcock, who would be Colavito's manager in 1967, was the most recent player to hit four in a game, which he did for the Milwaukee Braves against the Brooklyn Dodgers at Ebbets Field in 1954. Johnson, who gave up the fourth home run, witnessed two other four-home-run games. He was a teammate of Adcock's when he did it and was in the broadcast booth 32 years later when the Braves' Bob Horner hit four home runs at Atlanta-Fulton County Stadium in 1986.

Colavito hit four home runs in one day two seasons later, on August 27, 1961. He was playing for the Tigers at Griffith Stadium. He hit a home run in the first game of a doubleheader and added three in the second game, all to left field. Less than a year later, Colavito came within a foul ball of being the only player to hit four home runs in a single game twice, even as he notched his third three-home run game in four years. The July 5, 1962, game was in Cleveland, and Colavito launched his first two homers off Pedro Ramos, a 20-game loser that year despite a respectable 3.95 ERA. The third came off Frank Funk, who would win 11 games, lose 11, and save 11 that season. On Colavito's last at-bat, he sent a ball down the left-field line that landed in the upper deck, barely in foul territory. "It was hooking, and I stood there knowing it was a matter of fair or foul," Colavito said. "I was really sick. I knew I'd be the only one in history to hit four home runs in a game twice, consecutively no less." Instead, Colavito ended the at-bat by hitting the ball hard up the middle and was thrown out by the second baseman. "That one I really, really wanted," he said.

9

Going, Going, Gone

The four home runs in the Baltimore game did more than put Rocky Colavito in the record books—they kept him in an Indians uniform. Frank Lane and Red Sox GM Bucky Harris had hammered out a blockbuster trade the day before that would have sent Colavito, catcher Russ Nixon, and pitcher Cal McLish to the Red Sox for outfielder Jackie Jensen, catcher Sammy White, and pitcher Frank Sullivan. Despite Colavito's breakout 1958 season, Lane still wanted to trade him. "Harris loved the trade. He knew Colavito's tremendous potential at Fenway Park, and also knew that the colorful Colavito would bring in a lot of fans," a Boston sportswriter revealed later. The four-home-run game sank those plans. The next day, Lane called Harris to tell him the deal was off. "They'll run me out of Cleveland if I do [it]," he said.[1]

Meanwhile, the Indians were winning, and fans were coming to the ballpark in numbers not seen in years. This was in no small part due to the fans' adoration of Colavito. "The new-look Indians, off to a fast start, are within 200,000 of their entire 1958 attendance," *The Sporting News* observed in June. "Cleveland fans are enchanted by the hitting heroics of Rocky Colavito, one of the most exciting players to come along in years."[2] *Look* magazine gushed, "The likeliest heir to the American League line of Ruth, DiMaggio and Williams is Rocky Colavito, 25-year-old Cleveland right fielder."[3]

There were occasional sightings of Colavito at a restaurant or along Mayfield Road in Little Italy, said Thomas Rudar, Jr., who lived in the neighborhood. "All the tough Italian guys who boxed at the Alta House would melt like butter when Rocky was around," he said. Colavito, on a few occasions, made public appearances at Our Lady of Lourdes Shrine in Euclid, a suburb outside Cleveland where he spoke to the kids in a suit and tie.

I remember that he wasn't an imposing figure. As he spoke to us, he would squat down like a catcher so as not to hover over us, and look us directly in the eyes. Of course, the good sisters were standing over us to make sure we didn't ask any silly or inappropriate questions. I asked him about his four-home-run game, and he touched me on my right shoulder and said he wasn't hitting very well at the time, but it was only a matter of time before he caught fire.

Colavito handed out 75-cent tickets supplied by the Indians for seats near the right field foul pole for the upcoming Saturday game. "The seats were right across from our hero, where we were able to watch him camp under a fly, make throws with his great arm to the cut-off man, and play catch between innings with Jimmy Piersall in center field," Rudar said.[4]

Piersall, a two-time Gold Glove winner, was coping with bipolar disorder at a time when the disease was less understood. Piersall co-authored the 1955 book *Fear Strikes Out*, an account of his struggles that was turned into a 1957 movie starring Anthony Perkins. He had a 17-year career before becoming a coach and broadcaster. Colavito considered Piersall an outstanding center fielder and unforgettable character. "He was a pretty damn good player. He did a lot of screwball things, but you couldn't dislike him. I saw him go up in the stands in Boston—he galloped right in after somebody. Another time, in Detroit, he told me as he was running off the field that he had spit on a couple of guys who had been heckling him."

Tragedy struck the 1959 season when one of Colavito's young fans died in the stands during a June 23 game in Cleveland. "A fair-haired little boy who loved baseball more than anything else in his short life is dead today," the *Cleveland Press* reported.

Colavito kneels to speak to young fans (Colavito's personal collection).

He was Barry Stewart Packer, only 8 years old, who died last night at the stadium as his hero, Rocky Colavito, stepped to the plate. "I hope Rocky hits a home run," were the last words he ever spoke. Barry was the son of Mr. and Mrs. Bernard B. Packer, Beachwood. They had taken him to see his favorite Indians play Baltimore in sort of a post-birthday celebration. Barry's birthday was eight days ago. Barry suddenly slumped over in his seat at a high point in the game. "I thought he was playing," his father said today. "Then I just thought he had fainted." They carried him to the first aid station, and Barry was pronounced dead about 10 p.m. "He died at his happiest moment—at a baseball game," his grief-stricken mother Delores, who is under sedation, sobbed.[5]

When the 1959 American League All-Star team was announced, Colavito, with 24 home runs, was voted a starting outfielder. Making the team and being in the company of the game's best players was a dream come true. "It's something I'd been hoping for since I was a kid," Colavito said. "Having the players vote you on makes a fellow feel wonderful."[6] That day was special, he said years later. "I wanted to be a big-league ballplayer all my life. I was thrilled to be an All-Star and could never understand why someone wouldn't want to play. There was a meeting before the game, and you couldn't help but look around. You don't star gaze or anything like that; you don't want to seem like you're in awe of these guys because you're one of them. But I was thrilled to death." Colavito played in an era when players strongly identified with the league they played in. "I was proud to represent the American League. I heard Larry Sherry in an interview say in a braggart fashion that the National League was better, and I grinded my teeth," he said, referring to the Dodgers pitcher. "I never heard an American League player say something like that, never."

Without playing in the World Series, baseball's annual cavalcade of stars was Colavito's only opportunity to shine on a national stage. The lone exception was an occasional appearance on Major League Baseball's "Game of the Week," televised on Saturday afternoons. Playing in Cleveland, and not in a major media market like New York, made the All-Star Game exposure even more significant. Colavito started in right field in the first game, which the National League won at Pittsburgh's Forbes Field, 5–4. He batted fifth and went 1-for-3 with a single up the middle off Don Drysdale. When it was time for Colavito's fourth at-bat, he was pinch-hit for by Ted Williams. Colavito didn't like being taken out for a pinch-hitter—something commonly done in All-Star Games to help get players into the game—but being taken out for Williams cushioned the blow. "If I had to get pinch-hit for, I'm glad it was Ted—he's the best," Colavito said after the game.[7]

The second All-Star game was held on August 3 in Los Angeles Memorial Coliseum, where the Dodgers played four seasons before moving into Dodger Stadium. The field offered unusual outfield dimensions. It was just 250 feet down the left field line, with a 42-foot-high screen, and 300 feet down the right field line. The distance to right-center, however, was 440 feet from home plate. Roger Maris started in right field and went 0-for-2 before Colavito replaced him in the field in the fifth inning. He went 1-for-2, but the ball he hit off Elroy Face in the eighth inning landed far up in the left field bleachers.[8] A researcher later claimed that the ball traveled 455 feet, reaching the 33rd row.[9] The home run by Colavito and homers by Yogi Berra and Frank Malzone accounted for four of the five runs in the AL's 5–3 victory. A photo of the threesome's beaming faces, along with a reference to their Italian heritage, appeared in newspapers across the country the next day. "It's a great day for Italians," Berra said.[10]

Pennant fever started to take hold when the Indians swept a double-header against the Senators to regain first place over the White Sox on July 26. Colavito hit a three-run drive, his 30th, in the nightcap. His 36th and 37th home runs came off Whitey Ford on August 25 as the Indians won their seventh in a row. The 38th came the following day, one of nine he hit against the Bronx Bombers that year after hitting seven out in 1958. The go-ahead blast in the eighth inning gave the Indians a 5–4 victory. "They've found out they haven't found out much about him," Yankees manager Casey Stengel said of his pitchers in his imitable way.[11] That home run put Colavito nine days behind Ruth's single-season home run pace. Ernie Banks and Harmon Killebrew were one behind him. A chart in *The Sporting News* listed their chances of topping the Bambino, noting that the 17 home runs Ruth hit in September 1927 made breaking the record a steep proposition.[12]

An illustration of Colavito that appeared on an August cover of *Time* magazine was more evidence of his rising stature. The article heralded base-ball's new breed of home run sluggers.

> In Cleveland, the new star is a tall, trim (6 feet, 3 inches, 190 pounds), swarthy, hand-some right fielder that makes the bobby-soxers squeal and pulls seasoned fans into Cleveland Stadium two hours early to watch him take his cuts in the batting cage. With his long, right-handed swing, Rocky Colavito is the power man behind the Indians, a long-ball hitter in the tradition of Ruth and Foxx and DiMaggio.... Not even the dedicated Ted Williams approaches the game with more diligence—or more confidence—than Rocky Colavito, a man who lives baseball with the intensity of a Little Leaguer.[13]

Despite playing for an opposing team, the Bronx-born Colavito was popular in Yankee Stadium, where the city's large numbers of Italian-Americans often turned out in abundance. Stadium officials said ticket demand for seats in the lower right field stands were higher when the Indians came to town. "As he goes to his position, he always tips his cap to them and they respond with an ovation," a writer said. "Of course, Rocky, being a star now, does hear a few boos everywhere, but you'd think he played for the Yanks upon first hearing the reception he gets there."[14]

But even with the Indians' winning ways and Colavito's home run prowess, Frank Lane was critical of his star player for not producing enough. A reporter for *Sports Illustrated* who attended an Indians game with Lane in Yankee Stadium that summer described the GM second-guessing his manager, coaches, and players. Lane also exhibited a disturbed personality. With runners on first and second and one out in the eighth inning, and the team down by a run, Colavito strode to the plate. "It's over," Lane said. "Colavito will hit into a double play. Watch," sportswriter Walter Bingham quoted Lane as saying. Colavito lifted a fly into short left which led to a collision between Tony Kubek and Gil McDougald that allowed the tying run to score and landed Colavito on second with a bloop double. Kubek, a shortstop playing outfield that day, lay motionless on the ground. "'I hope he's knocked out,' shouted Lane deliriously," Bingham wrote. "'I hope that Yankee bum is knocked out.'" After Kubek was taken off the field by stretcher, Lane changed his tune. " 'He's a nice boy,' he said. 'I hope he isn't hurt badly.'"[15]

Colavito was used to Lane's derogatory ways. "We were in old Griffith Stadium one day, one of my favorite parks to hit in, and I'm pretty sure we were down 8–4. Anyway, and I say this in modesty, I hit a grand slam off Truman Clevenger, a good pitcher who got me out plenty. I came up a couple of innings later and just missed the ball, skying to short left. I heard later from some of the writers that Lane was in the press box, and when I made the out he called me every kind of SOB there was. That's the kind of guy he was," Colavito said.

First place was in reach for the Indians as the team began a four-game series against the White Sox on August 28, trailing the Pale Hose by 1½ games. The "Go-Go Sox," who relied on pitching, defense, and speed, finished last in the league in home runs but first in stolen bases, earned run average, and fielding percentage. Colavito was told by a White Sox pitcher that manager Al Lopez threatened to fine any hurler $500 for throwing him a first-pitch fastball. In the first game, played before 70,398 fans in Municipal Stadium, there were two outs and two on in a tie game in the seventh inning when White Sox catcher Sherman Lollar lofted a fly ball to left field to Minnie Minoso, who looked as if he was about to catch it. But that didn't happen. "Minoso caught his foot in the bottom of the cyclone fence," Colavito said. "The ball hit his glove and went over. Talk about heartbreaks."

After taking the first game, the White Sox's Dick Donovan pitched a 2–0 shutout, and the White Sox swept a doubleheader the following day, 6–3 and 9–4, with three of the Indians runs coming on a Colavito homer. It was just Colavito's second hit in 17 at-bats in the critical series. The Indians won seven of their next eight games to stay within striking distance of the White Sox, only to lose six of the following eight, finishing a disappointing five games behind the White Sox. "I think we should have won in '59," Colavito

said years later. "We had a better ball club than the White Sox. But I think
the pitching was better managed by Al Lopez. I think that's what beat us. We
just could not seem to beat them. Everything they did was right, and everything by us was wrong. Even the umpires' decisions seemed to go against us."

Differences between Frank Lane and Joe Gordon spilled out in the open
ten days before the end of the season, when the manager announced that he
was resigning after the final game. When the Indians were mathematically
eliminated four days later, Lane fired Gordon and offered the job to Leo
Durocher before reversing himself the next day. He then re-signed Gordon
to a two-year contract. "I'll never forget that," Colavito said. "It told me Lane
wasn't operating on all cylinders."

Colavito and Killebrew were tied with 39 home runs on September 1,
before both hitters' bats plunged into a deep freeze. Colavito's 42nd homer
came in the second game of a September 25 doubleheader against the A's,
two more than Killebrew. But after Killebrew homered in his next-to-last
game, his manager inserted him into the leadoff spot in a bid to get extra at-
bats, and he tied Colavito with a fifth-inning blast. It was the first time the

**Colavito finished one run batted in behind Boston Red Sox slugger Jackie Jensen
in 1959 (Colavito's personal collection).**

AL home-run title was shared since 1935, when the Tigers' Hank Greenberg and the Athletics' Jimmie Foxx each hit 36 out of the park. For Colavito, the home run crown was the first of three titles or awards he hoped to win some-day, along with the RBI title and MVP Award. He was only the ninth American League player to hit 42 home runs in a season, joining Babe Ruth, Hank Greenberg, Jimmie Foxx, Mickey Mantle, Lou Gehrig, Joe DiMaggio, Ted Williams, and Al Rosen, whose mark of 43 remained the most in a Cleveland uniform.

The Indians' 89–65 mark was the team's best record in four years. Colavito, playing every game, batted .257 and knocked in 111 runs, one behind league leader Jackie Jensen. Colavito was first in the American League in total bases with 301 and fourth in slugging percentage. He finished fourth in the balloting for the Most Valuable Player Award, behind Nellie Fox and two other members of the pennant-winning White Sox.

Several players shined for the Indians in 1959, starting with Tito Francona, who hit .363 with 20 homers and 79 RBIs after being acquired from Detroit. Francona came within 34 at-bats of qualifying for the batting title, won by Detroit's Harvey Kuenn, who hit. 353. Francona's outstanding season earned him the Indians' Man of the Year award. Minoso, a .302 hitter, Woodie Held, who slugged 29 home runs, and Jim Baxes, with 15 home runs in 247 at-bats, also excelled. Cal McLish, with 19 wins, and Gary Bell, with 16, led the way on the mound. Led by Colavito, the Indians hit a team-record 167 home runs, beating the previous high mark set in 1950 by three. It was also one more than the Athletics and four more than the Senators, two clubs that made their home parks more homer-friendly prior to the season.

Attendance at Municipal Stadium skyrocketed to 1,497,976. It was a dramatic turnaround after the past three seasons saw attendance decline to 865,467 in 1956, 722,256 in 1957, and 663,805 in 1958, causing the team to consider relocating to another city. The largest turnout of fans since 1951 put a halt to such talk. Lane also stood to gain personally from the surge in attendance. A provision in his contract allowed him to collect a nickel per person over 800,000. That resulted in a bonus of $41,708.55 to go with his $60,000 salary.[16]

After the season, Colavito was one of 19 power hitters to take part in the "Home Run Derby," a syndicated TV show in which two players faced off at a time in 26 half-hour episodes. The objective was to hit the most home runs in nine innings, with three outs per inning and an umpire calling strikes. When one batter was at the plate, the other chatted with broadcaster Mark Scott. The episodes were filmed in December 1959 at Wrigley Field, home of the Pacific Coast League Los Angeles Angels, said to be chosen for its uniform outfield dimensions for left- and right-handed batters. The shows aired from January 9 to July 2, 1960. Hank Aaron led the way with six wins in seven appearances, and Mickey Mantle hit the most home runs, slamming 44 over the wall. Colavito competed twice, losing first to Harmon Killebrew, 6–5, in ten innings, and then to Jackie Jensen, 3–2. He was flown to Los Angeles each time to participate and earned $2,500, the $1,000 loser's share for each contest plus a $500 bonus for hitting three home runs in a row.

It should have been the best of times for the Indians. The club was a pennant contender again, and attendance had scaled a height that until recently appeared out of reach. Colavito's offensive numbers compared favorably over the 1958 and 1959 seasons with Mickey Mantle and Willie Mays, widely considered baseball's best players. During those two seasons, Colavito hit 83 home runs, more than Mantle's 73 and Mays's 63. His 224 RBIs were also more than Mantle's 172 and Mays's 200. But Colavito's importance to the Indians, even after finishing third in the MVP voting one year and fourth

the next, was downplayed by Lane when contract negotiations began for the 1960 season. Lane still wasn't satisfied with the direction of the club, and he wasn't satisfied with Colavito. For the third year in a row, Lane argued that his star player didn't deserve much of a raise. Colavito's average dropped 46 points, and he had tailed off in September with a .207 average, three home runs and 13 RBIs when the team needed him most, Lane said. Tying for the American League home run championship and leading the league in total bases and extra-base hits seemed to carry little weight. Colavito said the GM claimed he left "375 runners on base, or something like that," over the course of the year. "I said, 'Frank, are you kidding? Tell me this: Did Joe DiMaggio and Babe Ruth and Lou Gehrig and Hank Greenberg knock in every run?' I kept going. 'Did Willie Mays? Mickey Mantle?

A publicity still from *Home Run Derby,* a syndicated TV show in which Colavito was one of 19 sluggers to square off in one-on-one contests in December 1959. The series aired in 1960 (Colavito's personal collection).

Stan Musial?' I said, 'If I knocked in every run, you wouldn't have enough money to pay me.'"

Lane brought contract negotiations out into the open in January 1960 when, speaking at a luncheon of the Associated Grocery Manufacturers, he claimed Colavito was seeking $45,000 and had issued a veiled threat of "or else" in a letter received the day before. Lane argued his case to the grocers that Colavito had shrugged off his decline in batting average as insignificant. It seemed like an odd gathering in which to go after Colavito, but Lane may have found the timing advantageous. Colavito charged Lane with "trying to turn the fans against me" by spreading false information. The amount Lane offered had been "ridiculously low," he said, and not the $33,000 reported in the press. Colavito countered Lane's proposal with an intentionally unrealistic figure, but less than the $45,000 Lane claimed. "He really blistered me in those letters, but not once did he mention anything on the positive side," Colavito told a reporter. "I honestly think he'd like to trade me. Maybe that's why he's trying to turn the fans against me. I always had the feeling he didn't like me, and now I'm sure of it." Lane denied trying to trade Colavito for Harvey Kuenn in the same article, as had been rumored. "I'd love to stay in Cleveland," Colavito said. "The fans have been wonderful to me. But ballplayers are like cattle. If we get traded, we've got to go, and that's how it will be."[17]

Discussions about trading Colavito for Kuenn were first broached between Lane and Tigers President Bill DeWitt at baseball's winter meetings in December. In early February—possibly as a negotiating ploy—Lane told reporters he was willing to trade Colavito. "Frank Lane indicates he wouldn't hesitate to trade his star slugger, Rocky Colavito, provided he could get another top-flight performer in return, say Harvey Kuenn," *The Sporting News* reported. But Lane added, "I think Rocky will be playing for us next season. Rocky is popular with the Cleveland fans, and also with me. But not at Rocky's price."[18] On another occasion with the press, Lane seemed to talk himself out of a trade. "Sure, I'd like to have Kuenn. Who wouldn't? I'm a Kuenn man. I like him. But I got to thinking of Harvey's 200 hits, of which maybe 40 would be doubles. The 150 hits for Colavito, well, 42 would be homers. I like the present margin in my favor. Also, Jimmie Dykes [the Tigers manager] wanted to make the deal. That scared me. He's pretty smart."[19]

Lane told reporters he would also be willing to trade Colavito for Mickey Mantle.

> If the Yankees offered Mantle for Rocky, I'd scratch my head. If they offered Art Ditmar and Mantle for Rocky, I would not have to scratch. The deal would be made. Don't forget that Rocky is Italian, and with the number of New York fans who are Italian and want a successor to Joe DiMaggio, Colavito would mean an extra 300,000 fans. Also, Rocky is three years younger than Mantle. Another thing, Rocky is going to beat Ruth's record of 60 homers.

Yankees GM George Weiss was dismayed by Lane's trade talk. "I'm not trading Mantle. I'm not looking for a trade. I don't know what he is talking about."[20]

Colavito wound up signing for $35,000, with a $2,000 bonus Lane insisted was contingent on the cleanup hitter hitting fewer home runs but for a higher average. "The contract incentive Lane put in would tell any half-knowledgeable baseball person that he knew nothing about the game. He was an idiot," Colavito said. Kuenn, who also went through difficult contract negotiations, signed for a reported $42,000. That put the trade talk to rest— or so it was said. "All negotiations to trade Harvey Kuenn for Rocky Colavito are off," DeWitt declared on March 6.[21] Meanwhile, Lane was up to his usual trading ways that off-season, sending 19-game winner Cal McLish, first baseman Gordy Coleman, and second baseman Billy Martin to Cincinnati for second baseman Johnny Temple. Colavito thought the Indians got the worst of it. "Billy Martin was every bit as good a second baseman as Temple. In fact, Martin was better defensively. In spring training of 1960, I played right field behind Temple. I thought at the time that Temple was over the hill. He didn't have Martin's range, and he seemed to be gun shy on double plays." Lane also sent Norm Cash, acquired that off-season from the White Sox, to the Tigers for third baseman Steve Demeter a week before the start of the season. Cash would lead the league in batting in 1961 with a .361 average to go with 41 home runs, played 15 years, and hit 373 of his 377 career homers for the Tigers. Demeter would bat five times for the Tribe and go hitless, retiring with two career hits.

It was during those discussions that Lane and DeWitt revived the on-again, off-again trade talks of Colavito for Kuenn. A new factor was Lane's excitement over the spring training play of 6-foot, 7-inch rookie outfielder Walt Bond who, in trying to make the jump from Class A ball that spring, hit .339 with six home runs and a team-leading 29 runs batted in. "Frank came up to [Hoot Evers and I] and said he wanted to trade Colavito for Harvey Kuenn," team adviser Bob Kennedy said. "And we said, 'Frank, you're gonna get killed if you do this.'" That was on April 16. Lane asked the men to think about it overnight and give him their opinion the next day. "We gave him our reasons for not doing it but said, 'If you think it's that important to you, and if you really want to do it, just go ahead and do it.'"[22] Lane, who was in Memphis, and Dewitt, who was in St. Louis, reached an agreement that day by phone, following eight days of negotiations and dozens of phone calls.[23] Lane announced the trade on April 17, 1960, about an hour after Colavito's eighth home run of the spring cleared the left field fence in the Indians' final exhibition game.

The trade ignited a prairie fire that infuriated and deflated Indians fans, casting a dark cloud that would hover over the franchise for decades. For many Cleveland fans, the date would live as a day of infamy. Colavito had a

Angry Indians fans hang Indians General Manager Frank Lane in effigy after Colavito was traded on April 17, 1960 (Cleveland Press Collection, Michael Schwartz Library, Cleveland State University).

special rapport with fans that was irreplaceable, said Lawry Babitt, who lived on a farm in Oberlin, 35 miles southwest of Cleveland. "Rocky related to people, and people related to him. I think they looked at him as someone who, if they had a kid, they'd want him to grow up like Rocky. In Cleveland, he's family," Babitt said.[24] Susan Grimm, who was 12 and living in Cleveland at the time, was crushed. "He was so good-looking, and my friends and I were all in love with him," Grimm said. "Elvis was big then, but we loved Rocky Colavito much more than we loved Elvis. Then he was taken away from us."[25]

Colavito's teammates were left scratching their heads. "That wasn't a good trade," Indians outfielder Jim Piersall said years later. "Kuenn did a good job for us, but Rocky was a local hero."[26] Gary Bell, the only Indian who played with Colavito during both of his tenures with the team, shared the fans' anger.

> I always really loved Rocky. He was just a super nice guy and a great teammate, and he took care of the fans. That's what I remember most about him, along with the home runs, a great arm, and being a great outfielder, too. Cleveland wanted to kill the GM when they traded Rocky off. He was an idol there, an idol for sure. Harvey was a good ballplayer, but Rocky was beloved in Cleveland. It was like a knife in the heart when they traded him.[27]

Yankees manager Casey Stengel thought Detroit came out better in the trade. "They got themselves a dandy in Colavito," Stengel said. Catcher Elston Howard agreed. "How can they give away a guy who hits 42 homers and knocks in 111 runs, even for someone like Kuenn?" Howard wondered. "Harvey doesn't hurt you like Colavito."[28] Hank Greenberg, now vice president and treasurer of the Chicago White Sox, sent Colavito his best wishes. "Congratulations on going to a club where your talents will be appreciated. Briggs Stadium is made to order for you. Good luck and continued success," Greenberg said.

Nate Dolin, an Indians vice president, was upset by the trade, though he didn't let it be publicly known at the time. "Rocky had almost everything you want in a ballplayer. He was an idol, he could hit the homer, and I was against trading him," Dolin said in 1962.[29] Lane insisted the trade was best for the club. "Rocky could beat Babe Ruth's home-run record," Lane told a reporter. "He's a good slugger; there's no question about that. But I'm for the Kuenn type for this reason: He doesn't strike out that often and he will move men up. Rocky doesn't do that…. People go out to see Rocky hit home runs. They don't go to see Kuenn hit singles. That's so, but people will go out to see a winning ball club."[30]

The trade shocked the baseball world and reignited a debate over who was more valuable—the singles hitter who hits for a high average and gets on base often or the power hitter who drives in more runs. (That could be more perception than reality. In 1958, Colavito had a .405 on-base percentage with a .303 average and 41 home runs, while Kuenn had an on-base of .402, a .319 average and 8 home runs.) The trade also highlighted the infrequency of home run and batting champions having to pack their bags. The only other American League batting champ traded before Kuenn was the Athletics' Ferris Fain, who went to the White Sox before the start of the 1954 season. Five batting champs were traded in the National League. Colavito was the tenth home run leader in the majors to be traded, five in each league. Future Hall of Famer Chuck Klein fulfilled both roles when he was traded to the Cubs after winning the Triple Crown for the Phillies in 1933 batting .368 with 28 homers and 120 RBIs.

In a deal overshadowed by Colavito's trade, Lane sent Herb Score, Colavito's roommate and an Indians favorite, to the White Sox the next day, reuniting the pitcher with former manager Al Lopez. Comedian Bob Hope, who grew up in Cleveland and was a minor investor in the Indians, captured how out of control many believed Lane was. "I'm afraid to go to Cleveland," Hope said. "Frank Lane might trade me."[31] Lane made 49 deals involving 108 Indians players during his three-plus seasons with the club.[32] The lone players on the 40-man roster when Lane arrived in October 1957 who remained in January 1961 when he left were Russ Nixon, who was traded to the Red Sox before the trade was nullified by Commissioner Ford Frick, and George Strickland, who retired for a year before coming back. Lane rarely expressed regret about a trade. "The only deals that irked me are the ones I didn't make," he once said.[33] Trading away Colavito followed him in notoriety to his death in 1981. A *Sports Illustrated* article nearly 30 years after the trade ranked it third-worst in sports history, and the first two were essentially cash transactions. The Red Sox's sale of Babe Ruth to the Yankees in 1919 for $100,000 plus a $300,000 loan, was followed by the sending of manager-shortstop Joe Cronin of the Senators to the Red Sox for $250,000 and shortstop Lyn Lary in 1935.[34]

Lane tried to ignore the public uproar over Colavito's sudden departure. "We've given up 40 home runs for 40 doubles. We've added 50 singles and taken away 50 strikeouts," the GM said. Lane also characterized the deal another way: "I swapped a hamburger for a steak," with DeWitt countering, "I like hamburger."[35] At the winter meetings in December 1964, nearly five years later, Lane continued defending the trade. "Rocky always does very well for Rocky, but has anyone ever won a pennant with him?" said Lane, who failed to win a pennant as general manager for five clubs. "Home run hitters are fine when they hit a home run, but one blast every 17 times at bat is expensive, if that is all he can do.... I still say it was a good deal."[36] In 1968, ten years later, Lane remained dismissive of Colavito after learning that outfielder Lou Piniella had been acquired by the Indians. "The fans in Cleveland will love Piniella, mark my words. Why? Because Piniella looks just like that dago fruit peddler, Rocky Colavito," he said, using an ethnic slur.[37]

After Lane hired Kuenn in 1971 to be a special batting instructor for Milwaukee, he acknowledged how despised he was in Cleveland. "Rocky was a teenage idol," Lane said. "He would stand for hours signing autographs. The fans hated me."[38] Lane continued his trading ways later in his career with the Athletics and Brewers. At Milwaukee, Lane's last stop as a general manager, he got rid of 33 players on the 40-man roster in his first year. When the team showed little improvement after two seasons, owner Bud Selig demoted him to a scout. Still, Selig, later baseball's commissioner who was denounced by many for failing to take action during the steroid era, thought highly enough of Lane to suggest that he belonged in the Hall of Fame.[39]

Colavito disliked Lane more than anybody he ever encountered in baseball. "Frank Lane was the biggest asshole who ever lived," Colavito said. He regretted not saying what he really thought about him in the biography *Don't Knock the Rock: The Rocky Colavito Story*, written in 1966 by longtime *Cleveland Plain Dealer* sportswriter Gordon Cobbledick. But back then, athletes and other public figures rarely spoke frankly about others, especially higher-ups.

Trading Colavito, Maris, and Cash left fans to wonder through the years about what might have been if all three players had come into their own in Cleveland. In 1961 alone, the three combined for 147 home runs and 413 RBI. For many fans, the loss of Colavito was the final straw. "I felt like most Clevelanders: I was depressed," said Bob Fitzpatrick, who was 18 when his favorite player was traded away. "It just ruined the atmosphere for baseball in Cleveland at the time. It took a long time for me to get over it."[40] Dale McMillin, 19 at the time, felt similarly. "Frank Lane made some bizarre trades, but a home run hitter for a guy who was a good leadoff hitter? That broke a lot of hearts in Cleveland," McMillin said. "Rocky was a good guy, and he deserved better, a lot better. Wherever Frank Lane is buried, let's find that tombstone and put, 'You dumb ass' on it. It was the worst trade in baseball."[41]

"For some reason, everyone loved Colavito," Kent Reinker said. "He simply touched a chord in the hearts of Clevelanders that other players did not. When Frank Lane traded him, Clevelanders were shocked, and the protest was universal and loud. He just hadn't understood Colavito's magnetism."[42] Emily Fitzgibbons said the Rocky Colavito Fan Club and its 633 members couldn't survive the trade. Its days were probably numbered anyway, since O'Connor's mother was pressuring her to resign from the club, and Fitzgibbon was gravitating to other teenage interests.[43]

Tito Francona, Colavito's teammate in 1959, said he was as mystified as everyone else by the trade. "Any team would want Rocky because he was a good leader," Francona said. "Everybody respected him. He never had a bad word for anybody—except Frank Lane. Rocky is number one in my book. Frank used to call Rocky the 'chocolate soda drinker.' He wanted men to drink beer. We used to say about Frank Lane, 'He had three teams, the one here, the one going and the one coming.'"[44]

10

The Motor City

A snarling tiger was on Rocky Colavito's jersey in place of the toothy grin of Indians mascot Chief Wahoo as he prepared to play in Municipal Stadium for the season opener on April 19, 1960. The No. 7 on his uniform, which most baseball fans associated with Mickey Mantle and Tigers fans with Harvey Kuenn, had replaced Colavito's familiar No. 6. Just 48 hours after the trade, and after nine years with the Cleveland organization, Colavito was unsure of what to expect when it came time to play on his former home field against the only team and organization he had known.

"I was in a state of shock," Colavito said. "I was born and raised in the Cleveland organization. I'd had a good year at Cleveland. I tied for the home run crown, and finished one behind in runs batted in. I had no reason to think I'd be traded and then—wham!—I was gone." Self-doubt crept in as he tried to come to terms with what happened. "I was really shook up. It's not that I thought I was a better ballplayer than Kuenn, but I was at home in Cleveland. I hit well in [the] Cleveland stadium. The trade made me feel like a failure. I knew Kuenn had led the American League in hitting the year before, but that still didn't soften the blow," Colavito said."[1]

There was no getting away from the trade, even if he could somehow take his mind off it. "It seemed like everybody in the world knew you were traded. It was traumatic, but I would never give Lane the satisfaction that he upset me," Colavito said. "Carmen loved Cleveland like I did, and she was devastated, too, but I know she wouldn't say it either. I was also still a major league baseball player, and I had to go on. You were a professional, and you acted like it."

The trade wreaked havoc on the Colavitos' family life. "We had a nice home in Cleveland, just 20 minutes from the ballpark and ten minutes from the airport," Colavito said. "We had no trouble getting baby sitters, and we had a lot of good friends. Everybody treated us well. All of a sudden that was gone, too."

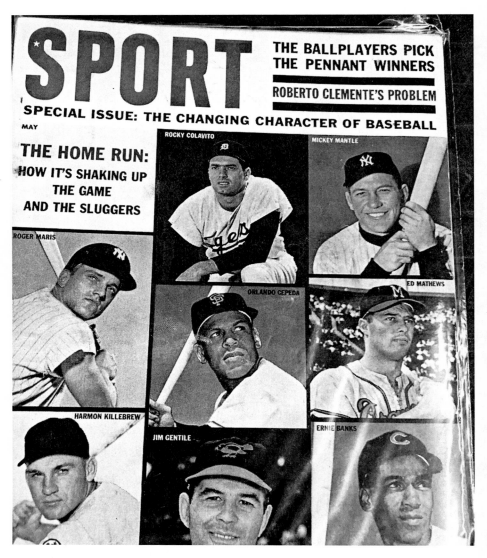

Colavito was featured in a *Sport* magazine article on home run hitters in a May 1960 cover story (Harvey Weber personal collection).

Sportswriters had a lot to say about the sensational trade. "Here was Rocco Domenico Colavito, the pride and joy of Cleveland, a super hero to every teenager in Cleveland, now suddenly a member of the opposition," one writer said. "The dastardly Frank Lane had done it—he'd traded away the beloved Rocky, and that aroused the ire of a whole community, a whole society, it seemed…. They wanted to lynch him."[2] Another sportswriter compared Colavito, the home run hitter, to a puncher and Kuenn, the singles hitter, to a boxer. "The fact is, Rocky simply is one of those rare characters who is born to be a star…. Rocky's glamour communicates itself to the fans, for this is the stuff of which they expect their stars to be made, and as Frank Lane found out when he traded Rocky from Cleveland to Detroit, it is less outrageous to knock motherhood and religion than it is to 'Knock the Rock.'"[3]

The Tigers had big plans for their newly-acquired slugger. The team was conservative when it came to trading away ballplayers, and swapping Colavito for Kuenn demonstrated that it was tired of being stuck in a holding pattern in the standings. Detroit had won and lost the exact same number of games over the past three seasons combined, stumbling along to fourth-, fifth-, and fourth-place finishes. With the addition of Colavito, the team, the fans, and the sportswriters who followed the Tigers were expecting the newly-acquired slugger to shake up the team, spark the offense, and bring more fans through the turnstiles. "The Tigers lost 30 games by one run last season due to lack of a long-ball hitter," wrote Edgar Hayes, the *Detroit Times'* sports editor. "Colavito hit eight home runs in spring training this year while the entire Detroit club hit only 14. This trade makes the Tigers a pennant contender."[4]

Tigers General Manager Rick Ferrell made it clear what the team wanted to see by eliminating the $2,000 bonus Lane had made dependent on the slugger hitting fewer home runs and for a higher average. At the same time, some of Colavito's new teammates were reeling from Tigers mainstay Kuenn's departure. "None of us are safe now," pitcher Jim Bunning said. "Anything can happen now. Anyone can go." But Bunning also thought Colavito could be an outstanding acquisition for the Tigers. "You never know how a deal will work out, but I'll say this—if both players have the same kind of year they had last year, it'll be a good deal for us. Harvey will get his share of hits. There is no way to stop him. But Rocky is going to put the fear of the Lord into the other pitchers when they face us. I don't know why he shouldn't hit 50. The background is better in Detroit, and the ball carries farther."[5] Second baseman Frank Bolling was in a state of shock. "I don't believe it. I can't believe it," he said.[6]

Al Kaline was the Tigers' unquestioned leader and star. He had been the Tigers' golden boy since going straight from Southern High School in Baltimore to Detroit in 1953 without playing a single game in the minors. In Kaline's second full season in 1955, at age 20, he won the American League batting title with a .340 average, 21 points higher than runner-up Vic Power. Kaline was also one day younger than Tigers great Ty Cobb was when he won his first batting title in 1907. Though Kaline would never duplicate that league-leading average again, there were three more .300 seasons, three seasons with 27 home runs, and two seasons topping 100 RBI by the time Colavito joined the team. Kaline also earned three consecutive Gold Gloves in the outfield, two in right field and one in center. Colavito said the trade probably strained his relationship with Kaline at first. "Al and Harvey Kuenn were very good friends, so in my mind, I think, he resented me a little but he didn't really show it," Colavito said. "He didn't say I don't like you or act like that, but let's face it, if one of my best friends gets traded, and we get the other guy, there might be a little resentment. But I never held that against him, and he was a damn good ballplayer." Kaline knew it was a difficult transition for Colavito.

> I know Rocky was a tremendous hero over in Cleveland, and it had to be very disappointing for him. I don't know this for a fact, but it had to be hard to leave a place where he was loved by the people over there and to come to another team who had some stars over here, too. But it is baseball, and you have to do your best every time you put the uniform on, no matter whose uniform you have.[7]

Colavito's roommate was pitcher Pete Burnside, whom he considered "a gentleman from the word go, and a class act." When Burnside was traded in the off-season, Colavito roomed the next three seasons and became good friends with Bunning. The right-hander was the Tigers' ace while Colavito was on the team, went on to pitch a perfect game with the Philadelphia Phillies, won 224 games, and was inducted into the Hall of Fame. After his baseball days were over, he launched a new career as a Republican congressman and then senator from Kentucky. Manager Jimmie Dykes was starting his first full season with the Tigers. He replaced Bill Norman in 1959 after the team lost 15 of its first 17 games, and they went 74–63 the rest of the way. Dykes played 22 seasons and was the White Sox's all-time winningest manager by the time he took the helm of the Tigers. The team's veteran starters included Frank Bolling at second base, Eddie Yost at third, Charlie Maxwell in left field, and Kaline in center. On the mound were Bunning, Burnside, Frank Lary and Don Mossi. New additions to the team besides Colavito included minor league first baseman Norm Cash, acquired from the Indians five days before Colavito, and shortstop Chico Fernandez, who came over from the Phillies.

As the 3 p.m. game time approached, the Cleveland ballpark had a charged atmosphere. Fans cheered Colavito's name in pre-game introductions and when he came to the plate. "Welcome Home Rocky," with the word "Home" x'd out, and "Lost Rocky and Pennant" were among the signs and banners around Municipal Stadium, especially Colavito's familiar right field stands.[8] One spelling-challenged fan held a sign that read, "Bring Back Covalita." "When I came out onto the field, there were quite a few banners. I thought this is unbelievable," Colavito said. "These fans are so loyal, and they didn't forget. It really thrilled me. I probably should have had someone take a movie of it, just panning the stadium, especially where things hung from the upper deck." The reception made it even harder for Colavito to be playing for a team other than the Indians, but he rededicated himself to doing just that. "I was with a new team and wearing a new uniform, so I had to give it my best shot, which is what I did," he said.

Colavito and Kuenn posed for pictures, holding their bats in uniforms and numbers worn by the other two days earlier. "It wasn't fair to Harvey, either," Colavito thought to himself. Kuenn had his supporters in Cleveland, too. The reigning batting champion received more cheers than Colavito when the lineups were announced, according to one account, and they became more pronounced as the game wore on.[9] Boos were noticeable when Colavito made an out, and he gave the boo-birds plenty of opportunities. In a 15-inning game won by the Tigers, Colavito struck out four times in six hitless at-bats, along with a walk. After Kaline put the Tigers ahead with a two-run single in the top of the 15th inning, Colavito capped his disappointing return by grounding into a double play. Kuenn, on the other side of the diamond, didn't get his first hit until the tenth inning, finishing 2-for-7 before suffering a pulled leg muscle. "I had the worst day I ever had in baseball, anywhere and anyhow, from the sandlots to the minors to the majors," Colavito said. "It was all from the pressure of trying to do too much." Dykes gave the right fielder a pat on the back after the game. "Forget about today," Dykes told him. "The important thing to remember is that you were on the winning team."[10] Cash lightened the mood the next day at the ballpark. "Say, Rocky, how about playing for our side today?" he said.[11]

Colavito recovered from his inauspicious debut the following day by driving a 2–1 pitch off the facing of the second tier in left field in the top of the fourth inning, helping the Tigers win, 6–4. He homered again in the team's third straight winning effort, this time against the White Sox, while the Indians went down to a third straight defeat. A cartoon in the *Cleveland Press* several days later depicted Frank Lane haunted in bed by images of ballplayers he had traded away. Hovering over him were likenesses of Colavito (.318 average, 3 homers, 8 RBI), Roger Maris (.421 average, 2 home runs, 6 RBI), and Minnie Minoso (.292 average, 3 homers, 9 RBI).[12]

With a 5–0 start, the Tigers were the major league's only unbeaten team. At Detroit's home opener, Colavito received a standing ovation when he came up to the plate for the first time. "Not since Kaline himself flashed across the horizon at Briggs Stadium in 1955 has a player captured fandom's fancy the way Colavito has," a Detroit reporter wrote. "Even the Tigers say freely that his arrival has made the difference between just another ball club and an undefeated team with five straight victories. One who says it the loudest is Kaline, no less."[13] As in Cleveland, Motor City fans liked watching Colavito stretch his back in the on-deck circle by lifting his Louisville Slugger over his head with both hands and pulling it behind his shoulders. They grew accustomed to the way he set himself at the plate and pointed his bat at the pitcher, and they appreciated his friendly personality, the way he hustled, his cannon of an arm, and his long home runs. Colavito, as usual, showed his gratitude by tipping his hat to the fans and signing autographs after games. A Rocky Colavito Fan Club formed in Detroit.

Christine Williams was ten when the trade happened. But unlike suffering Cleveland fans, she was a Tigers fan living in Detroit. Williams was smitten by Colavito's appearance.

> I remember seeing Rocky Colavito's picture in the paper next to Harvey Kuenn when the trade was announced, and I fell in love with his looks then and there. There wasn't much more to the analysis than that. I grew up in this narrow German Lutheran environment, and here was this dark-haired Catholic who always made the sign of the cross when he went up to the plate and stretched the bat across his back. It was probably akin to what someone might have felt about the Beatles later. He was so different, and he rocked our little world.[14]

Colavito said he had never expected to be as popular in Detroit as he was in Cleveland. "I could never receive the affection Detroit had for Harvey, who grew up in the Tigers' organization, any more than Harvey could replace me in Cleveland for the same reason," he said later. "And in the same way, I could never have been as close to the fans as an Al Kaline, a great ballplayer who also was one of their own. Make no mistake, though—Detroit fans were good to me." Cleveland fans also continued to be good to him when he played in Cleveland, even in a Tigers uniform. "What you really are aware of is the fans' reaction," Kuenn said. "Rocky was so very popular in Cleveland that it's only natural they'd still be pulling for him, and when he hits a home run, they cheer more than they cheer when any other Tiger hits one. You become aware that these are your fans cheering him, and yes, maybe you do feel that you'd like to do something to match him."[15]

The fast start by the Tigers came to a screeching halt when the team lost its next ten games in a row. Colavito's bat also cooled down, and the 340-foot distance down the foul lines in Tiger Stadium, compared to 320 in Cleveland, was a contributing factor. Colavito was getting out in front of pitches, and when he pulled them toward the left field corner they would curve foul at the last minute because of the 20 extra feet to the foul pole, rather than landing in the seats for home runs at Municipal Stadium. The fence in Detroit was also eight feet high down the line in Detroit, compared to five in Cleveland's park. "Don't think it wasn't in the back of my mind that they would have been home runs in Cleveland," Colavito said. He also struggled with the hitting background in Tiger Stadium. "Sometimes I'd have to step out of the box or make believe I had something in my eye, because the vendors in Detroit wore white shirts in center and they were distracting," he said. "I'd wait for them to get out of the way."

Colavito hit a ninth-inning home run to give Detroit a 1–0 victory on May 10, but that was a rare bright spot. After his average dropped to .161 on

May 22, he was benched for nine games and called on to pinch-hit only twice. "I was pressing, but I don't know why I was trying to impress anyone, since I hit 42 home runs the year before," Colavito said. "I liked Jimmie Dykes, except he took me out of the lineup. The guy he put in for me, Neil Chrisley, was doing pretty well, to be honest. I understood that in a way, but I wasn't liking it." Colavito's tailspin prompted a May 24 letter from Father Gambone of Holy Guardian Angels Rectory in Reading, where Colavito attended church. "We're still rooting and pulling for you at the Parish. Keep plugging away and know that you are backed by our prayers. If things get to look a little low, say a prayer to St. Sebastian, the patron saint of athletes. May God bless you and keep you well. And I shall pray that the Angels will carry that ball hit from your bat a long, long way."

Colavito got untracked after a suggestion from third-base coach Billy Hitchcock to open his stance. In a four-game series in early June, he smashed three home runs and had seven hits against the Indians in Cleveland. Colavito recovered by the All-Star break to have 17 home runs and 43 runs batted in to go with a .255 batting average. But the slow start cost him a chance to be an American League All-Star a second year in a row. Roger Maris, Colavito's friend and former teammate in Cleveland, started in right field in his first season with the Yankees, on his way to winning the 1960 American League MVP award. Kaline, despite hitting 96 points lower than at the 1959 All-Star break, was named to the team as a reserve. Kuenn, who was batting .305 with five home runs and 36 RBI, was also chosen.

Colavito felt more comfortable at the plate as the season wore on, swatting two round-trippers and knocking in six runs against the Athletics in the last game before the first All-Star break. He also put together a 12-game hitting streak. "I was trying too hard that first year, and about midway the season I just settled down," he said. Colavito also learned that playing in the Motor City, home to the Big Three auto makers, came with a special perk. The Ford Motor Company provided each player with the car of his choice to use during the season. If they wanted to buy the vehicle after the season was over, they could do so at a discount by paying the reduced dealer's cost. Colavito drove a Lincoln, Mercury, and Thunderbird in his seasons with the Tigers. The program eventually ended several years after he got to Detroit, because some players didn't pay their parking tickets. Colavito became friendly with Lee Iacocca, Ford's president. After Iacocca left Ford to become chairman of Chrysler Company, Gar Laux, Chrysler's vice president, told Colavito to call if he ever needed a car, even if he played for another team. When Colavito found himself on the White Sox later in his career, a brand-new Cougar was waiting for him at the airport.

With the Tigers' record sitting at a dismal 44–52 on August 3, Indians General Manager Frank Lane and Tigers President Bill DeWitt engineered another one-of-a-kind trade. This time it was for managers. "Jimmie, a lot of funny things happen in this game," DeWitt began, before telling Dykes he had been swapped for Indians manager Joe Gordon.[16] Colavito had become enamored of Dykes during the less than a full season he played under him. "Jimmie Dykes was the greatest, he was the best by far," Colavito said when asked at the end of his career which of the 14 managers he liked playing for most. "He was a gentleman, and that's only part of it. He was the most inspirational manager I have known. He would run a clubhouse meeting, and when he was done you really wanted to go out and break your neck for him."[17] Colavito wasn't happy about having Gordon as a manager again. He had been stung by a comment made after his trade to Detroit, as well as by Gordon's ringing endorsement of it. "Gordon claimed I had said, 'Kuenn and who else?' when I was told of the trade, and I never said anything like that, ever. I had too much respect for Harvey. He was a good player," Colavito said. "I hit 83 home runs in two seasons. What did Gordon want? I don't think that was all that bad. I was hurt by what he said."

Colavito also became a favorite target of *Detroit Free Press* columnist Joe Falls. He began compiling a record on Colavito for "runs not batted in" (RNBI), which the ballplayer resented. They feuded after Falls, also an official scorer, gave Orioles outfielder Sam Bowen an error for losing a ball in the sun on a ball Colavito hit that landed ten feet away. "When I joined the Tigers the players all told me to be careful of him," Colavito said. "They said he's a snake in the grass. He'll stab you in the back." Colavito didn't speak to Falls during his last three years on the Tigers. He also told reporters who came to his locker that he would stop talking if the columnist joined them. Later, after Colavito was no longer on the team, he agreed to bury the hatchet at the urging of close friend and Detroit businessman Eddie Robinson. "I caught holy hell from Kaline and Cash," Colavito said. "Nobody liked him." Later, after his playing career, Colavito was up for a job hosting a sports show on a Michigan station. Falls wrote a column slamming him again, Colavito said, and he didn't get the job.

The Tigers weren't much better with Gordon at the helm, going 26–31 to finish the season in sixth place with a 71–83 record. Colavito rebounded to end up with 35 home runs, fourth in the league behind Mickey Mantle with 40, Roger Maris with 39, and Jim Lemon with 38. He was just the fourth Tiger to top 30 in a season in the franchise's 60-year history. But Colavito's 87 RBIs were a disappointment, as was his .249 average, the lowest of his professional career. He had an outstanding year with the glove, leading all American League right fielders with nine assists and turning five double plays, with the league's second-best fielding percentage of .976 for right fielders. Cash's .286 average was good enough to lead the Tigers. Kaline hit .278 with 15 home runs and 68 RBIs, his worst season to date. Bunning went 11–14, and Lary won 15 but lost the same number. "The whole team was dismal," Colavito said. "We couldn't put it together after the first few games."

In Cleveland, trading Colavito away for Kuenn didn't have the effect Lane predicted. The club lost 13 more games in 1960, and saw attendance drop by 546,991. Without Colavito's power in the lineup, the Indians hit 40 fewer home runs and scored 78 fewer runs. Kuenn hit .308, 59 points higher than Colavito, but managed only nine home runs and 54 RBIs. Colavito hit 26 more home runs than Kuenn and knocked in 19 more runs. It was Kuenn's one and only season in Cleveland. Barely eight months after the trade, Lane shipped him off to the San Francisco Giants. In return, the Indians obtained slugging outfielder Willie Kirkland and starting pitcher Johnny Antonelli. "I think it's the best thing that ever happened to Harvey," Colavito told a reporter. "And I admit that it should help me, too. Now people won't be comparing us all the time. Harvey can start life anew, and he'll be hitting ahead of some pretty good sluggers."[18]

Cleveland's trade of Kuenn to San Francisco after one season left no doubt which team got the worst of the trade. Making matters worse, Antonelli lost all four decisions with the Indians in 1961 before being sold to the Milwaukee Braves, where he won his lone decision and retired after the season. Kirkland averaged 21 home runs in his three seasons with the Indians, with a high of 27 in 1961 that included four home runs in a doubleheader. But over the three seasons, he batted .259, .200 and .230. Lane traded Kuenn away because he said, in part, that the Indians needed a home run hitter. "All of a sudden they needed a power hitter?" Colavito said a half-century later, still dumbfounded. "What happened to the one they had?"

Colavito took a modest pay cut for the 1961 season that left him in the $30,000 range, but confident he was going to return to the batting form he showed in Cleveland. A big change in Major League Baseball was also afoot. The American League was expanding from eight to ten teams with the addition of the Los Angeles Angels and Washington Senators (the original Senators team relocated to Minnesota, where it was rechristened the Minnesota Twins). The Houston Colt .45s and the New York Mets entered the National League as expansion teams in 1962. Whether because of expansion or coincidence, home run records fell by the wayside in 1961. Roger Maris's 61 home runs were the most ever in a season, a mark that would stand for 37 years. But he was hardly alone in mounting an assault on the record books. Mickey Mantle, Maris's teammate, clubbed 54 out of the park. Forty-one players hit 20 or more homers, the most in one year, and six slugged 40 or more. The Yankees' 240 round-trippers were the most ever by a team. Home run records were set by the American League, with 1,534, and by both leagues combined, with 2,730. The Yankees' reserve catcher, John Blanchard, was representative of what happened that year. He hit four home runs in a row over three games, two as a pinch-hitter, en route to 21 for the season in just 243 at-bats.

The Tigers had a new manager for the 1961 season, Bob Scheffing, who had led the Cubs for three seasons. And Colavito had a new position, moving to left field so Kaline could return to right. Colavito said the change was made because Kaline, after two seasons in center, felt he wouldn't be picked to start in center fielder for the American League All-Star Game as long as Mantle played the position. But Colavito took the change in stride. "Anybody who plays the outfield should be able to play all three positions. The only difference is the way the ball comes off the bat. That shouldn't be any problem," he said.[19] In spring training, Colavito met DiMaggio, the player he idolized as a youth and emulated as an adult. Colavito told him he had been his favorite player growing up. They talked for a little while until someone told DiMaggio that ex-wife Marilyn Monroe was on the phone, causing him to end the conversation abruptly and rush out of the room. Colavito and his baseball idol would meet a few more times over the years.

There were several new faces to start the 1961 season. Billy Bruton was acquired from Milwaukee in a trade to patrol center field. Dick Brown was behind the plate, Jake Wood was at second base, and Steve Boros at third. Shortstop Dick McAuliffe emerged as a starter later in the season. Jim Bunning and Frank Lary were back to anchor the pitching staff. Colavito expressed guarded optimism for the season. "We can't be as bad as last year, so we must be better," he said. "I look for Al Kaline to have a great season. I feel good, too."[20] After the Tigers lost their season opener, the team went on an eight-game winning streak. Colavito got off to a good start, too, with four home runs in his first 14 games. Then a bizarre incident occurred in the May 14 day game in New York, with Colavito in the middle of it. So, too, were Carmen Colavito, Rocky's father Rocco, his brother Dom, and sister Clara.

As the Tigers were leaving the field after the bottom of the eighth inning, Colavito suddenly vaulted over the low fence by the visitor's dugout and started to go into the stands on the third base side, shocking the 23,556 fans in attendance. Catching a glimpse of what appeared to be his father throwing a punch, Colavito rushed to his defense. He sprinted up an aisle about 12 rows before security, ushers, and teammates stopped him. At that point he could see that Dom had intervened. When he returned to the field, Colavito was ejected by umpire Ed Hurley for leaving the field of play. "I'm sorry it happened, but I would do it all over again," Colavito said after the game. "My father is 60 years old, and I'm not going to let anyone take a swing at him, whether it happens to be Yankee Stadium or anywhere else."[21] He also said to the press, "I think you gentlemen all would do the same thing I did."[22]

Colavito later learned that two men sitting behind Carmen were intoxicated and that one of them was blowing in her hair. Distressed, Carmen caught Dom's attention, and he went over and told the two men to leave her alone. When one asked Dom what he was going to do about it, Rocky's older brother knocked him out with one punch, leading the other guy to raise his hands to indicate he didn't want to fight. Rocky's father wasn't assaulted, as the ballplayer thought. "My father comes over, and you know how the seats collapse, and his foot was caught in the seat and he was swinging at air," Colavito said.

The newspapers had a field day. "Colavito's act is without a precedent in modern major league baseball," one article said.[23] "One of the mad, mad scenes of Yankee Stadium history exploded like an atom when Rocky Colavito virtually catapulted into the third-base box seats behind the Tigers dugout. Pandemonium ensued," read another.[24] Hurley, the veteran umpire, said he had never seen anything like it before. "I've heard about players going up into the stands, but this is the first time I ever saw it," he said.[25] American League President Joe Cronin didn't fine or suspend Colavito, as some expected. "It wasn't the right thing for the boy to go up into the stands. But I guess it was natural for him to want to help his father," Cronin said.[26]

Clara Colavito said she had hoped her brother wouldn't notice what was happening in the stands for fear he might do something. "The family didn't want to make a scene, because we knew if Rocky saw it, he'd be right in here."[27] The elder Colavito, interviewed the next day at his Bronx home, said he had not needed help. "I could have handled myself all right," he said. "After all," he said, grasping a reporter's hand in an iron-like grip, "I'm no weakling. I told Rocky the important thing was that he got a triple and the Tigers won. We could have taken care of our end of the night by ourselves."[28]

Colavito became the first player to hit home runs in ten ballparks in one season, thanks to expansion, accomplishing the feat in Fenway on July 5. He was also the first to do so against each team in his home ballpark. Colavito made a strong impression on second baseman Jake Wood. "On the field, the Rock was very, very intense," Wood recalled. "He was the type of guy who would do anything to help promote his team and win. We were very fortunate in 1961 to have Al Kaline, him and Norm Cash hit back-to-back-to-back. If Billy Bruton, who batted second, or I as the leadoff man, got on base that year, chances were that we were going to score." Wood was also Colavito's pinochle partner. "When we were on the road, Rocky was an impeccable dresser," he recalled. "The Rock always looked professional and acted that way on and off the field."[29] Pitcher Paul Foytack was also impressed by Colavito. "He was a real nice guy, he had a great arm and was a good outfielder," Foytack said. "And he could hit a ball about a mile."[30]

With the Tigers' record at 55–30, Colavito was named as a starter for the 1961 American League All-Star team. He started in left field in San Francisco's windy Candlestick Park in the first of that year's two Midsummer Classics. The outfield featured Colavito in left field, Mickey Mantle in center and Roger Maris in right. Norm Cash was at first, Johnny Temple at second, Tony

Kubek at shortstop, and Brooks Robinson at third, with Jim Bunning on the mound and John Romano behind the plate. Colavito went hitless in four at-bats as the NL won in ten innings. In the ninth inning, he was at bat with Maris on second and Kaline on first when the All-Star Game's most famous non-pitch occurred. Giants reliever Stu Miller, in the game in place of Sandy Koufax, went into his stretch when a gust of wind blew him off the mound, resulting in a balk.[31] Colavito then reached base on an error that scored Kaline and tied the game. He had narrowly missed a home run in the fifth inning on a long fly to center. "Willie Mays was looking at the ball, kind of watching it go out," Colavito recalled. "At the last second, he leaped and caught the ball. I know when I hit a ball that well it should be a home run, and that should have been. The wind definitely hurt me."

In the second All-Star Game, in Fenway Park, Colavito batted second between teammates Cash and Kaline and again played left field. In the first inning, he lofted a changeup from NL starter Bob Purkey over the Green Monster in left for what proved to be the American League's lone run. The game ended after nine innings in a 1–1 tie due to heavy rains. Colavito found Fenway Park to be both a blessing and a curse during his career. The 37-foot-high wall in left was only a reported 315 feet from home plate, though some claimed the distance measured even closer. But the Green Monster just as easily took homers away on hard-hit balls that lacked height. "I hit bullets there that I know would have gone out in other places," Colavito said.

The Tigers led the league until July 25, with Cash having a career year in all three major offensive stats. Earlier that month, Commissioner Ford Frick declared that Babe Ruth's record of 60 home runs in a season would stand unless broken in 154 games, not during the eight more games added to the schedule due to expansion. Frick, who had been a friend of Ruth's, made his announcement as Maris and Mantle were in pursuit of the record. Colavito disagreed with Frick in an interview that summer, although he doubted the home run mark was in danger. "Several guys in our league are capable of it, but I don't think Ruth's record will be broken," he said. But Colavito said breaking the record would be well-deserved if it happened. "Switching from day ball to night ball and back again is rough," Colavito said. "Ruth never had to do that. If [someone] hits 61, he deserves it. The extra one takes care of the extra games."[32]

On August 27, Colavito hit four home runs in a day for the second time in two years. This time they were spread over a doubleheader in Washington. In the first game, Colavito lined a pitch from the Senators' Bennie Daniels into the front row of seats in the left field bleachers. In the nightcap, he blasted a 400-foot shot halfway up the bleachers off Dave Sisler in the fourth inning, hit another off Sisler over the Detroit bullpen in the fifth, and added his third home run of the game in the eighth off Mike Garcia into the left field bleach-

Rocco Colavito, Jr., 5, with his father prior to the Tigers' annual fathers-sons game in 1961 (Colavito's personal collection).

ers. The home run outburst gave Colavito 38 for the season, eclipsing the 35 tallied by Rudy York, the Tiger who spurned his autograph request in the 1940s. In a lighter moment at Tiger Stadium, Rocco Jr., was photographed holding his bat behind his back and stretching like his father at the annual Father-Son Day.

When the Tigers went into New York on September 1 for the start of a ten-game road trip, they were just two games behind the Yankees. It was the only other time beside the 1959 season that Colavito was on a team in contention in September. But the Tigers lost all three games to New York, the next three in Baltimore, and three out of four in Boston. The team woke up on September 12, 11½ games out of first. Fourteen wins in the team's final 19 games did little to change their final placement in the standings. The Tigers ended the season with a 101–61 record, 30 wins more than the previous season and 40 wins over .500. That was more than good enough most seasons to win the pennant going away. But the Yankees, with six players topping 20 home runs, led by Maris's 61 and Mantle's 54, finished eight games ahead of Detroit.

"We were up against the best team I ever played against," Colavito said. The Yankees' explosive offense also overshadowed a terrific defense the team didn't get enough credit for, he felt. "Mantle was a hell of an outfielder and he ran like an antelope," Colavito said. "If he made a mistake, he could outrun it. Roger [Maris] was a terrific defensive outfielder with a strong arm. What Clete Boyer had over Brooksie [Brooks Robinson] was a better arm, and Bobby Richardson could turn the double play as well as anyone I ever saw. Yogi Berra and Elston Howard were also outstanding defensively behind the plate." Colavito felt the Yankees' pitchers were also underrated. "If I had one game to win, it would be Whitey [Ford] for his stuff and for his demeanor," Colavito said. "He had a much better fastball than anyone ever gave him credit for. And [Ryne] Duren was as good a reliever as there was." Five of Colavito's ten favorite ballplayers he played against, or mostly against, in his career played on that 1961 club—Mantle, Maris, Boyer, Howard, and Bill Skowron. The other five were Willie Mays, Hank Aaron, Roy Sievers, Hank Bauer, and Don McMahon.

The 1961 season was a banner year for the Tigers at the box office, with 1.6 million in attendance, second highest in the league. Cash led the league with a .361 batting average, to go with 41 home runs and 132 RBIs. Kaline hit

Left to right: Colavito, Al Kaline and Norm Cash were the heart of the Detroit Tigers' batting order from 1960 to 1963 (Baseball Hall of Fame).

.324 and compiled a 22-game hitting streak. Lary went 23–9, with Bunning winning 17 and Don Mossi 15. Colavito's season ranked with 1958 as his most complete. He hit 45 home runs, which placed him well behind Maris and Mantle, and one behind Jim Gentile and Harmon Killebrew. Colavito's .290 batting average was third on the team and represented a 41-point improvement from the year before. His 140 RBIs were one shy of Maris's and Gentile's league-leading 141. (The Baltimore slugger was awarded a share of the title in 2010, 49 years later, after a baseball researcher found that an official scorer mistakenly awarded Maris a second RBI in a June 5 game.)

Colavito believed he would have won the RBI title if not for the umpiring team of Charlie Berry, Bob Stewart, Joe Linsalata, and Frank Umont. "They were the four worst umpires in the league, and they were all together," Colavito said. In one game, he hit a ball he said landed in fair territory in the upper deck for what should have been a home run. Instead the third-base umpire called it foul. "I'm hollering at the plate umpire. I said, 'You saw it went around the pole and it was a fair ball.' He said, 'I know, Rocky, it was fair.' I said, 'Overrule them.' He said he couldn't do that, and he wouldn't." In all, Colavito believed the umpiring crew cost him five RBI in a season in which he missed tying for the league by one. Over the course of his career, Colavito would miss tying for the RBI crown twice by one RBI, in 1959 and 1961, and the home run crown by one in 1958. He would later wonder if having two home run titles and three RBI titles would have boosted his credentials for the Hall of Fame.

Colavito finished fourth in the American League in total bases with 338 and third in runs scored with 129 and walks with 113. He also played in every game, tying Brooks Robinson. Colavito even stole a base off Angels pitcher Art Fowler, who didn't bother to hold him on at first base, accounting for one of his 19 career steals. Colavito also led all AL outfielders in assists for the lone time in his career with 16. Colavito's home run total was second all-time in Tigers history to Hank Greenberg's 58 in 1938. There wasn't a home-field advantage, either, with just 18 of his 45 homers clearing the fences in Tiger Stadium. Colavito finished the season with 209 career home runs, good for 26th on the all-time list.

Colavito and Cash combined to knock in more runs than Maris and Mantle—the famed "M&M Boys." Still, Colavito was disappointed the Tigers didn't make it into the World Series. "The bottom line was to win. I had never been on a winner, and I wanted to be on a winner," he said. "I never thought about being in contention for the home run or RBI crown. I just thought about catching the Yankees and beating them when we had a chance, so we could get some leverage in the standings."

In San Francisco, Harvey Kuenn's year with the Giants was a forgettable one. In 131 games, he hit .265 with five homers and 46 RBIs. In Cleveland,

Willie Kirkland found taking Colavito's place was no easy matter. The team had just 15 home runs in its first 28 games, and Kirkland, expected to provide some firepower, received his share of boos. "That's not because of the way Willie is playing," said Gabe Paul, Frank Lane's successor as Indians general manager. "It's because he's playing in Rocky Colavito's old spot, and the fans haven't forgotten Rocky."[33]

11

Motown Discord

Although Jackie Robinson broke baseball's color barrier in 1947, racial segregation was still in full force in the South when Rocky Colavito arrived in Lakeland, FL, east of Tampa, for spring training with the Tigers in 1960. It was the first time Colavito encountered such extreme racism, though he was certainly aware of racial disparities in baseball and society at large.

Colavito began his professional career just four years after Robinson stepped onto Ebbets Field for the first time as a Brooklyn Dodger. His first game in April 1951 came only weeks after Brown v. Board of Education was filed in U.S. District Court, leading to the landmark Supreme Court ruling in 1954 that found "separate but equal" schools in Topeka, KS, to be inherently unequal. Colavito's debut with the Indians in September 1955 came three months before Rosa Parks refused to sit in the back of the bus in 1955, sparking the Montgomery Bus Boycott that dismantled segregated public transportation in Alabama's capital.

When Colavito came up to the majors for the last month of the season in September 1955, he even played alongside Larry Doby, who had followed Robinson by 11 weeks to the major leagues in 1947. Doby signed with the Cleveland Indians, becoming the first black ballplayer in the American League. To Colavito, Doby was a veteran ballplayer he looked up to. "I liked Larry, and he was good to me," Colavito recalled. "He was sort of quiet, but he took to me in the sense that he treated me just like any other player on the team. There was none of that crap like I am a veteran, and you're a rookie." Colavito played with Doby again in 1958. Both Robinson and Doby came from the Negro Leagues, which existed in response to Major League Baseball's refusal to accept African American ballplayers. Other former Negro Leagues players Colavito played with on the Indians were Al Smith, Harry "Suitcase" Simpson, and Davey Pope. "I know they went through a lot of shit, but I didn't hear it," Colavito said. "A lot of that happened before I came on the team." It took baseball 12 more years, until 1959, before every team followed the example set by Dodgers GM Branch Rickey and Indians owner

Bill Veeck to integrate baseball. It took even longer for spring training facilities in the South.

The sit-ins at a Woolworth lunch counter in Greensboro, NC, in February 1960, were another catalyst in the civil-rights arsenal for change in a resistant South. They occurred two months before Colavito was traded to Detroit. Colavito didn't have African American teammates during parts of his first two seasons as a pro when he played in the South, but he witnessed the effects of segregation on his teammates in Lakeland in 1960 and again in 1961. Black players had to have meals brought to them on the team bus because they weren't allowed inside whites-only restaurants. Nor could black ballplayers sleep in hotels where white players slept.

> I remember in spring training stopping at restaurants or truck stops, and they wouldn't serve the black guys. That really made me sick. I always made sure to ask them what they wanted and bring it out to them. It was so unfair, but there was nothing I could do about it except get them something to eat. They were as hungry as we were. They weren't bothering anyone. Imagine good players like them not even being able to stay with their own teammates.

Lakeland was also the first encounter with segregation for second baseman Jake Wood, a black teammate of Colavito's "I grew up in New Jersey in an integrated environment," Wood said. "It was like a culture shock going to Lakeland. The team bus would let the black ballplayers off at a certain point because they weren't wanted in other parts of town." African Americans were restricted to designated seating sections in the ballpark and at the local movie theater. Signs for segregated drinking fountains and bathrooms were visible, and cab hailing for black players was restricted to a single corner.[1] Tigers outfielder Willie Horton remembered having to stay in a segregated hotel and finding it difficult to go back and forth to training camp several miles away. "I had to walk sometimes from downtown to the ballpark because no taxi would stop," Horton said.[2] Things finally changed in 1962, when the Tigers moved to a new Holiday Inn in Lakeland that housed the entire team, ending the segregated accommodations. Outfielder Billy Bruton and the team's four other "Negro" ballplayers, as blacks were then commonly called, approved of the new arrangements, according to an article in *The Sporting News*.[3]

Colavito learned of the Tigers' integrated living quarters after reporting to spring training camp following contract negotiations with General Manager Rick Ferrell. Colavito rejected three contracts offered by Ferrell before signing for $48,000, reportedly $1,000 less than Al Kaline. "I felt like I deserved double [the raise] considering I hit .290 consistently all year, with 45 home runs and 140 runs batted in," Colavito said. He and Carmen now had a third mouth to feed with the arrival of their second child, Marisa Ann Colavito, on November 21. He also learned over the winter that the Indians had attempted to reacquire him. The team offered six players to get him back, but the Tigers rejected the deal.[4]

The Tigers were returning in 1962 with practically the same starting nine, with Jim Bunning, Frank Lary, Hank Aguirre, Don Mossi, and Paul Foytack again expected to carry the pitching load. Expectations were high for Colavito, but he got off to a slow start, hitting less than .200 after 27 games and being demoted briefly to seventh in the batting order. It took 28 games and 101 at-bats before Colavito hit his first home run on May 16, an upper-deck blast to left field off the Twins' Camilo Pascual. But that first home run got Colavito untracked. He hit over .300 with 13 home runs over the next month. During that time, Colavito also met President John F. Kennedy, who was sitting behind the dugout for a game at D.C. Stadium. A Secret Service agent nearly stopped him as he walked over to shake the president's hand.

On June 24, Colavito rapped out seven hits in ten at-bats in a 22-inning game, boosting his average 15 points to .285. The Tigers lost the marathon contest to the Yankees, 9–7. "I didn't have a thing to eat for 12 hours except for a candy bar between innings," Colavito said. "It was tough. I snuck into the clubhouse for the candy bar."[5] The concession stands saw a steady parade of fans, selling some 32,000 hot dogs and 41,000 bottles of beer before closing early to accommodate Michigan labor laws. The Yankees' Yogi Berra caught all 316 pitches of the seven-hour contest.[6]

Colavito walked a lot and struck out less than many power hitters in his career, averaging 84 free passes and 77 whiffs over a 162-game season. The Tigers recognized his good eye at the plate by giving him the green light to hit on 3–0 counts. By July 2, Colavito's 17 home runs were close to his 1961 pace, and he was selected to the American League All-Star team by Yankees manager Ralph Houk. Colavito added three more home runs in a game for the third time in four seasons, giving him 20 as he headed to the Midsummer Classic. The Tigers, with a 43–40 record, were in second place but far off their record of the year before. Norm Cash led the team at the break with 23 home runs, but the Tigers were without Kaline, who broke his right collarbone on May 26 and missed 57 games. Jim Bunning was 9–4, Paul Foytack was 7–1, and Hank Aguirre was 7–3, but Frank Lary, hampered by shoulder trouble, was limited to a 2–6 season.

In the first All-Star Game in 1962, in Washington, D.C., Colavito entered the game in the fourth inning to pinch-run for Mickey Mantle. He went 0-for-1 with a walk as the National League won, 3–1. In the second game, at Chicago's Wrigley Field, he started in right field after Mantle was scratched due to an injury, moving Roger Maris to center. In the seventh inning, with Brooks Robinson and Maris on board, Colavito ripped a line drive off Dick Farrell over the left field wall. He added a fourth RBI on a sacrifice fly in the ninth as the American League won, 9–4. Colavito, along with winning pitcher

Ray Herbert, who threw three shutout innings, and Leon Wagner, who had a home run among his three hits and made the game's best defensive play, shined brightest, with Wagner narrowly named the winner of the Arch Ward Memorial Award as the game's best player. A wire service photo in newspapers the following day showed Wagner, Colavito, and Pete Runnels, who had each homered, touching a bat.[7] The home run was Colavito's third All-Star Game clout in four years, the fourth player to reach that mark after Stan Musial, Ted Williams, and Ralph Kiner. The four RBI were one shy of the record set by Williams and Al Rosen.

The second half of the season was only slightly better for the Tigers, with the team finishing 10½ games behind the Bronx Bombers. After the Tigers' 1961 season, in which they went 101–60, the fourth-place finish and 85–76 record was a big disappointment. Colavito had another strong season, leading the American League with 309 total bases. He finished with a .273 average, and his 37 home runs and 112 RBIs were both good for third in the league. He also played in 161 games and had a career-high 601 at-bats. The 37 homers solidified Colavito's stature as Detroit's biggest home run threat

Colavito and Tigers pitcher Frank Lary were in a good mood after a Tigers victory (Baseball Hall of Fame).

since Hank Greenberg. He also had exactly 200 home runs over the past five years, an average of 40 a year going back to 1958. That was more home runs hit over the same period than the other leading sluggers of the day, including Mickey Mantle, Roger Maris, Willie Mays, Hank Aaron, Ernie Banks, Harmon Killebrew and Frank Robinson. "Rocky was one of the top power hitters of his era," said Jim Kaat, the eighth-winningest left-handed pitcher in baseball history. Kaat gave up five home runs to Colavito in 78 at-bats during the 1960s. "He was one of those hitters that no matter where you pitched, he'd pull the ball. I can't remember Rocky hitting the ball in the opposite direction. From my perspective, he was the prototypical right-handed hitter. You had to pitch him down and away and try to get him to hit the ball on the ground to the shortstop."[8]

Norm Cash led the 1962 team with 39 home runs, but his average plummeted some 118 points, from .361 to .243, one of baseball's largest dropoffs ever. He remained a home run threat but never hit more than .283 the rest of his career and admitted years later that a corked bat helped him win the batting title. Kaline, in 398 at-bats, led the team with a .304 batting average. Anchoring the mound were Bunning, with a 19–10 record, and Aguirre, who went 16–8.

After the season, the Tigers played a series of exhibitions in Japan and the South Pacific. But the Colavitos were having a new house built, and with construction nearing completion the outfielder joined Frank Lary as the only Tigers not going. The team asked Colavito not to say anything publicly out of concern that the Japanese promoter might cancel the trip. Colavito was also looking forward to staying home with his family. Being away from home and living the life of a ballplayer took a toll on him, his wife and kids. In an interview that off-season, Colavito talked about how hard it could be to maintain a private life and a sense of normalcy.

> "Home run sluggers, of course, are the most popular of baseball's stars. They attract swarms of fans, young and old, male and, if the slugger is handsome, female," the article said. "Rocky Colavito, for one, is as big a hero with teenage girls as Fabian, Paul Anka or any of the rock 'n' roll singing idols. But today Rocky is troubled by another difficulty as he tries to live a private life that at least approaches normalcy. 'I have two kids, one of school age,' he said recently. 'Rocco, who's six, calls me 'that man who plays ball.' I hardly ever see him. I want my children to grow up like other kids who attend the same school from kindergarten to graduation. I live in Temple, PA, nearly a thousand miles from Detroit. While I'm playing ball, Carmen must stay home to take care of the children. I saw her for only one week this year between February and July, and then only because she was able to park the kids with a relative and drop in on me unexpectedly after the Tigers' first road trip to California."[9]

Before heading off to spring training in 1963 for another season away from home, Colavito had contentious contract negotiations with General

Manager Jim Campbell, who had succeeded Rick Ferrell. The divide extended five days after players were to report, with their disagreement spilling into the press. Campbell's refusal to allow a company to film Colavito in his Tigers uniform for a lucrative commercial unless an agreement was in place hardened their positions. "I made up my mind it was him or me," Campbell said a decade later. "What I offered Colavito was fair. But he had a lot of ideas about contracts that were way out of line. At the time, I was just fed up with all the nonsense. I figured now was the time to get it all over with."[10] Colavito eventually signed for $54,000, but he carried his grudge against Campbell throughout the season, refusing to speak to him even when the two men found themselves alone in an elevator.

Some news reports suggested that Colavito resented and was jealous of Kaline, because of an unwritten rule that Detroit management wouldn't pay anyone more than the long-time Tigers star. But Colavito said he didn't feel that way, respecting Kaline as a ballplayer and never mentioning him in contract talks. "I wouldn't do that because it wasn't my business," Colavito said. "I was only interested in my contract, not his." Kaline said he didn't consider his relationship with Colavito to be contentious. Paul Foytack, Kaline's roommate for nine years, never heard him suggest it either.[11] Colavito and Kaline weren't close, but Colavito said that was simply because their personalities were different. Colavito held a high regard for Kaline's playing ability. "Al Kaline was Detroit's darling, and the team catered to him," Colavito said. "But he was a great talent. He could run, he could throw, he could steal, hit, and hit with power. He was a complete player. Al didn't have the charisma of a Mickey Mantle or Willie Mays, but he could do it all, and I respected that." Kaline, in turn, appreciated Colavito as a teammate and as a ballplayer. "He was a great teammate. He came to the ballpark every day ready to play. He worked hard, and was a great home run hitter," Kaline said. "He probably had one of the best arms in the history of the game, although it wasn't the most accurate there was. I had a lot of respect for him."[12]

The Tigers didn't make many changes gearing up for the 1963 season. Gus Triandos, obtained from Baltimore, was behind the plate, and Bubba Phillips was acquired from Cleveland to start at third base. Returning were Cash at first, Jake Wood at second and Dick McAuliffe at shortstop. Colavito, Bruton and Kaline were once again the starters in the outfield, while the team was counting on Bunning, Lary, and Mossi to rack up wins. Colavito got off to another slow start in 1963, this time going 66 at-bats before hitting his first home run on April 26. He was still struggling on May 22 with a batting average of .237 when manager Bob Scheffing benched him. Colavito was upset. He didn't like to sit, plus he had played 458 consecutive games and was about two months shy of the team record of 511 straight games set by Charlie Gehringer in 1931.

The team stood at a disappointing 24–36 on June 18 when Scheffing was replaced by Chuck Dressen, whose managing career reached back to 1934 with the Cincinnati Reds. Colavito, hitting .231 with eight home runs, had to convince Dressen not to bench him for Gates Brown after the minor league call-up homered in his first at-bat. Colavito's season mirrored the season the Tigers were having. The team was mired in the second division at the All-Star break, and attendance was in decline. Colavito knew as his season wore on that it was going to be his last in a Tigers uniform. "Campbell came out in the papers saying he hoped I had a good second half of the season so my market value would be higher," Colavito said. "Boy, is that supposed to make a ballplayer happy or feel at home?"[13] He contributed with his glove and arm when his bat fell silent. In an August series with the Indians, Colavito caught Joe Azcue's long drive with a leaping catch above the left field wall for the game's final out. A few weeks later, he made a throw to keep the winning run at third against the Indians after snaring Max Alvis's foul fly above the bullpen roof in left field.

Outfielder Willie Horton debuted with the Tigers in 1963, playing in 15 games. Years earlier, Colavito had seen Horton and a friend, then in their teens, stopped by security after sneaking into the ballpark. Colavito was on the Indians then and saw what happened as he was coming off the team bus. He took the boys to see the Tigers' clubhouse manager, who at Colavito's request gave them a job. "From that day on, Rocky was my hero," Horton said. "Later, when he came to the Tigers he took me under his wing when I joined the team and helped me become a major leaguer. He also told me that I would one day take over from him in left field. I will never forget what he did for me."[14] Colavito later heard stories of how DiMaggio, his boyhood idol, was not helpful to Mickey Mantle, his successor in center field, though he never discussed the subject with Mantle. "I hate to say this, but it seems to me that DiMaggio was a little jealous of Mickey. Why? He was such a great player. I just don't understand that. Why couldn't he compliment Mickey? Willie Horton was heir apparent to my job, and I knew they were going to move me, but I did whatever I could for him. I wanted to help him. It was the same with Gates Brown, who was a good kid and a helluva pinch-hitter," Colavito said. Horton said Colavito was a caring person. "Rocky is a quality human being, an Abraham Lincoln–type person because of the way he was concerned about equal living for everybody," Horton said. "He always wanted to help people. He was a good person, a people-type person."[15]

Tigers reliever John Hiller also felt a debt of gratitude to Colavito. He didn't play for the Tigers until after Colavito was no longer on the team, but he had a fond memory of him. "When I first came here, right out of high school, they introduced me to a lot of people, but I was scared and didn't have much to say," Hiller said. "Colavito came over to my locker and sat down and talked to me for about 20 minutes. I never forgot that."[16]

Horton, Brown, McAuliffe, Bill Freehan, and pitchers Denny McLain and Mickey Lolich all played for the Tigers in 1963 and became part of the nucleus that brought Detroit a World Series Championship in 1968. But Colavito was long gone by then. He finished the 1963 season batting .271, with a career-low 22 home runs and 91 RBIs. The team fell to fifth place with a 79–83 record, and attendance dropped to almost half of what it had been just two years earlier. After the ugly contract negotiations and low home run production, the only question that remained for Colavito was which team he'd be traded to. "I had a steak dinner bet with Jim Bunning that I'd be traded first, and I was traded right before him," he said.

Colavito was traded to the Kansas City Athletics on November 18 with pitcher Bob Anderson and $50,000 for second baseman Jerry Lumpe and pitchers Ed Rakow and Dave Wickersham. The Tigers called Colavito's house to inform him, but he was in a car with Dom and two uncles, driving back from a hunting trip in New Hampshire. Instead, Colavito heard about the trade over the car radio. "I'm glad to get away from Detroit," he told a reporter. "I'm glad to get away from the front office. I like to feel appreciated."[17] In another interview, Colavito said, "I wasn't too surprised," before adding, "I know I'll hit more homers in Kansas City. That left field is a much better target than the one in Detroit."[18]

During the four years he batted cleanup between Al Kaline and Norm Cash, Colavito averaged 35 home runs and 107 RBIs. He was a productive and popular ballplayer, though he didn't reach the level of acclaim enjoyed with the Indians. "In Cleveland, the Rock was the king," one writer wrote. "When he went to Detroit, he found that all loyalties were concentrated on Kaline. Kaline was the king, and Colavito only a minor prince during his four-year stay with the Tigers."[19] Colavito's trade came four days before the assassination of President Kennedy, a calamitous event that would devastate the nation. Looking toward spring training, he had some inkling that playing for the Kansas City Athletics and Charles O. Finley, the team's maverick owner, would be a departure from the relative normalcy of other clubs. But little did he know just how much.

12

Joining the Circus

When Rocky Colavito became a member of the Kansas City Athletics on November 18, 1963, he joined a last-place team with an owner who was a pariah in Kansas City and to fellow American League owners. Playing for Charles Oscar Finley was one of the most challenging seasons of Colavito's career, and the strangest.

Finley had made his fortune as a health insurance broker, developing a nationwide group plan for doctors. He bought a controlling interest in the Athletics before the 1961 season, following unsuccessful attempts to buy the team several years earlier. He had also failed in efforts to buy the Detroit Tigers, the Chicago White Sox, and the Los Angeles Angels. Finley, who would soon gain a reputation as baseball's most eccentric owner, made a promise to Athletics fans upon buying the team.

> My intentions are to keep the A's permanently in Kansas City and build a winning ball club. I have said and want to say again I have not thought of moving the franchise…. When I was chasing the Detroit Tigers, I wasn't going to move the Tigers out of Detroit. When I was chasing the White Sox, I wasn't going to move the White Sox out of Chicago. And when I got a place to roost in Kansas City—brother, I mean to tell you, I'm here to stay![1]

Only he wasn't. Finley first tried to move the team the following year after becoming embroiled with city officials over terms of a lease for Kansas City's Municipal Stadium. A sticking point was his insistence that he be allowed to move the team if attendance dipped below a certain figure. From 1963 to early 1964, Finley tried to strike deals to relocate the team to Atlanta, Louisville, Milwaukee, and Oakland, only to be thwarted by American League owners who unanimously opposed him and threatened to wrest the franchise from his control.[2]

All Colavito needed to know about Finley's judgment was the man the owner chose in December 1960 to be his general manager, three days after taking the reins: Frank Lane. The hiring came eight months after Lane engineered

the trade of Colavito to Detroit. That decision had proved to be the nail in
the coffin for Lane's tenure in Cleveland, after Indians attendance without
Colavito plummeted by 446,991 fans. Cleveland's board of directors rebuffed
Lane's request after the 1960 season for a new contract, and Indians Vice
President Nate Dolin advised Lane to take the Athletics offer. "I'm trying to
tell you that your days [in Cleveland] are numbered and to take that job,"
Dolin said.[3] Finley praised his new GM's record for trading ballplayers when
he announced his new hire. "I know what he did to revive the interest in the
White Sox and what he had done at Cleveland, and I believe he can do as
much or more for Kansas City," Finley told the press, reportedly with a
straight face. "I can't think of anyone who could do a better job of pumping
life into a ball club than Frank Lane."[4]

Lane signed an eight-year contract beginning with the 1961 season and
lasted eight months. He still managed to make nine trades during his short
duration, involving 36 players. One trade he was unable to make was acquiring Jim Piersall from Cleveland as a box-office draw, which he blamed on the
backlash from the Colavito trade. "They're afraid of bobby-soxers," Lane said,
recalling the uproar following Colavito's departure.[5] Finley had his hands in
every aspect of the baseball operation and clashed frequently with Lane before
removing him.[6] Pat Friday, Lane's successor, lacked baseball experience and
was chosen on the basis of his success in overseeing one of Finley's insurance
offices. Joe Gordon, Finley's first manager, lasted even less time, getting the
pink slip after 60 games.

As the 1964 season and Colavito's debut with the Athletics drew near,
American League owners rejected Finley's formal request to move the team
from Kansas City to Oakland by a 9–1 vote. Two days later, they directed Finley to agree to the City Council's proposed four-year lease without an attendance clause, calling it "fair and reasonable." The vote authorized American
League President Joe Cronin to call a special meeting to consider expelling
Finley if he didn't sign it. Cronin sent Finley a telegram advising him to sign
the lease or face league action. He signed it.[7]

Colavito was a huge power upgrade for an outfield in 1963 that was led
by George Alusik's nine home runs. Finley turned to the acquisition of home
run hitters in a bid to gain a winning record and boost attendance. The team
had finished eighth in the ten-team league, 16 wins below .500. It was also
eighth in scoring runs and tied for dead last in homers. Gino Cimoli, the
team's Opening Day right fielder in 1963, only hit four. The Colavito trade
was the club's biggest since the seven-player deal that sent Roger Maris to the
Yankees in 1958, but the Athletics didn't stop there. They added a second
power hitter by acquiring Jim Gentile from the Orioles, nine days after getting
Colavito. Gentile had hit a career-high 46 home runs in 1961, one more than
Colavito, and 33 home runs in 1962. But like Colavito, his home runs took a

big drop in 1963, when he hit 24. "Ed Lopat, our manager, thinks we gave up a lot of young pitching for them," Finley said. "But we had to have hitting, and we had to have gate attractions."[8]

After Finley traded for Colavito, his freshly minted star player flew to Chicago at the owner's request to do interviews and discuss a contract. Colavito had earned $54,000 the previous year with the Tigers, but Finley sought a pay cut of $4,000. Angered, Colavito became a holdout on March 4, staying home in Pennsylvania as spring training got under way. Finley responded by offering to trade Colavito to the White Sox for outfielders Jim Landis and Dave Nicholson, but Ed Short, the White Sox general manager, turned the A's down. "We have some interest in Colavito, but we wouldn't pay that price for him," Short said. "We're not about to make that trade."[9] Colavito's brother Dom offered to pay his younger brother the $4,000 difference so he could get off to a good start in spring training, but Colavito agreed to the pay cut and ended his holdout. Before the 1964 season got under way, Colavito moved his family into an apartment with a swimming pool near the ballpark, where he and Carmen occasionally socialized with pitcher Moe Drabowsky and his wife.

As a showman, Finley used novel promotions and innovations to boost attendance and shake up the baseball establishment. He received permission from the league to use sleeveless, vest-type uniforms of Fort Knox gold trimmed in Kelly green, with Kelly green sweatshirts. The two-toned uniforms were worn with "kangaroo white" shoes. Finley added a "sea-foam" green and "wedding-gown" white to complement the gold uniforms the year Colavito joined the team. "I hated that green and gold uniform. It was gaudy, and it felt heavy," Colavito recalled. "The white with the green trim was nice, and the gray with green numbers was a very nice uniform. Why in God's name did they stick in the yellow?"

The Athletics' Municipal Stadium took on a circus atmosphere. Kansas City players would autograph the first three dozen balls used at home, providing autographed souvenirs early in the game when fouled into the stands.[10] Finley put sheep and a shepherd on an embankment beyond right field, which lasted until one of the sheep was killed after being beaned by a home run. Another died of a heart attack following a chase up the hill by a relief pitcher before a game. The shepherd didn't last long, either; he was supposed to ring a bell after an Athletics home run but fell asleep and was fired.[11] A small menagerie beyond the left field fence included six capuchin monkeys, six China gold pheasants, six German checker rabbits, and two peafowl.[12] At home plate, a compressed-air device installed below ground blew dirt away, and a mechanical rabbit named Harvey popped out of the ground to hand new baseballs to the umpire. There was also a team mascot, a Missouri mule named Charlie-O. The animal was draped in a Kelly green and gold blanket

The Athletics' unpredictable owner Charles O. Finley with team mascot Charley-O the Mule (Baseball Hall of Fame).

and bridle at the games, with a matching A's cap atop its head. Charlie O. was occasionally paraded onto the field with Finley, as the mule and the owner became synonymous with the Athletics' unconventional way of doing things.

Finley also wanted to introduce three-ball walks, colored bases and foul lines, and orange baseballs, but those ideas fell on deaf ears with league officials.[13] "We used an orange ball once in an exhibition game, and you couldn't see it as well as a white ball," Colavito said. Finley proved prescient, though, in his advocacy for the designated hitter, interleague play, and night-time World Series games. He also had a clock installed in the scoreboard to time pitchers to try to make umpires enforce a long-ignored rule that pitches needed to be delivered in 20 seconds. It was something former maverick owner Bill Veeck had also tried to do. The minor leagues at the Triple A and Double A levels would adopt the 20-second clock in 2015.

In another of Finley's antics, the owner hired a taxi cab with the meter running to take a relief pitcher to the mound after being summoned from the bullpen. Reliever Ted Bowsfield, in his haste to get into a game, forgot to wait for the taxi. He got the last two outs to seal the team's 2–1 victory, but

Finley laced into him after the game, leaving Bowsfield to wonder how much the owner cared about winning.[14] On "Automotive Industries Day," Finley wanted the team to ride on a fire truck decked out in team colors and fire hats. Colavito thought it was silly and balked at wearing something on his head, but Finley threw one of the heavy hats at him anyway, bruising his thumb and hurting his ability to bat for the next week.

Finley turned concert promoter on September 17, 1964, when he brought the Beatles to Kansas City's Municipal Stadium on their first tour of the United States, seven months after the band's maiden appearance on "The Ed Sullivan Show." The Beatles were paid $150,000 to perform a half-hour set of 12 songs in front of 20,280 fans—the most ever paid for a concert.[15] Jimmy Piersall, then with the Angels, added to the zaniness three weeks earlier by coming to the plate in Kansas City wearing a Beatles-style wig and strumming his bat like a guitar before the home umpire made him stop. On the day after the concert, Finley put Betty Caywood, a 32-year-old Chicago weather forecaster, in the broadcasting booth, the first woman to broadcast a major league game.[16] Colavito even got into the swing of things that season by taking part in a throwing contest prior to an Athletics-Angels game on July 24. He threw a ball from home plate over the center field fence, 410 feet away.[17] In 1965, Finley, always the attention-seeker, hired Bobbi Johnson, the reigning 1964 Miss USA titleholder, to be a bat girl and brought back 59-year-old Negro Leagues legend Satchel Paige to pitch one game.

To bring more excitement to the ballpark, Finley installed loud horns and flashing Kelly green and gold lights over the auxiliary scoreboard in left-center field in 1964, which went off when a Kansas City player hit a home run. He also brought the fences in at what was already considered to be a hitter's park. The center field fence was moved ten feet closer to home and given a shorter, five-foot height with the installation of a wire inner fence, compared to one that had stood almost 25 feet at its highest point. The distances to right field and right-center were also shortened to make the ballpark more homer-friendly.[18] This was nothing new: The 1964 season marked the sixth time in the team's ten-year Kansas City history that the outfield dimensions were changed. Balls traveled well to left field thanks to a recurring wind, and Finley proposed to Colavito moving in the left field fence prior to the season. The slugging outfielder urged him not to. "I think the fences are fair to everyone just as they are," Colavito told the owner. "You don't get any cheap home runs in Kansas City, but if you hit the ball right, it will go." He also had another reason not to see them brought in. "If they had moved the fences in and I had had a pretty good season, everyone would say I was hitting cheap home runs," he said.[19]

Believing Yankee Stadium's dimensions gave the perennial front-running team an advantage, Finley attempted to recreate the short right field porch by making the distance to the right field foul pole 296 feet. Finley was rebuked by Commissioner Ford Frick, who pointed to a rule that went into effect after June 1, 1958, requiring a minimum distance in new or remodeled parks of 325 feet down the left field and right field lines, and 400 feet to center field. Parks built prior to then with shorter distances, such as Yankee Stadium, were grandfathered in. To conform, Finley shortened the distance to the right field foul pole to 325 feet, with a homer-friendly distance of 360 feet in right-center. The new outfield dimensions produced an immediate power surge, with 43 balls leaving the park in Kansas City's first 11 home games.

Eddie Lopat was in his second season as A's manager in 1964, having gone 73–89 in 1963. The team's players were a mixed bag. Rookie second baseman Dick Green played stellar defense, and after a slow start, caught fire midway through the season, hitting at a .320 clip to finish with a higher average and more home runs than Jerry Lumpe, the player he had replaced. Wayne Causey was solid in the field at shortstop and at the bat, hitting .281 with 170 hits. Third baseman Ed Charles had a good year with the glove and contributed 16 home runs. Doc Edwards caught the bulk of games, batting .224. In the outfield with Colavito, who wore No. 7, the same number he had worn in Detroit, was center fielder Nelson Mathews, who set a team record with 143 strikeouts. Left field was patrolled by committee, with Alusik, Ken Harrelson, Jose Tartabull, and Manny Jimenez all seeing playing time. On the mound, Orlando Pena's 12 victories were enough to lead the team. Behind him were John O'Donoghue with ten wins and John Wyatt with nine. Workhorse Wyatt held down the bullpen, appearing in 81 games to break a major league record for appearances to go with his 20 saves. Wes Stock appeared in 50 games with a 1.94 ERA, and rookie Ken Sanders posted a 3.67 ERA.

Colavito had a good year with the Kansas City Athletics in 1964, but the team still finished in last place (Colavito's personal collection).

Colavito got off to an unusually fast start for Kansas City, ripping nine home runs through May 9, more than he had at the All-Star break the year before.

His first eight were hit out of the A's ballpark, showing how much he had found Kansas City's dimensions to his liking.[20] Colavito played in the 1964 All-Star Game as a substitute for Al Kaline at Shea Stadium, ripping a pinch-hit double to left-center in the seventh inning for his lone hit in two at-bats. Colavito was in right field with two outs and two on in the bottom of the ninth inning when Johnny Callison crushed a winning home run to right off Dick Radatz. "Callison's ball hit the wall separating the upper deck facing and bounced right back onto the field," Colavito recalled. "I picked the ball up and gave it to Jim Bunning, who was his teammate, to give it to Callison." The 7–4 victory put the National League ahead of the American League in wins for the first time since the Midsummer Classic began in 1933. The American League wouldn't take the lead over the National League again until 2018, when a record ten home runs were hit as the American League won, 8–6, in ten innings. Colavito, watching on TV from home, rooted for the American League, but fell asleep before the 3¾-hour game ended.

Colavito quickly became a fan favorite in Kansas City, continuing his practice of signing autographs after home games for every kid who stood in line. But despite the A's high hopes in the off-season, the team got off to a slow start and before long was firmly entrenched in last place. Eddie Lopat received a pink slip one-third of the way into the season, after compiling a 17–35 record. Replacing him was coach Mel McGaha, a former minor league ballplayer who had the distinction of playing basketball in the NBA for one season. McGaha promptly named Colavito team captain, only the second player to hold that honor since the club was in Kansas City. "It's a fine honor for Rocky, and he was very pleased about being named," McGaha said. "Rocky is well respected not only on our team but throughout the league. He'll be a fine example for our players on and off the field."[21] Colavito was deeply appreciative. "It was very prestigious, and I was honored," he said. Despite the team's losing ways, Colavito was praised in *The Sporting News* by a *Kansas City Star* beat reporter for making "a major contribution to the team's morale. Even though the Athletics are going nowhere, Colavito has hustled as if a pennant were at stake in each game."[22] The same writer noted how much Kansas City fans had taken to him. "The greatest source of Colavito's popularity is his never-ending hustle. Colavito has developed a rapport with the fans who sit in Charles Finley's pennant porch in right field. Youngsters display signs professing their loyalty to Colavito, and they faithfully applaud his every action."[23]

Colavito roomed on the road with fellow Italian Jim Gentile and felt that Gentile was treated poorly by the team. "Jim was supposed to get a bonus if he hit 27 home runs, and when he was getting close the team sat him down for several games," Colavito said. "I thought that was really lousy of them." So did Gentile. "When I signed, Finley calls me up and says what did you weigh when you hit 46 home runs? I said 215. He said you weigh 213 and

Italian ballplayers Colavito and Jim Gentile of the Kansas City Athletics and Tom Satriano and Jim Fregosi of the Los Angeles Angels posed for the cameras in 1964 (Wilborn & Associates Photographers).

under and I'll give you $125 on Tuesdays, and for every home run you hit over 27 I'll give you $1,000. I had 28 and was going for 30, but they didn't play me," he said.[24] It didn't help either player's relationship with management when they were the only players on the team to pass up a mid–July party held by Finley at his home in Chicago, when the Athletics were in town to play the White Sox. "We had a doubleheader the next day, and Rocky said, 'I'm not going to go to the party,' and he didn't either," Gentile said. "Neither did I. I think that put us on the wrong side of Finley."[25]

Gentile said Colavito was the best person he ever roomed with. "All the other years, with other guys they went their way, and I went my way," he said. "But with Rocky I was just glad to be around him, and l learned things." It also kept him out of trouble. "There are only three guys in baseball that I really was friendly with—Brooks Robinson, Gus Triandos, and Rocky Colavito," Gentile said. "They were guys you just felt great around and could talk to about anything. It was great to call him a friend. Everybody liked Rocky. He was one of a kind."[26]

Colavito reached a major milestone when he hit his 300th career home run against the Orioles. The accomplishment meant a lot to him, and he pressed at the plate as he drew closer to the mark. "We had a ten-game home-stand, and in those ten games I got two good balls to hit that I thought could be home run balls," Colavito said. "One I fouled off, and one I hit off the fence for a double." Finley wanted to present Colavito with 300 silver dollars flown in from a Las Vegas hotel for the occasion. He hired an armored Brink's truck with a driver at the ready at a daily cost of $21. The truck was parked behind a visible section of the chain-link center field fence, and play was to be halted after the home run to present Colavito with the bonus. But all the attention served to make pitchers more aware of the accomplishment—and that much more careful with their pitches, Colavito said. Gentile, batting in the lineup after him, said it worked to his advantage. "Nobody would pitch to Rocky," Gentile said. "He got a lot of walks, and it was great for me, because I think I drove in eight runs that week."[27]

After 16 days, Colavito deposited his 300th home run on September 11 over the left field fence in Baltimore in the first inning, with Wayne Causey aboard. The 380-foot blast came off hurler Dave Vineyard and produced Colavito's 900th career RBI. With the home run, in the second game of a doubleheader, Colavito became just the 24th major leaguer to reach the mark, eight of whom were still active. In his ninth full season, Colavito had become the fifth-fastest ever to reach 300 homers. Only Eddie Mathews, Jimmie Foxx, Ernie Banks, and Willie Mays got there sooner. "If Colavito, now 31, can avoid injuries, he has an excellent chance to finish among the greatest home-run hitters of all time," *The Sporting News* said. "Colavito appears almost certain to hit 400 homers, a total only ten men have achieved. If he has a reasonably long career, he could top the 500 mark. Only four players have broken through 500."[28]

Finley wanted to present a plaque with the silver dollars to Colavito, but it came with a hitch. Finley wanted to make the presentation at Brown University, where the A's owner was to give a speech. Colavito balked. "Finley was all about publicity for Finley, and he exploited anything and anyone he could. I said there is no way I am going to come up there. It has nothing to do with baseball. If you want to give me that plaque, you send it to my home, and if not, you keep it," Colavito said. Finley agreed on the condition that a photographer was there for publicity. The plaque arrived at Colavito's house in the off-season, and two photographers took pictures that appeared in newspapers the following day. The 125-pound mahogany memento featured metal strips under each silver dollar, listing the number of each home run, the date on which each occurred, and the city where it was hit. The plaque cost $1,800 in addition to the $300 in coins, with the 300th home run ball mounted on top. "To Rocky Colavito, an outstanding athlete and a great credit to the game of baseball," the inscription read. "The Kansas City Athletics are proud to make this presentation to you, Rocky, in honor of hitting your 300th major league home run—the 24th player in baseball history to accomplish this rare feat. Congratulations, Charles O. Finley." "It was gorgeous," Colavito said. "If he only kept up what he represented in that message he would have been all right, but he just didn't. Somebody must have written that for him."

Colavito had a scare late in the season when his daughter, Marisa, cut her right foot and had to be rushed to a hospital in Kansas City. After learning about it from a phone call, Colavito dashed to the hospital from the ballpark without stopping to change out of his uniform. "I could hear his cleats on the hospital floor as he entered the room," Marisa McGrath recalled. "He got close to reassure me that everything was going to be OK."[29]

The Athletics finished with a 57–105 record, 16 more losses than the year before and dead last in the league, 42 games behind the Yankees. Despite several successful promotions, attendance dropped by 119,886 in 1964 to 642,478. The A's dismal record came despite a boost in power that saw 239 home runs hit out of the Kansas City ballpark, nine short of the major league record. The team jumped to third in the league in home runs, led by Colavito's 34 round-trippers, four short of the record by a Kansas City player and fourth in the league. His 102 RBIs were fifth-highest, and his .507 slugging percentage ranked seventh. Colavito was also tied for first in the league with 11 winning hits. His season totals came closest to his career average over 162 games of 33 home runs, 102 RBIs and a .266 average. Gentile, slowed by a severe leg pull halfway through the season, hit 28 home runs, good for tenth in the league, and knocked in 71 runs. The shorter outfield dimensions also contributed to the pitching staff's 4.71 ERA, the league's worst. The 220 home runs the pitching staff gave up was a dubious league record until the Orioles topped it in 1987.

Despite Colavito's comeback season, it was one of the most frustrating of his career. "We didn't have a good team. We lost so many games, and I hated losing," he said. "We had a good infield, but the outfield was not as consistent. We had a good second baseman and shortstop in Dick Green and Wayne Causey, and a good first baseman in Jim Gentile." Despite the losing record, the fans who did attend games treated the players well, Colavito said. But after one year under Finley, he was ready to leave.

Charlie Finley was a nut case and a clown, and he wasn't a nice man. He exploited anything he could, and he wanted publicity for himself in any way, shape or form he could get it. And he and what passed as the brass knew nothing about baseball and showed no respect for baseball players. He was another egomaniac in the class of Frank Lane. Down deep I hoped I would be traded. I wanted to get away from Finley and from that organization. The team wasn't good, and everybody wants to be on a winner.

Finley convened the board of directors—himself and his family—after the 1964 season to discuss moving the team. Afterward, he reiterated his intention to leave Kansas City after the lease ran out following the 1967 season, and he stopped promoting season ticket sales. He also reversed course in 1965 by pushing back the outfield fences. The abrupt move away from power to defense, pitching, and speed made no difference in the standings, as the Athletics finished last again. A 40-foot screen was mounted atop the right field fence in 1966, helping to depress home run totals even further to 45 that year and 57 in 1967. Almost overnight, Kansas City's Municipal Stadium went from being one of the best home run-hitting parks ever in 1964, when 51 home runs were hit in the first homestand alone, to one of the stingiest. When the lease expired, Finley moved the team to Oakland and its new multi-purpose Oakland-Alameda County Coliseum for the 1968 season. The Athletics would become the best team in baseball in the early 1970s, winning the World Series three years in a row from 1972 to 1974, and claiming five consecutive division titles from 1971 to 1975, though Finley would never stray far from controversy.

Finley left behind a turbulent period in Kansas City, intruding on players, alienating and angering fans, infuriating local politicians, fighting with the media, and going through five general managers in seven seasons while delivering losing teams at or near the bottom of the standings in front of smaller crowds every year. "This loss is more than compensated for by the pleasure resulting from our getting rid of Mr. Finley," Missouri Sen. Stuart Symington said after the Athletics announced they were moving.[30] Comments from Finley, including "This is a horse-shit town. No one will ever do any good here," hadn't helped.[31]

But Colavito was long gone by then. After a five-year absence, he was returning to his true baseball home—the Cleveland Indians. He got the call at his Temple, PA, home from A's General Manager Pat Friday. "I was putting snowshoes on Rocco Jr., and Marisa before they left for school," Colavito said. "I thought it was about my contract. When he told me, I had to sit down.... Every year I thought this might be the year I go back. I could not be happier than I am right now."[32] The Indians announced on January 20, 1965, that they had reacquired Colavito as part of a three-team trade. Outfielders Jim Landis, a five-time Gold Glove winner, and Mike Hershberger, another outstanding defender, were obtained by the A's from the White Sox to patrol the outfield's newly-enlarged dimensions, along with up-and-coming pitcher Fred Talbot. The Indians sent budding pitcher Tommy John, who went on to win 286 of his 288 victories after the trade, outfielder Tommie Agee, the 1966 Rookie of the Year, and starting catcher John Romano to Chicago. The Indians also received catcher Cam Carreon from the White Sox.

The Indians, in a state of free-fall since Colavito's trade five years earlier, hoped his return would turn things around on the field and at the box office. "Cleveland went baseball batty at exactly 9 a.m. January 20," a reporter said. "Indians president and general manager Gabe Paul announced to an unbelieving city that Rocky Colavito was coming back."[33] "I liked the people in Kansas City—they were very good to me," Colavito said. "I liked the town, too. But I'm glad to be home in Cleveland, and I do mean home."[34] He had wondered over the past five years what it would be like to play for Cleveland once more. "Every year, when I went into Cleveland with the Tigers and Athletics, I'd say to myself, 'Wouldn't it be nice to be playing here again?'"[35]

The news of Colavito's return triggered a flood of emotions from Indians fans, who couldn't wait to see him wearing the team uniform in Municipal Stadium. That extended from older fans who grew up with him to younger fans who heard stories about the now-legendary player from their families or others. "They weren't exactly dancing in the streets. There was too much snow in Cleveland that day," *The Sporting News* said. "But don't bet the fans wouldn't have done just that if the weather had been better. That was the immediate reaction to the Indians' biggest trade of several winters—the one that brought back Rocky Colavito and righted the 'wrong' committed by Frank Lane almost five years ago."[36]

In announcing the trade, the A's lavished praise on Colavito. "It was with a great deal of reluctance that we traded Colavito," Friday, the general manager, said. "He is a great player, and he was a favorite with the fans here. I never have known a player who hustled as consistently and as much as Colavito."[37] The A's followed their trade of Colavito by selling Gentile to the Houston Astros for $150,000, another nail in the coffin for the team's one-year power-hitting experiment. Gentile would close out his career in 1966 as a teammate of Colavito's in Cleveland.

Hank Peters, an Athletics front office executive who followed Colavito to the Indians in 1965, said trading the team's star slugger away didn't go over well with Kansas City's fans, including one family member. "I thought for a while my son Steve would never speak to me again after Rocky went to Cleveland in that three-cornered swap with the White Sox," Peters said. "In the one season he was there, the Rock had taken the kids by storm, and they were plenty unhappy when he left."[38]

13

The Return

The Cleveland Indians had been a troubled franchise since April 17, 1960, when the Tribe traded away Rocky Colavito just as his career was in full flight. The Indians failed to compete in a pennant race for the next five seasons, and fans abandoned the team in droves. Home attendance increased by 125 percent in Rocky's last season, to 1,497,976. It plummeted by almost 550,000 the next season and continued to sink like the *Titanic*. In 1964, the Indians' 81 home games drew just 653,293 fans to the stadium, fewer than those who attended the nine Cleveland Browns games. Colavito's popularity and home run prowess had helped Cleveland retain its franchise in 1959 by putting fans in the stands when the team was considering leaving for another city.[1] Now, in 1965, he was being called on to do it again.

The Indians' board of directors had authorized Gabe Paul, who held the titles of president, general manager and treasurer, to explore moving the club to Oakland, Dallas, or Seattle. That remained a possibility even after the club signed a new lease months before reacquiring Colavito. Bringing Colavito back to revive interest in the Indians came at a steep price, with the team surrendering three players who factored into its plans.[2] Paul said it was difficult to lose so much talent, but the club had its back up against the wall. "We needed Colavito to save the franchise," he said. "We got him back on January 27, and the phones have been ringing every business day since, with people telling us it was the best move we ever made. Rocky always was something special in Cleveland."[3]

Colavito made $50,000 with the Athletics, and after hitting 34 home runs with 102 RBI for the last-place team, he asked for a $20,000 raise. Paul said the team was nearly bankrupt and couldn't afford that much, and Colavito agreed to sign for a lot less. His $55,000 salary still made him the team's highest-paid player.

Fans interviewed by the *Cleveland Plain Dealer* after the trade was announced were thrilled by Colavito's return. "We love Rocky. It's great to have him back. Best thing to happen in the last ten years," Bill Martieau of

South Euclid said. "The Indians are sure to draw a million," predicted Richard Barnett of Shaker Heights. "This will be great for the box office. Rocky will do for the Indians what Jim Brown does for the Browns," offered Bonnie Meyer of Brooklyn, Ohio. "Rocky is an idol in Cleveland," added Sandy Maniche of Aurora. "It is a great deal for Indian fans."[4]

Herb Score, Colavito's former roommate now working in the broadcasting booth, was thrilled to learn of his friend's return. "He called me as soon as he heard about the deal," Colavito said. "Both of us couldn't be happier. I'm in fine shape and hope I have four or five good years of baseball left."[5] For some fans, though, something had been lost in the intervening time between Colavito's trade and his return. "Rocky was like 'the man' for Cleveland—like Mickey Mantle was for the Yankees—and he was still pretty good when he came back, but the years he missed were what I missed," said Bill Jonke of Maple Heights, a small city south of Cleveland. "I was only 12 when he was traded, and I was 17 when he came back."[6]

Colavito asked to wear No. 6 again when he returned to the Cleveland Indians in 1965 but General Manager Gabe Paul said it had to be a number in the 20s (Barcroft Media).

Colavito wore No. 6 for the Indians for three years after switching from No. 38 in 1957. He asked to wear the number again, but Paul insisted on No. 21 instead. Colavito was unhappy about it, but the GM believed No. 6 was more appropriate for infielders, and numbers 21 through 30 were best suited for outfielders. The Indians opened the 1965 season losing three of their first four games on the road, but around 300 fans still showed up at the airport to greet the team. The largest Opening Day crowd in the majors that year turned out for Colavito's return, with 44,335 people pushing through the turnstiles on what the *Cleveland Press* dubbed "Welcome Back Rocky Day." It was Cleveland's best-attended home opener since Colavito suited up as a Detroit Tiger at the stadium, two days after the trade in 1960.

"The return to Cleveland was a fantastic day, a beautiful day," Colavito said. "The fans went bananas. They brought banners that hung from the stands saying things like, 'Welcome back, Rocky.' There were standing ovations, and it was very, very heartwarming." Pitcher Sam McDowell enjoyed taking in all the hoopla. "When he did come back to Cleveland, it was like the second coming, and I don't say that in a facetious way," he said. "The fan reaction was so fantastic when it was even announced he was coming back. I just sat there and watched the whole scene."[7] Colavito didn't disappoint on the field, hitting a sixth-inning round-tripper as the team won the season opener, 6–5, over the Los Angeles Angels. "Rocky's two-run homer in the sixth inning shook the ballpark like it hasn't been shaken in years," a press account said.[8] *Sport* magazine's Bob Sudyk described Colavito's effect on the crowd this way:

> As the ball landed in the left-field stands 400 feet from home plate, Rocky jogged around the bases. Down from the stands swept the mammoth roar from 44,335 fans. Rocky pulled hard at the peak of his cap several times in humble thanks. Then he was swallowed up in a mob of his teammates in the dugout. When the inning ended, he burst out of the dugout in his customary headlong dash for his right-field position. The entire crowd joined in a standing ovation that made the hair stand on end on the necks of the most cynical members of the audience. Rocky's homer put the Indians in front in a game they eventually won in ten innings on Leon Wagner's second home run, 6–5. Much more importantly, he had single-handedly brought the game into the heart of a city that seemingly had lost all feeling for baseball. Just last fall Cleveland was fighting apathy to keep the franchise from moving. The magic Rocky projects in Cleveland is as strong as ever, despite his five-year exile to Detroit and Kansas City. Everywhere you go, baseball fans agree that Cleveland is where he belonged and the place he never should have left. Seldom has a professional athlete and a city wanted and needed each other so much.[9]

Opening Day was a deeply heartwarming experience for Colavito. "I've thought about this day for a long time—a long time," he said. "When you come back after all these years, and before so many wonderful people, you wouldn't be human if it wasn't special. I would say it was one of the most memorable home runs in my career. What made everything perfect was that we won. I'll always remember this game." Afterwards, Wagner said, "I almost would feel bad about hitting those home runs if Rocky doesn't get one, too. He's one of the nicest guys I've met. Now I understand why all the fans here like him so well and wanted him back."[10]

Opening Day reviews overflowed with hope for the team's future. "The attendance shows first that when the management stocks the team with bona fide stars and keeps them around, the fans will come around, too," a reporter wrote. "The greatest move Gabe Paul ever made to prove his desire to stay in Cleveland was to bring Colavito back where he belongs."[11] An accompanying photo showed Colavito about to step on home plate after hitting

Colavito visited Sister de Montford and the children at Parmadale Children's Village of St. Vincent de Paul in June 1965 (Barcroft Media).

the home run under the headline, "Rocky's Home Again." A *Cleveland Plain Dealer* editorial also celebrated the Indians' large turnout and Colavito's return. "They saved their loudest, heartiest cheers for an old hero now back in local uniform, Rocky Colavito."[12] Colavito, at Paul's request, even posed with Frank Lane before the game, accepting a fruit basket to make light of the general manager's dismissive "fruit peddler" remark five years earlier.[13]

The Indians were coming off back-to-back 79–83 seasons, but the team had considerable promise, especially its young pitching staff. The hurlers included Sam McDowell, the 21-year-old southpaw, and 23-year-old Luis Tiant. Both had reached double figures in wins for the first time in 1964. Sonny Siebert, at 28, also showed considerable potential. Others on the staff being counted on were Jack Kralick, who won a team-leading 12 games the year before; newly acquired veteran Ralph Terry, who won 23 and 17 games for the Yankees before having a down year in 1964; and Don McMahon, a workhorse out of the bullpen whose 70 appearances in 1964 earned him the Indians' Man of the Year award. Gary Bell, a starter-turned reliever, was the only player still on the club that Colavito played with in the 1950s.

Colavito liked the hitting background and field dimensions in Cleveland's ballpark. "I loved playing in Municipal Stadium," he said. "I was kind of raised in that park" The Stadium was home to both the Indians and pro football's Browns (The Cleveland Press Collection, Michael Schwartz Library, Cleveland State University).

Unlike the pitching staff, the Indians were counting on several first-time starters among position players on the 1965 team. Joe Azcue was the catcher, Fred Whitfield was on first base, Pedro Gonzalez was the new second baseman, Larry Brown was moving over to short, and Max Alvis was at third. Joining Colavito in the outfield were left fielder Leon Wagner, who led the team in 1964 with 31 home runs and 100 RBI, and Gold Glove winner Vic Davilillo in center. Chuck Hinton was acquired from the Senators to come off the bench. The team's manager was Birdie Tebbetts, starting his third season at the helm. Colavito was named captain of the Indians, just as he had been in 1964 with the Athletics. The post was an indication of the stature he enjoyed. "You get respect by example," Colavito said. "Your peers see that you run out every ball and that you play as hard as you can, and they respect that." In early June, the *Cleveland Plain Dealer* published a photograph of Colavito showing Sister De Montford how to hold a bat while surrounded by some of the 220 children in attendance at Parmadale Children's Village of St. Vincent de Paul. "I'll help you get a grip on the bat if you'll help me get a grip on the man upstairs," Colavito was quoted saying in the caption.[14]

The Indians played .500 ball over the first two months of the 1965 season, but improved to 22–7 in June, moving from fifth to first place by the end of the month. McDowell won five of six to go with a sparkling 0.89 ERA. Terry shut down the opposition to go 4–0, and Siebert and Tiant won three games apiece. Colavito and Alvis each had eight home runs. One of Colavito's was a tape-measure shot in Cleveland on June 18 as the Indians beat the Angels, 3–2. "Rocky Colavito unloaded one of the mightiest home runs ever hit at Municipal Stadium," the *Cleveland Plain Dealer* reported.[15] "I never hit a ball harder," Colavito said of the sixth-inning home run off lefty Rudy May. "I've hit balls in the upper deck here, and some pretty good shots out beyond the fence. This was hit as hard as any of them. Maybe the hardest of all," he said of the 450-foot blast that cleared the fence in left-center.[16]

Colavito hit a bunch over the fence in that vicinity during his career. Baseball researcher Bill Jenkinson concluded that Colavito launched 14 balls into the left field upper deck at Municipal Stadium.[17] He also determined that Colavito drove 19 home runs into the upper deck in Tiger Stadium, one into the upper deck in Yankee Stadium, and two in the upper deck in Chicago.[18] Colavito thought the longest ball he ever hit in Cleveland may have been the one he sent into the upper deck off a breaking ball from the Orioles' Connie Johnson on July 12, 1957. "I knew it was about as good as I could hit a ball," he said.

Colavito was glad to have the Cleveland ballpark to hit in for half of his games again. "I loved Municipal Stadium," he said. "The dimensions—320 down the lines, 365 in left center and 410 in center—were good. I was kind of raised in that park." Although Municipal Stadium was located on Lake Erie, the wind was seldom a factor unless the weather was stormy. But the 78,000-seat stadium—baseball's largest—could feel vast and empty when attendance was poor. "There were times when there were like 6,500 people, and in that size ballpark it's like no one is there," Colavito said. "That wasn't fun. But there were times when there was a full house."

Fourteen-year-old Ida Pocci sat in the right-field seats at Municipal Stadium with her sister and their friends to see Colavito close-up. After the game, they would join other kids in the parking lot seeking autographs from ballplayers as they left the clubhouse. "Some would sign, and some wouldn't, or they would do it for a while and then stop," Pocci said. "Rocky was different. He would line the kids up—we had to make an orderly line, and there couldn't be any pushing or shoving—and we had to say, 'Thank you.' Rocky would always stay until we all got autographs." Pocci made Colavito a birthday cake when August 10 rolled around and gave it to a policeman standing outside the clubhouse. To her surprise, Colavito came out and thanked her for the cake. "He said it was delicious, and the guys ate it up in no time," Pocci said. "It was a thrill for a 14-year-old. Not only did I get to give him the cake, but he appreciated it." (Colavito said he typically received eight to ten cakes from fans on his birthday, which he would put on a table in the middle of the room for the players to eat, keeping one or two for himself.) The next season, Pocci wrote a letter to a newspaper defending her favorite player when she read he was having trouble with his manager. "He actually saw me in the stands the next day, said he had seen the letter and wanted to thank me for writing it," Pocci said. "He was so thoughtful in so many ways, no matter how popular he was, or how many people were seeking his attention."[19]

Colavito was helpful to players on other teams, in the same way Ted Williams was for him. Tony Conigliaro, the Red Sox slugger who at age 20 was on his way to leading the American League in home runs with 32 in only his second major league season, raved about Colavito after seeking batting advice during a mid–July series at Fenway Park. "He's the greatest guy I ever met," the fellow Italian-American star exclaimed. "I went and asked him if he could or would help me. He spent more than an hour with me," Conigliaro said.[20] Jerry Michalek was typical of Northeast Ohio Indians fans who worshipped Colavito for his likeability and skill. "I was a kid in the '60s, and he was my favorite player. He was my dad's favorite player, too," Michalek said. "I loved his batting stance, with the bat held real high and how he just stared

Left to right: Posing before the start of the 1965 season are Dick Howser, Chuck Hinton, Leon Wagner, Rocky Colavito, Max Alvis, Vic Davilillo, Larry Brown, Joe Azcue and Camilo Carreon (Ray Matjasic/Colavito's personal collection).

down and intimidated the pitchers. I lived for baseball, and I liked Vic Davalillo, Chico Salmon and Max Alvis—but I loved Rocky."[21]

At the All-Star break, the club's record was 48–34, and Colavito was batting .298 with a league-leading 20 home runs and 61 RBIs. Davalillo was hitting at a .321 clip, good for third in the league, and Terry, McDowell, and Siebert each had nine wins, one behind the league leader. Colavito and Davalillo were voted starters, and Alvis was picked as a reserve in the 1965 All-Star Game. Playing right field and batting cleanup, Colavito went 1-for-4 with a run-scoring single as the National League won in Minnesota, 6–5. McDowell pitched two innings and was saddled with the loss.

The second half of the season for Colavito began with an injury. He suffered a back spasm that made it difficult to hit for power. "I had 20 home runs in the first half, and in my mind, I could have wound up with 40 or more," Colavito said. "But I hurt my back, and it really messed me up. I never really regained my power." The injury happened while running from first base toward third on a single, causing him to be taken out of the game. The back injury limited Colavito to six home runs in the second half of the season, when he typically hit best, but he still drove in runs at a good pace. In September, Colavito reached a personal milestone with his 1,000th career run batted in. His defensive contributions included a game at Yankee Stadium when he ran back to the low bleacher wall in right field, crouched in front of the 344-foot marker, and leaped to rob a batter of a home run.[22] Playing all 162 games despite the back injury, Colavito went errorless in right field in 274 chances, becoming the first American League player to play every game of a season without an error, and only the second major leaguer after Danny Litwhiler of the Philadelphia Phillies in 1942. It was quite a feat for a player who had learned to compensate for a lack of speed and an at-times erratic throwing arm with preparation, anticipation, and experience.

But the injury continued to take its toll on Colavito at the plate. In the last month of the 1965 season, he batted .310 but with just one home run. Like Colavito, the Indians fared worse in the second half of the season, finishing in fifth place with 87 wins and 75 losses. Even so, it was the Indians' most wins since Colavito's last season with them in 1959, and the team's best record from 1960 to the strike-shortened season of 1994. Colavito batted .287 with a league-leading 108 RBIs and 26 round-trippers, fifth in the league. He was also first in walks, second in on-base percentage, third in hits, fourth in total bases, and fifth in runs scored. Davalillo hit a team-leading .301, and four Indians hit 21 or more home runs, led by Wagner with 28. Siebert blossomed with 16 wins and a 2.43 ERA, while Terry allowed only 1.2 walks per nine innings, fewest in the league. But the team's most dominant pitcher was McDowell. In a breakout season, McDowell won 17 games with a stingy 2.18 ERA and 325 strikeouts, second-most in team history behind Bob Feller's

348 in 1946. It was the first of McDowell's five league-leading strikeout seasons, and the first of four seasons that he won 15 games or more. In 1968, McDowell posted a 1.81 ERA. But the six-time All-Star also suffered from wildness, leading the league in walks five times and losing 14 or more games four times at the height of his career. The pitcher, who battled alcoholism during his playing career, had a record with the Indians of 122–109, averaging slightly more than a strikeout per inning and compiling a 2.99 ERA.

"Sam McDowell had a great arm," Colavito said. "He had a great fastball and a great curve ball, and a very good slider and an excellent changeup. He wasn't afraid to throw the changeup on a 3–2 count. He did it to me three times in a row once, and that was unheard of. With all that ability, he could have been even better than he was, and he was a helluva pitcher." Colavito left a lasting impression on McDowell.

> He was probably one of the classiest acts in baseball. He wore a suit and tie and dressed like that every day at home and on the road. The rest of us only wore one when we traveled on a plane and couldn't wait to take it off and put on work clothes. He always shined his shoes—he would sit there with his shoe kit before the game and spit shine them—and had the same attitude with his uniform. He made sure his bats were polished and clean before he took them out and put them in the bat rack before the game. You might say he was a little obsessive-compulsive with cleaning, but he was just first class. When he was at the plate, Rocky had the same exact mannerisms of Joe DiMaggio. You would swear it was DiMaggio up at bat.

McDowell also marveled at Colavito's throwing ability. "The outfield was big in Municipal Stadium, but I saw him throw runners out from the right-field corner. He had the most amazing arm from the outfield I ever saw. He'd throw it on a line all the way to third base, right on the spot. I saw him pitch, and he was unbelievable. I personally believe he could have been a great pitcher if he wanted to." Colavito's character also left a lasting impression on the pitcher. "Rocky was a very quiet leader. The way he went about his job made him a leader. He wasn't boastful—in fact he was very humble—and I never heard him say anything bad or negative about anybody. He was very genuine and extremely proud. I would have to say that if you wanted to design a perfect athlete in ability and personality, Rocky probably was the most perfect."[23]

The fans responded to the Indians' season and Colavito's return by coming back to the ballpark in numbers not seen since the trade. The Indians had 934,786 ticket buyers, compared to 653,293 the previous season. Bringing Colavito back had worked; talk of relocating the newly revived franchise was laid to rest. Colavito finished fifth in the voting for the Most Valuable Player Award and was voted the Indians' Man of the Year by the Cleveland chapter of the Baseball Writers' Association, with McDowell a distant second. Colavito was the first Indian to win the award twice, having done so in 1958. A silver-engraved serving tray was presented to him at the annual "Ribs and Roasts" affair held in a hotel in downtown Cleveland. A columnist added to the swooning over Colavito's return. "There have been some pretty fair love affairs in our time.... But the greatest of them all has never made the gossip columns. One must be there and see it to believe it. It is pure, undying and unbelievable—the romance between Cleveland and Rocky Colavito."[24] But as Colavito, his fans, and his adopted city knew all too well, love stories don't always have happy endings.

14

Breakup

The Indians were coming off their best season in half a dozen years in 1965, and Rocky Colavito, after a productive and satisfying season, was thrilled to be back in a Cleveland uniform. He was also healthy again, now that the back injury that had sapped his power over the second half of the season was healed. He signed a contract for $68,000 for the 1966 season, the most he ever earned in his career. (That had the buying power of about $530,000 in 2018, accounting for inflation.)

In spring training in Tucson, Colavito posed for photographs with Paul Newman, the great actor from Shaker Heights, and teammates Leon Wagner and Chuck Hinton. The same starters and most of the pitchers were back, and confidence in the blend of seasoned veterans and emerging stars was validated when the club sprinted out of the starting gate in April. The Indians won their first ten games, outscoring opponents, 43 to 23, though it was matched by the Baltimore Orioles' equally fast start. Colavito hit .302 in the opening month but hurt his throwing shoulder in a game against the Yankees on May 4. The injury happened when Colavito fielded a line drive off the bat of Roger Maris that went down the right field line in Yankee Stadium. "I went into the corner, where it said 296 feet," Colavito said. "I cut it off and should have turned to my left. Instead, I put the brakes on, straightened up and threw to second because I knew Roger would try for two. That's when I felt something go in my shoulder." It was Colavito's first arm injury, and he received cortisone shots to take away the pain. But he believed he permanently lost velocity on his throws—perhaps ten percent—due to the injury. Colavito's bat went into a tailspin afterward, hitting just .189 with only two home runs and nine RBI in May. Colavito's fourth round-tripper of the season, on May 18, was his only career pinch-hit homer. It came with two on and two outs in the ninth at Cleveland to spoil a shutout bid by the Senators' Pete Richert.

The month of May also saw the publication of *Don't Knock the Rock: The Rocky Colavito Story*, written by veteran *Cleveland Plain Dealer* columnist

161

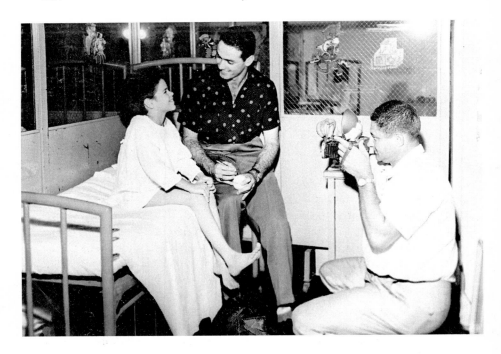

Colavito visited a Cleveland hospital on August 15, 1956 (Colavito's personal collection).

Gordon Cobbledick to capitalize on the player's triumphant return to the Indians. "The star that came home. A public idol, an athlete credited with the single-handed revival of baseball enthusiasm in Cleveland," was how the book was hyped in an ad that ran in Cleveland newspapers.[1]

As ever, Colavito could be found after home games, lining children up and signing autographs for each one. "When I first came to the big leagues, there was a Saturday afternoon game and he had a crowd of about 200 people," catcher Duke Sims recalled. "The rest of us usually got in our cars and left. I watched him. What I learned was how you make people feel good and keep them in control. I remember being on the bus a lot of times, or in my car, and seeing Rocky coming out there. All of a sudden here comes 50 kids, and he'd sit there and sign them all. He didn't want anyone to go away disappointed."[2]

Colavito rebounded in June, hitting .297 with 10 home runs and 23 RBIs, including three home runs in a doubleheader against the Red Sox on June 22 and two more in a game against the Athletics two days later. In the middle of the month, the Indians acquired Jim Gentile, Colavito's power-hitting roommate with the Athletics. But Gentile was used sparingly in what was his last season, batting just .128 with two home runs. June also saw Sonny Siebert pitch a no-hitter against the Senators at home, winning 2–0. Colavito started the game but was taken out for a pinch-runner and replaced in right by Jim Landis, now a teammate after going to Kansas City in the three-way trade that brought Colavito to Cleveland. That month also saw Colavito's errorless streak halted at 234 consecutive games on June 16, setting an American League fielding record. The streak had begun on September 8, 1964, as a member of the Athletics. Colavito had come a long way since Mike McNally, who signed him, told Hank Greenberg, then the Indians GM, that Colavito's flat feet made him unsuitable to be an outfielder.

Colavito was named to the American League All-Star team in 1966 for the sixth time and the third year in a row. "It's a great honor," he said at the time. "Sure, it's nice to have the time off, but anytime they pick me, I'll be there."[3] Playing in his ninth and final All-Star Game, in St. Louis, Colavito flied out to Hank Aaron in the eighth inning as a pinch-hitter in a game the National League won, 2–1, in extra innings. For his All-Star Game career, Colavito had six hits in 25 at-bats for a .240 average, including three home runs, hit in 1959, 1961 and 1962. The three blasts were, as of 2019, tied for third-most, and his eight RBIs were tied for fourth.

Many of Colavito's teammates during his second tour with the Indians were struck by how the team captain carried himself. "Rocky was probably the finest gentleman I ever played baseball with," Max Alvis said.

> He had high moral character and was a friend, a gentleman, a good family man and a great ballplayer and teammate. You could expect 110 percent from Rocky Colavito every time he put the uniform on. It was a pleasure to be a teammate of his because you knew you could depend on him. He had your back. As I look back on my career, I wasn't a star by any stretch of the imagination, and he was, and for him to have conversations and to show interest in me was special. He was as good an individual as I ever played ball with or against.[4]

Luis Tiant, who came from Cuba to the United States to play baseball, also had a deep affection for Colavito. "For me he was my best buddy, the only person who really took me under his wing when I came to Cleveland," Tiant said. "That's something you keep in mind the rest of your life. He's like a brother to me. Rocky was a straight shooter who didn't care about someone's color or any of that. He got along with everybody."[5] Joe Azcue got to know Colavito well because their lockers were side by side. Colavito's locker, he said, was immaculate. "Everything was always in its place, and looked perfect," Azcue said. He was impressed by Colavito's prowess at the plate and his powerhouse of an arm. "They put ballplayers in the Hall of Fame who are not in the same caliber of Rocky," he said. But Azcue was struck more than anything about how Colavito represented himself. "You say classy, that's Rocky," Azcue said.[6] Larry Brown also held Colavito in high esteem. "You hear your whole life in sports about guys being leaders," he said. "I kind of disagree with what a lot of people say a leader is. A leader is a guy who produces. Rocky was a leader on and off the field. He was like a class above everybody else. It's like he wore a better suit than everybody else. He was a star but didn't act like one."[7]

Ballplayers who were beginning their major league careers found Colavito friendlier and more approachable than most veterans. That was Sonny Siebert's experience. "When I signed with the Indians, they sent me to Cleveland, and I got to take infield and outfield practice with Rocky. My wife was with me, and although Rocky was a star, he took time to show us around downtown Cleveland. He was very friendly and showed us a good time. I was really impressed by him."[8] Pitcher George Culver experienced Colavito's generosity, too. "Rocky treated us younger guys like veterans, and he never talked down to us," Culver said. "I had the ultimate respect for Rocky. He would have made a great manager."[9] Dave Nelson, an African American minor leaguer trying to make the club that year in spring training, also found Colavito to be more welcoming than other veterans. "He introduced himself and said, 'Let's play some catch.' He made me feel welcome. He was a genuinely great person and humble for a great star," Nelson said.[10] Duke Sims said Colavito was the ultimate role model for a young player "I remember how Rocky carried himself, and really what a star he was within American League baseball. Everywhere he went, he was Rocky Colavito. He was in the Al Kaline class, the Mickey Mantle class. If you were a young ballplayer, that's who you looked up to."[11]

The second half of the 1966 season began poorly for the Indians, with the team going 11–19 in July. The summer was also a period of intense social unrest in Cleveland. A riot that lasted for six days erupted on July 18 over issues of racism and social and economic inequality in the black neighborhood of Hough. Cleveland was one of several major cities across the United States that saw similar eruptions in the mid–1960s. Yet, as Cleveland was reeling from violence that saw four people killed, 50 injured, 275 arrested, and numerous incidents of arson and firebombing, Colavito said the riot wasn't discussed in the clubhouse. "Ballplayers didn't talk about it," Colavito said. "We just went on with our daily routine and about our business." Carl Stokes was elected mayor of Cleveland the following year in response, the first African American mayor of a major city.

Colavito hit nine homers in July, giving him 23 at the end of the month. After going 15–17 in August, the Indians fell 15 games behind the Orioles. Birdie Tebbetts wasn't around to see the end of the season. He was fired on August 19, elevating coach George Strickland to interim manager.

Colavito wasn't sad to see Tebbetts depart. Their relationship had hit rock bottom after the manager accused the ballplayer in the clubhouse of being a "showboat" on a throw to the plate in a game in early August. It was another case of Colavito's short fuse leading him to lose control with an authority figure when he felt mistreated, and then carrying a grudge afterward. "I was livid. It's the worst thing he could have called me. I charged him and said, 'You can call me anything you want, but you can never call me a showboat.' All the guys jumped in front of me, and I would not talk to him after that, even though I knew he regretted it."

Colavito was fined $500 by the league, which the team reimbursed him after Tebbetts' departure. The change of managers made little difference in the team's play. Cleveland ended the disappointing 1966 season with an 80–80 record, 17 games behind the Orioles.

Despite the team's poor showing, attendance remained steady at 903,359, a drop of just 31,427. Colavito, playing through the shoulder injury, slumped to .129 with only two homers and three RBIs for the final month, including a stretch of 29 straight hitless at-bats. He was kept out of the starting lineup in eight of the final twelve games, believing it was at Gabe Paul's direction.[12] Colavito hit 30 home runs, good for sixth in the league. It marked the 11th year in a row he hit 20 or more home runs in a season, and the seventh time with 30 or more. But his 72 RBIs were the fewest he had over a full season, and his .238 batting average was a career low.

Colavito also hit into a league-leading 25 double plays. Little did he know that the 1966 season would mark the end of his career as a full-time player.

The off-season brought a new addition to the Colavito family—Steven James Colavito, Rocky's and Carmen's third child, was born on November 21, 1966. But the joy felt in the Colavito household was tempered by a changed attitude toward Colavito from the Indians' front office. Gabe Paul, who brought Colavito back to Cleveland two years earlier as a savior for the team, now tried to cut his salary 25 percent, the maximum allowed. Colavito balked and held out until March 7, before accepting a 15 percent pay cut that lowered his pay to $58,000. Colavito expected to have a better 1967 season and make the money back and more in his next contract negotiations. But things were about to get worse.

Colavito's new manager was Joe Adcock, a power-hitting first baseman who hit 336 home runs in a 17-year career with the Braves, Reds, Indians, and Angels. Adcock hit several memorable home runs in the 1950s. There was the titanic shot in Ebbets Field that landed on the double-deck roof in left center; the first of only three home runs ever hit to center field at the Polo Grounds; four home runs in a game at Ebbets Field; the ball he hit to become the first right-handed hitter to clear the 60-foot-high scoreboard in right-center at Connie Mack Stadium in Philadelphia; and the fence-clearing blast to break up the perfect game Harvey Haddix took into the 13th inning that was changed to a double after passing Hank Aaron on the base paths. One might have thought Adcock and Colavito, as power hitters, would have had a lot in common, if only for being in the select group to hit four home runs in a game. Colavito's accomplishment in 1959 was the first since Adcock did it in 1954. When the two ballplayers set foot on a field on opposite teams in April 1963, *The Sporting News* saw fit to point out the historic occasion: "For the first time in the history of the American League, two players who have hit four home runs in one game in the majors were members of opposing clubs when the Indians and Tigers clashed here, April 11," the article said.[13] But Colavito said he and Adcock never discussed hitting four home runs in a game. "I didn't like him, and he didn't like me," Colavito said.

Their mutual dislike started in a spring exhibition game in 1956. Colavito singled off Milwaukee's Juan Pizarro, and Adcock held him on at first. Red Kress, a first-base coach Colavito said could be surly at times, made a remark that bothered him, and he let the coach know it. That's when Adcock entered the picture. "Adcock stuck his two cents in and said I shouldn't talk like that to my coach," Colavito recalled. "I said, 'Why don't you mind your own fucking business?'"

In 1964, Colavito was on first base against the Angels when Adcock, in his last year as a player, asked him how many career home runs he had. "He was jealous because I had passed him in home runs," Colavito said. "He took it personal. Adcock and Neil Chrisley—who I didn't think was a team player and hardly ever had a good thing to say about anybody—were the only two players I disliked my whole career." Colavito spotted Gabe Paul eating breakfast with Adcock in Anaheim, where the Indians were closing out the 1966 season. He hoped Adcock wasn't going to be offered the manager's job. "I thought, 'Oh my god, no,'" Colavito said. "Later, I heard Gabe Paul admitted right after he signed him that he knew he made a mistake. He told Adcock that managers and general managers were expected to attend the World Series to make trades and that sort of thing, and Adcock told him he wasn't going."

The rookie manager promptly announced in spring training that Colavito would hit better if platooned in left field with the left-handed-hitting Leon Wagner. Chuck Hinton was named the starting right fielder. "He's the same kind of hitter I was," Adcock said of Colavito. "He hits the fastballers real good, but some of those guys with the good curve and change-ups give Rocky some trouble."[14] Colavito's lack of speed in the outfield and Wagner's defensive lapses were also offered as reasons why the two men would take turns playing. "Platooning, of course, means more splinters for Rocky than Wagner," a writer observed. "If the switching continues, the Rock will be in the dugout about three quarters of the time, or else become one of the game's all-time highest paid pinch-hitters."[15]

Colavito received a jolt on Opening Day. "I didn't know I wasn't starting in Kansas City until I looked at the lineup card," he said. "I couldn't believe I wasn't going to play." In the month of April, Colavito had just 12 at-bats in 15 games, appearing in only seven. Hinton led the team with a .317 average, but starting wasn't easy on him, either. "The fans hated me because they thought I had stolen Rocky's job," Hinton said. "Colavito and I got along fine, but it put a lot of pressure on me and created a bad situation on the club." Hinton was batting over .300 when Adcock suggested he change his batting stance by moving up on the plate. "I had never hit that way in my life, but he was the manager. I wound up hitting .245. You tell me who was right."[16]

Sitting on the bench, Colavito got to observe Adcock's decisions up-close, and he couldn't believe

Colavito didn't like Indians manager Joe Adcock, and the feeling was mutual (Barcroft Media).

what he was seeing. "He was the all-time worst manager I ever played for," Colavito said. "He was so bad I just assumed he was the worst manager in baseball ever. He made mistakes a Little League manager wouldn't make. Plus, he was a sour-looking, miserable human being."

Adcock fined players for all kinds of on-field infractions, such as walking a leadoff hitter after the seventh inning or not driving home a run in certain situations. Knowing how much players resented it, the team captain went into Adcock's office to tell him, thinking it would be helpful for the manager to know.

> I walked in and said, "Can we have a man-to-man talk?" He said sure. I said, "I just want you to know that a lot of our young pitchers are really shook up about the fines. It's putting pressure on them and not making them pitch as well as they can." He had a fit. I said, "Joe, I just asked if we can have a talk, and if you don't want to, we don't have to." He said something like, who was I to come in his office, and I said, "I'm not trying to do anything but help the team." Finally, I said, "You're a fucking asshole."

Before leaving, Colavito challenged Adcock to a fight outside the office, which Adcock declined.

Culver said it wasn't just Colavito who didn't get along with Adcock. "I remember how uncomfortable guys were in the clubhouse with him. Joe had this thing about older guys. There was something that bugged him about them. Joe didn't like Jim Gentile or Leon Wagner. He and Max Alvis went at it all the time, too. That's why he only lasted one year."[17] Siebert said he had a run-in with Adcock because the manager refused to believe he was suffering from an inner-ear problem, a life-long affliction.[18] Sims also said players and Adcock were often at odds. "That whole ball club didn't have a good relationship with Joe. There were several different meetings where guys expressed disgust with the way he managed," with and without management present. "In my case, he wanted to completely change how I hit and how I approached hitting. He also didn't run the pitching staff well, and that's key."[19] Infielder Vern Fuller said it was pretty clear where the team stood when it came to the Colavito-Adcock rift. "We all respected Rocky, of course. He was an icon. Joe Adcock was as dumb as a pole."[20]

Colavito didn't hit his first home run of the 1967 season until May 3, and he started only 18 games during the month, appearing in two others as a pinch-hitter. Wagner complained about being platooned, but Colavito stayed quiet until blasting Indians management on May 16. An article with his comments was splashed across the top of the *Cleveland Plain Dealer's* front page.

Rocky Colavito, fed up with his role as a part-time outfielder, finally broke his silence here last night and issued a public complaint against the Indians' management. In a prepared statement to the newspaper, the 33-year-old Bronx-born slugger hinted that manager Joe Adcock was under orders by General Manager Gabe Paul not to play him regularly. He also said he would retire if he felt he couldn't do well as a regular, and the ball club would have a better chance of scoring runs if he and Wagner were in the lineup at the same time. "I'm not asking them to trade me because I love Cleveland, and I've always been treated wonderfully by the fans. But I'd be better off leaving than sitting on the bench," Colavito said.[21]

Another low point came when Colavito was pinch-hit for in Fenway Park, a haven for right-handed power hitters. The only other time that happened to him was in the 1959 All-Star Game, when he was taken out for Ted Williams. With one out and the bases loaded, Adcock sent the left-handed-hitting Wagner to hit for Colavito against right-handed reliever John Wyatt. Colavito reacted by firing his bat at the rack, which hit the concrete back wall and bounced back into the dugout. He also exchanged words with Adcock. Some sportswriters complained afterward that Colavito was not being a "team player."

Colavito's last home run in an Indians uniform came on June 14 off the Angels' Clyde Wright. His playing career in Cleveland ended on July 29, when he was dealt to the Chicago White Sox. In exchange, the Indians received

$50,000, aging reserve outfielder Jim King, batting .188, and a player to be named later, who turned out to be journeyman infielder Marv Staehle. King would get three hits in 21 at-bats for Cleveland before being released in his last season, and Staehle never wore an Indians uniform. It was clear the team no longer wanted Colavito or his high salary. "When Adcock called me into the office to tell me I had been traded, I made a 180-degree turn to get the hell out of there. I don't remember shaking hands with him or anything," Colavito said. "I never looked at it as the team didn't like me anymore. I looked at it that Adcock and Paul didn't want me. I knew the fans always cared about me, and that overruled any other thought."

Colavito batted .241 with five home runs and 21 RBIs in 63 games, 13 as a pinch-hitter on an Indians team mired in the second division with a 45–53 record. The news devastated Colavito fans in Cleveland and throughout Northeast Ohio. Gerry Nemeth was one of many youths shattered by the news. "When I was a kid growing up in the Sixties, every kid wanted to be either Rocky Colavito or Mickey Mantle. I would do the Colavito stretch on deck, and then strike out on three pitches, but I was still Rocky Colavito," Nemeth said. "When he got traded the second time, we cried."[22] Brent Kecskemety, who grew up in Cleveland, said Colavito's sudden departure hit hard in a family that was always ready to spit at the mention of Frank Lane's name. "When Rocky returned from Detroit, he was a returning hero," Kecskemety said. "It was just awesome. He was my first favorite player, and 21 became my favorite number. It was sad when he was traded. People knew he wasn't the same that year, but they still really wanted him to stick around. The Indians tried to build up Ken Harrelson a couple of years later as Rocky's replacement, but it didn't work."[23]

"Rocky was handled poorly this season," a columnist wrote. "Even before he arrived in Tucson, plans had been made to platoon him. It seemed this was the way to punish the outfielder for his holdout.... The Rock is gone but it will take a long time before he's forgotten here."[24] In the *Cleveland Plain Dealer*, Colavito said, "I'll always have a warm spot in my heart for this city. It's been real good to me. But the situation being what it is, I guess it's better that I leave. However, I am leaving with a certain amount of sadness."[25] Gabe Paul, for his part, denied that Colavito's holdout earlier in the year and his inability to get along with Adcock had anything to do with the trade. Adcock concurred. "I agree with what Gabe told you. As far as I'm concerned, we had no problems," he told a reporter.[26] Colavito remained convinced the platooning was a set-up to trade him. "Gabe Paul wanted to soften the blow for himself before trading me by all of a sudden making me a part-time player," he said. "[Former Indians GM] Hank Greenberg told me to watch out for Gabe Paul. He said the wider his smile gets, the worse he'll put a knife in your back."

"That was the worst thing," Joe Azcue said, recalling the trade years later. "Colavito was Cleveland."[27] Max Alvis was also upset. "I remember 'the Rock is back' [excitement], and how hopefully we were going to experience his great production as a Cleveland Indian again, and maybe bring a pennant to the Indians because of our good pitching. If we could get Rocky to do those things, maybe he'd put us over the edge and bring a pennant to Cleveland. The rest of us didn't do our part, I guess."[28]

Rocco Jr., cried at the news that his father had been traded. His father was feeling low, too. He felt hurt by the rejection and saddened by how things turned out. "I didn't want to get dealt. I always felt that was my town," Colavito said. He wondered through the years what it would have been like if he had never been traded from Cleveland, believing his career statistics would have been better. Unlike some ballplayers, Colavito never wanted to leave. "Your name becomes synonymous with the team you started with or played the most with," he said. "People still think of me as a Cleveland Indian. I would have liked to have stayed my whole career in Cleveland."

15

Back to the Bronx

Rocky Colavito never particularly liked the Chicago White Sox. Suddenly, in the middle of the 1967 season, he was wearing their uniform. After returning to Cleveland and thinking he would finish his career there, Colavito instead found himself on his fourth team in five years. "Your job is to go and report to the new team, and do whatever they ask of you," Colavito said. "You're going to play as hard as you can against the Indians or anyone else. But making that switch is the hardest adjustment for any ballplayer. Another hard part is if you went down in the standings." That wasn't the case here.

The White Sox were in first place with a 56–41 record, 12 games ahead of the seventh-place Indians. If there was an upside to the trade, it was that Colavito had suddenly been thrust into the middle of a pennant race. He also admired Eddie Stanky, the team's scrappy manager. One of the coaches was also a familiar figure in Colavito's career—his former manager, Kerby Farrell. Colavito played under him at minor league stops in Reading and Indianapolis, and in 1957 with Cleveland, where Stanky was one of Farrell's coaches. "I was on the same club as Rocky, and I know nobody with so much pride," Stanky said upon Colavito's arrival. "Rocky'd give his paycheck just to be with a champion."[1] Despite the White Sox's perch atop the American League, Colavito was joining a team with an anemic offense that he expected to bring a charge to. The White Sox finished the 1967 season with a .225 team batting average, the lowest for a first-division team since 1909. They scored only 463 runs and got shut out 23 times, new lows for a 162-game season. The team-leading batting average was a paltry .241, from both right fielder Ken Berry and third baseman Don Buford.

The team's strength was its pitching, led by starters Joel Horlen (19–7, 2.06 ERA) and Gary Peters (16–11, 2.28 ERA). The team's ace in the hole was its dominating bullpen of Hoyt Wilhelm (1.31 ERA), Don McMahon (1.67), Bob Locker (2.09) and Wilbur Wood (2.45). Colavito roomed with McMahon, a veteran pitcher and fellow New Yorker who came over to the White Sox in a trade with the Red Sox in June. The two former Indians hit it off. Colavito also became close with veteran third baseman Ken Boyer, acquired the week before in a trade with the Mets. Colavito was already friendly with Ken's brother, Clete, and later coached alongside Cloyd, a third Boyer brother, in Kansas City. "That power-hitter [Boyer] from the National League hits a big home run for us, and now one of the big sluggers in the American League [Colavito] is joining us," Stanky said, predicting that the image of the White Sox as a weak-hitting team would change.[2]

After Colavito joined his new team in Chicago for a doubleheader, the White Sox played the Indians in Cleveland. He was in the lineup against Luis Tiant and hit a game-winning home run in the tenth inning, after Boyer's single tied the score. After the game, Colavito told the press he wasn't seeking vengeance against the Indians. "It's nothing against my former teammates. They're a great bunch of guys. I'm not trying to hurt anyone," he said. "But being traded and everything, I just wanted to help my new club win."[3] Colavito received a warm reception from the Cleveland faithful. "The Cleveland fans cheered Colavito when he was announced as the clean-up hitter, and when

he came up to bat," a reporter wrote. "They unleashed some boos when he made an out and gave a standing ovation when the game-winning, two-run homer left the ballpark."[4]

The game-winning blast was among seven runs Colavito drove home for the White Sox in his first 11 games. It was also the first of three game-winning hits he had against the Indians, including a ninth-inning single in the same series. He later singled to knock in the only run in a 17-inning game between the two teams. But as in Cleveland, Colavito saw only limited playing time in Chicago. He believed it had less to do with diminishing skills than perception. "In those days, when you were 34 or 35 they thought you were finished," Colavito said. "It was like a stigma they put on players." Tommy John, traded to

Colavito joined the Chicago White Sox in mid–1967, when the team was in the thick of a pennant race (Baseball Hall of Fame).

Chicago from Cleveland in the three-way trade that brought Colavito back to the Tribe, appreciated the way his new teammate carried himself on and off the field. "Rocky played the game the way it's supposed to be played," John said. "He was also a gentleman. He dressed like a gentleman and behaved like a gentleman."[5] Ken Berry also thought highly of his new teammate. "He was a classy guy," Berry said.[6]

The 1967 pennant race in the American League was one of the most thrilling in baseball history. The White Sox, Twins, Tigers, and Red Sox were all in contention going into the final weekend of the season, when Chicago lost its final five games to the sixth-place Washington Senators and the last-place Kansas City Athletics, both with losing records. The "Impossible Dream" Red Sox, propelled by Carl Yastrzemski's late-season heroics and Triple Crown season, finished on top. It was the closest Colavito ever came to being on a pennant-winning team and reaching the World Series. "All the years in the league, and I never played on a pennant winner," Colavito said. "No matter what you do individually, you want once, just once, to know what it's like to win it all."[7]

But Colavito also felt the White Sox didn't deserve to win. That's because the team sought questionable advantages in playing to its strengths of pitching and speed in Comiskey Park, considered by Colavito to be a graveyard for hitters because of its far-away fences. A published report claimed that the White Sox stored balls in a dark, dank area for months at a time to deaden them. It was done so that the mildewed balls were harder to hit out of the park for home runs. The boxes the balls came in decayed, so the balls were transferred into new boxes retaped to escape suspicion by umpires.[8] There was also a belief that the balls were frozen, which is what Colavito believed.

> I'm up to bat at Comiskey Park and I really hit the ball to left center, only for it to be caught at the wall. I'm thinking, "What happened to my power?" I look at my brand-new bat, and I see the ball mark is right in the middle of the sweet spot, and I'm annoyed. Walter "No Neck" Williams, sitting at the end of the dugout, says, "Rock, don't you know?" I said, "Know what?" and he says, real quiet-like, "The balls are frozen." I said, "What?" and he said, "Yeah, the balls are frozen." I looked at him in dismay, threw my bat in the rack and sat down.

Catcher J. C. Martin said he had his suspicions about the balls being frozen. "I will tell you this, the balls that year were the heaviest and had the highest seams I've ever seen. When a ball is moist the seams pop up, and that went on all year," Martin said that Harmon Killebrew hit a double to right center that he was certain was going to be a home run. On his next at-bat, Killebrew told him, "J. C., there's something going on with those balls." Martin also saw Gene Bossard, the head groundskeeper, drill two holes in the dirt in front of home plate and put a hose in them to flood the whole area, turning the dirt to mud. "You couldn't have driven a ball past our infield with a cannon," Martin said. "The ball would hit that mud ... and just die."[9]

The White Sox also watered down the infield grass to slow ground balls in the infield. "I hit three balls one night that were hard up the middle, and the ball went splat each time and Gary Bell had to go in to get them," Ken Berry recalled. "He laughed at me all the way to first base each time. We had good pitching and good defense, so the team was willing to forego the hitting to let the pitchers hold the opposing teams to one or two runs so we would always be in the game."[10] It was also reported that someone in the center field scoreboard used high-powered binoculars to steal signs from the catcher and relay them to third-base coach Tony Cuccinello, using a small flashing light hanging in the back of the stands. Cuccinello remained still if the pitch was a fastball and jumped around if it was a curve.[11]

Colavito, however, said he never saw it, and he doubted it could have happened without him knowing it. But something, he said, was clearly amiss. "The White Sox were always up to some kind of espionage," he said. "In my mind, there was no way we were going to win with these bastards cheating. It dampened my enthusiasm." Yet while it bothered Colavito, he never spoke up about it or raised an objection. "You don't do that because it would sound like you were against your own team," he said. "It also wasn't one of those things you discussed with other players. But I knew it wasn't right. And I always felt we could beat someone fair and square."

Colavito's tenure with the team was a disappointment. With one fewer at-bat than he had on the Indians, Colavito hit .221 with three home runs and 29 runs batted in, batting an even-lower .202 in September. Combining both teams, his season totals for 123 games were a .231 batting average with eight homers and 50 RBIs in 381 at-bats. It was the first time Colavito didn't have at least 21 home runs in a season. The sharp and sudden decline in power, together with losing his starting job in Cleveland and failing to become a starter in Chicago, marked the worst season of Colavito's career.

Colavito's salary for 1968 was slashed 20 percent. He signed his contract just two months after the season ended and was determined to prove he could still play at a high level. But he had some doubts about whether the White Sox had him in their plans, and his sporadic opportunities to play in spring training at Sarasota, FL, provided further evidence of that. On March 26, Colavito learned he had been put on waivers, ending a short-lived tenure with the White Sox. He was claimed by the Los Angeles Dodgers for well above the waiver price of $20,000, according to General Manager Buzzie Bavasi.[12] The Colavitos had rented a house with an indoor pool near the White Sox spring training camp, but Rocky had two days to join his new team, and Carmen, her mother, and the kids had two days to pack up.

The 1968 season was a strange one for baseball, with pitchers dominating hitters more than at any time in the modern era. An expanded strike zone begun in 1963 in response to the home run surge in 1961 was to blame. Bob Gibson set a modern earned run average record of 1.12, while the Indians' Luis Tiant compiled a 1.60 ERA in the American League while allowing a batting average of .168, a record low. Don Drysdale pitched six consecutive shutouts en route to setting the consecutive scoreless innings mark. Carl Yastrzemski was the only American Leaguer to bat .300, winning the batting title with the all-time low mark of .301. After the season, baseball's Rules Committee restored the pre–1963 strike zone and lowered the height of the pitching mound from 15 to ten inches, helping return the balance between pitching and hitting in 1969.

Colavito reported to the Dodgers, his first National League team, with high hopes. "I should be able to play 150 games, but I'm sure it will depend on whether I do the job," he said after arriving in spring training.[13] The Dodgers, like the White Sox, were known for pitching, speed and defense— and decidedly not home runs. Outfielder Len Gabrielson led the team in 1968 with ten, followed by third baseman Bob Bailey with eight. The whole team hit 67, only six more than Roger Maris alone hit seven years earlier. "It is unusual and somewhat startling for a writer covering the Dodgers to be talking to a genuine home run hitter, especially one belonging to the Dodgers," a Los Angeles writer said of Colavito.[14]

If the situation seemed once again made to order for him, Colavito's hopes of playing every day and adding a home run threat to the Dodgers' offense were soon dashed. He found himself relegated to occasional starts in the outfield and pinch-hitting. Colavito worked hard to stay ready, including watching film of his swing that revealed he had been holding his hands too high. Dodger Stadium, with its far-away fences where balls didn't travel well at night, could be unforgiving for a power hitter. Willie Mays advised Colavito on the difficulty of hitting home runs there before a game against the Giants.

Colavito also didn't develop a comfort level with the Dodgers. His dislike for manager Walt Alston had a lot to do with it. "I thought he was the second-worst manager I ever played for, behind Adcock," Colavito said. "He was not a good manager in the tactical running of the team, and he was aloof. Later, I saw that Maury Wills, the Dodgers' longtime shortstop, said something similar to how I felt. It made me feel good, although I never said it for publication." Alston, in an early-season team meeting in Atlanta, singled out Colavito for praise while talking about the importance of playing proper baseball. Colavito had backed up a throw at third from left field and made a heads-up play that the manager pointed to as he blasted the team for lackadaisical play.

But Colavito believed an angry exchange he had with an umpire later changed the manager's opinion of him. "Alston didn't like that I blew my cork," he said. Colavito was batting against the Phillies' Woody Fryman when home umpire Tony Venzon called him out on a pitch low and outside. Colavito erupted in anger, claiming it was a pitch he couldn't even reach. Venzon, after tossing him out of the game, referenced a dust-up between them that happened in a minor-league game in Spartanburg, SC, back in 1952, when Colavito was 18, which he had no recollection of. The next day, Phillies pitcher Chris Short asked Colavito what he had done to the umpire, because the pitch wasn't even close to a strike.

The low point for Colavito came in a game in which he was the last player left on the bench. Alston told him to grab a bat and pinch-hit with two outs in the ninth, but the batter before him made the final out. Colavito could barely contain his anger. "I was never that close in my whole career to not doing what the manager asked me to do," he said. Denied playing time, Colavito went to Alston's office and asked to be traded or released.

When the team plane landed due to turbulence in Platte, Nebraska, Carmen told Rocky she was in pain from bursitis and was having difficulty taking care of the kids. Doctors said surgery was a possibility. Colavito told the Dodgers he was going home, and it was there that he learned of his release while Carmen recovered. He wasn't without a team for long. Four days later, on July 15, the Yankees signed Colavito, three weeks shy of his 35th birthday, to a $40,000 contract. He had been making around $50,000, but the severance payment the Dodgers were obliged to make made his pay about the same. The Atlanta Braves also showed interest in signing Colavito. Paul Richards, the Braves' general manager, called Colavito's house, but the call came after he had already agreed to terms with the Yankees.

"Rocky Colavito, a Bronx boy who grew up rooting for the New York Yankees, finally made the team today," the *New York Times* reported.[15] An accompanying photograph showed Colavito practicing with the Yankees' Tom Tresh. The two went way back. When Colavito began his professional career at Daytona Beach playing under Mike Tresh, he would often see Mike's 12-year-old son, Tom, at the ballpark. Tresh grew up to be the 1962 Rookie of the Year at shortstop before moving to the outfield. "When Rocco Domenico Colavito was growing up in the Bronx, near the intersection of 174th Street and Third Avenue, he dreamed of playing for that baseball team in the Bronx, the Yankees," the *New York Times*' George Vecsey wrote. "Instead, the boyhood Yankee became an idol in Cleveland and, later, another baseball nomad, growing older in that terminal baseball way. Then in the month before his 35th birthday, which was yesterday, Rocky was given a chance to return to the borough and the team of his youth, only to find that all of them—the Yankees, the Bronx or himself—are not quite what they used to be."[16] Vecsey recalled Colavito favorably decades later. "Rocky was such a humble guy when he came to the Yankees. He was a hero in Cleveland and extremely well-received by Yankee fans. He was very old-school, no strut to him at all, an honest working man giving you his best shot. Mantle, who was a great teammate by all testimony, welcomed him."[17]

Marty Appel, who was later the Yankees' public relations director, had an entry-level job that summer working primarily as Mickey Mantle's mail clerk, but also opened the mail for Colavito and several other players.

> I was the kid doing the fan mail, so no one paid any attention to me. When we got Rocky during the summer, I made a point to introduce myself as a member of the PR staff, and he remembered my name. There were only four players who remembered my name as I went about my daily chores in the clubhouse, but it was a kick for me that the great Rocky Colavito did. Everybody on the clubhouse staff and in the front office really admired him.[18]

Putting on the pinstripes was special for Colavito, considering how he had dreamed of playing for the Yankees while growing up in the Bronx. "I was always a Yankees fan until I played against them," he said. "They were my team. I would have to say it was a thrill to be on the Yankees, but it wasn't as special as it could have been when they were winning." Baseball's most storied franchise had gone from consecutive American League pennants from 1960 to 1964 to sixth place in 1965, a humiliating tenth-place finish in 1966, and one rung up from the cellar in 1967. Gone from the great Yankees teams of the 1960s were Roger Maris, Elston Howard, Whitey Ford, Ralph Terry, Bobby Richardson, and Clete Boyer. But several key players were still playing under manager Ralph Houk. Tom Tresh, Joe Pepitone, Mel Stottlemyre, Jim Bouton, Al Downing, and Steve Hamilton all remained from the 1964 team. So, of course, did one of the greatest Yankees of all-time: Mickey Mantle. The Mick, hobbled by injuries, closed out his career that year batting a career-low .237, with a team-leading 18 home runs and 54 RBI.

Colavito admired Mantle and enjoyed being his teammate. "We had always got along, played in All-Star Games together and talked around the batting cages a bit," he said. "Mickey was a great player. What I found out about Mickey was that he was very shy. He was a good guy who everybody liked, and who always gave 100 percent even if he wasn't feeling up to par." Colavito appreciated something Mantle said to him the year before, when he was on first base and Mantle was holding him on. "'You know, Rock, now I know how you feel,'" Colavito recalled Mantle saying. "I said, 'What do you mean?' He said, 'When my legs were good, if the ball bounced twice they couldn't throw me out. Now I can appreciate guys like you. When I hit a ball in the hole, they play deep because I can't run as well, and they throw me out. I've lost a lot of hits that way.' I appreciated that Mickey recognized that," Colavito said.

Colavito watched from the dugout when Mantle hit his next-to-last homer under peculiar circumstances, breaking a tie with Jimmie Foxx on the career home run list. The pitch came off Denny McLain at Tiger Stadium after catcher Jim Price asked Mantle where he wanted the ball thrown. McLain had won 30 games at that point, and with a 6–1 lead in the bottom of the eighth inning, was on his way to his 31st. He put the ball where Mantle wanted it, and the 535th home run of his career landed in Tiger Stadium's upper deck in right field. Mantle's last home run came the following day. Colavito said he could tell something was going on before the home run, but knowing where a pitch was going to be and connecting was still no sure thing. "I bet you could get ten major leaguers and tell them fastballs are coming, and I bet you eight or nine of them don't hit it out."

Colavito thought Mantle hit the ball harder than any batter he ever saw, followed by Frank Howard and Ted Williams. He would sometimes gaze up in awe at a couple of spots in Yankee Stadium where Mantle hit king-sized home runs. One landed deep in the left field bleachers, and the other nearly cleared the ballpark high above right field. "I wish the ball he hit off the facade in right field that almost went entirely out would have happened," Colavito said of a fastball Mantle crushed in May 1963 off Kansas City's Bill Fischer. "It would have been nice to know someone hit it all the way out of Yankee Stadium." Regarding the great debate over who was the greater player, Willie Mays or Mickey Mantle, Colavito said they were very close.

> Willie Mays was the greatest all-around player I ever saw, and Mickey Mantle was a close second. Mays could do everything well, better than well. He could run like a son of a gun, throw like one, too, and play the outfield as well as anyone I ever saw. So could Mickey. Mickey could fly—out-and-out fly—even with his bad knees. If he hadn't got hurt, there's no telling how much he could have done. Both had charisma, and to me that is a very important item for a superstar. You have to have charisma, and though Mickey was shy, both of them had it.

The Yankees in 1968 finished four games over .500, representing a modest climb back to respectability. The roster was stocked with fading stars, prospects, and journeymen, including three infielders—Gene Michael, Dick Howser and Bobby Cox—who would achieve greater success as managers or in the front office. The mound was anchored by Stottlemyre, who went 21–12 with a 2.45 ERA, Stan Bahnsen, who was 17–12 with a microscopic 2.05 ERA, and Fritz Peterson, who had a 12–11 record with a 2.63 earned run average. The Yankees' commitment to a youth movement meant finding playing time for outfielders Bill Robinson, Andy Kosco, and Roy White. Once again, Colavito had to settle for infrequent starts in right field. He made his first game as a Yankee a memorable one by lofting a three-run homer at home that barely went 300 feet, landing just inside the left field foul pole. That gave his new roommate, Steve Barber, all the offensive support he needed in tossing a 4–0 shutout. Colavito's next home run came 36 days later, when he drove a pitch from Jim Kaat into the first row of the left field stands in Minnesota for his 371st career home run. The blast gave him sole possession of 15th place in career round-trippers. But Colavito's most memorable moment in Yankees pinstripes came when he pitched. It was his idea. "When I first joined the Yankees, I knew the pitching staff was on the thin side. I said to Ralph (Houk), 'If you need somebody to mop up, I'd be glad to help out,'" Colavito said. "Houk said, 'Do you mean that?' And I said 'Sure.'" Colavito was summoned to pitch in relief against the Yankees' top minor league team on July 25 in Syracuse, ten days after joining the team. He threw two innings of relief and was followed to the mound by shortstop Gene Michael. That proved to be a tune-up for what was to come.

The Yankees were scheduled to play three doubleheaders in a five-day period in late August, and eight games in all. They defeated the league-leading Tigers on a Friday in the first game of a twi-night doubleheader on a Tresh home run, but the two teams played to a 19-inning tie in the second game, which in those days had to be replayed in its entirety. Colavito was lifted for a pinch-runner, and Houk gave him permission to leave early, allowing him to grab a bite to eat with his brother Dom while watching the end of the game in a restaurant. The makeup game was scheduled as the second game of a doubleheader on Sunday, now making it nine games, including one that went 19 innings, and four doubleheaders in five days for the pitching-strapped team. Houk approached Colavito about pitching. "Did you mean what you said when you first joined us?" he asked. When Colavito said he did, Houk said, "You're my number one man today." Barber, combating the after-effects of the flu, started the first game of the August 25, 1968, doubleheader at Yankee Stadium, surrendering two runs in the top of both the first and third innings. In the third, Colavito was told to go out to the right field bullpen and warm up. Barber walked the opposing pitcher with one out in the fourth, and after two singles followed to produce another run, increasing the score to 5–0, Houk signaled for Colavito. It was only his second pitching appearance in a major league career that spanned 1,784 games. The other time was in 1958, when he also faced the Tigers and threw three scoreless innings.

The crowd roared as Colavito ran in from right field to the pitcher's mound. "They went bananas when I came in," Colavito said. "They also had gone bananas when I headed out to the bullpen." Right fielder Andy Kosco was no different from most people on the field, in the stands or listening on the radio, in not knowing what to expect. "I was wondering how hard he could really throw, and if the hitters could get around on him," Kosco said. "It was a treat. It was very exciting."[19]

Colavito inherited runners on first and second with one out. At the plate was the dangerous Al Kaline, his former teammate in Detroit and the only batter he had faced ten years earlier. Colavito induced him to ground out, and then retired Willie Horton, whom he had mentored, on a fly ball, drawing a standing ovation as he headed to the dugout. Colavito worked without a windup and threw hard. His slider, which seemed to be working well in the bullpen, abandoned him in the game, but his fastball was on the mark. Colavito struggled with his control in the fifth inning, walking two, but still set the side down without a hit. In the sixth inning, his last, he rang up his first strikeout before surrendering a double to Kaline that fell in front of Joe Pepitone in center. Colavito got out of the inning without a run being scored, giving him 2⅔ innings of one-hit ball while throwing 55 pitches in 92-degree heat. Yankees fan Bob McCarthy, 14, was glued to the TV with his mother in Scotia, NY, surprised by what was taking place. "I remember the excitement as the broadcaster noticed Rocky heading to the bullpen, and the oddity of someone of Rocky's hitting prowess possibly coming in as a pitcher," McCarthy said. "But he was terrific. He had a real good command of his pitches, like he knew what he was doing. He was so effective that it made you wonder why he didn't pitch more often."[20] In the bottom of the sixth, Colavito walked and scored what proved to be the winning run in a 6–5 game.

Colavito offered to pitch the seventh inning, but Houk wanted him fresh for the second game against tough lefty Mickey Lolich. Dooley Womack was brought in from the bullpen instead. "When he came out, they booed the shit out of him. It wasn't his fault," Colavito said. Womack and Lindy McDaniel pitched three shutout innings to preserve Colavito's win. In Colavito's two combined appearances with the Indians in August 1958 and the Yankees in August 1968, he faced 23 batters in 5⅔ innings and allowed no earned runs, one hit, struck two and walked four. He was excited to get the win. "This is the only time I've ever won as a pitcher in professional baseball," Colavito said. "It was a little strange. When you've been an outfielder all your life, it has to be. I was very fortunate, though. Guys were hitting the ball up in the air."[21] Colavito was the last non-pitcher to win a game in the 20th century. The next time it occurred was in 2000, when catcher Brent Mayne pitched a scoreless 12th inning to notch a win for the Colorado Rockies. The next day, shortstop Gene Michael pitched 3 innings, allowing no earned runs.

In the second game, Colavito unloaded a third-inning home run off Lolich to knot the score at 3–3 in a game the Yankees won. The win gave the team 12 victories in 15 games despite their grueling schedule. The next day, Houk moved Michael from the shortstop position to the pitching mound, where he struck out three and allowed no earned runs. "I have had people say to me from all over New York that they remember when I pitched," Colavito said. "Years later, when I was coaching in Cleveland, I told manager Frank Robinson, in jest, that he should let me pitch again. I said, 'I pitch every ten years, and the ten years are up. What do you think?' He just gave me a look."

Colavito with Yankees shortstop Gene Michael (left) and Manager Ralph Houk after both ballplayers pitched in relief in successive games on August 13 and 14, 1968 (Colavito's personal collection).

The Bronx-born Colavito was always warmly received by the Bronx faithful, who saw him as one of their own. Phyllis LaVietes, who decades later started the Rocky Colavito Fan Club on Facebook in 2008, which had over 1,300 members a decade later, was one of them. "Rocky was a good player and a handsome guy. He was a native New Yorker like me, and when he joined the Yankees, I was overjoyed," LaVietes said. She had a chance to meet Colavito, and her time with him confirmed what she thought. "When you see a lot of celebrities up close, they're not what they seem like from far away. But Rocky is as good a person as he was a player. He's personable, he's a family man, and a gentleman through and through. He's a real role model."[22] Pepitone, who like Colavito was an Italian-American and native New Yorker, in his case from Brooklyn, thought well of his teammate during the 2½ months they played together. "I had few moments with Rocky professionally, but he was a gentleman and a good teammate when he was a Yankee. I admired his home run power and the strength of his arm," Pepitione said.[23]

On September 24, the Yankees and Indians split a doubleheader at Yankee Stadium. "There was nothing remarkable about either game," a *New York Times* sportswriter wrote.[24] But there was: Colavito's 374th home run, the last one of his career, was hit 422 feet into the Indians' bullpen in left field off Cleveland's Mike Paul, a blast a baseball researcher ranked as the ninth-farthest for a player's last career home run.[25] It came in the second inning of the second game before 13,453 people in the stands. Colavito, who also hit a ground-rule double in the ninth inning, attached no special milestone to it at the time. His last at-bat came against the Red Sox on September 28, striking out as a pinch-hitter against the Red Sox's Jim Lonborg in Fenway Park. Mickey Mantle played his last game that day, too, with Houk letting them both skip the final game of the season to fly home. In 39 games with the Yankees, Colavito went 20-for-91 for a .220 average, with five home runs and 13 runs batted in. Combined with the Dodgers, he batted .211 for the season with eight home runs and 24 RBIs in 204 at-bats over 79 games. It meant the second season in a row that Colavito finished with eight home runs. After the season's final game, Colavito drove home with his family, wondering if his career was over. After being a starter and cleanup hitter going back to his sandlot days, being relegated to a part-time role the past two seasons—even though he believed he could still be a productive hitter—was a bitter pill to swallow.

The Yankees agreed to Colavito's request when they signed him to put him on waivers at the end of the season so he could be released. That occurred on September 30. But before that date, Colavito proposed a deal to General Manager Lee MacPhail that would allow the team to put him on the list of Yankees players available for selection by the two expansion teams coming into the league in 1969, the Kansas City Royals and Seattle Pilots. The new teams had to pay every major league club $125,000 for each player drafted, allowing the club to withdraw three names prior to its next selection. Colavito wanted the Yankees to give him $50,000 of the $125,000 that the team would get, which would allow them to protect a player in their plans for 1969. He thought it was a good deal for him and for the team, and that going to an expansion team might prolong his career. But MacPhail didn't go for it.

"There was an excellent chance I would've been selected," Colavito believed. "I was far from done. I could have played. But I never got that opportunity. In the end, I thought the hell with this, plus my wife wasn't feeling that good. I called it a career, but I never felt like I was done." Colavito never announced his retirement. A photograph in the *New York Times* showed him sitting in front of his locker in street clothes, with his bag packed. The article said Colavito considered his time with the Yankees "a very happy one," and he was undecided whether he was going to play ball in 1969. "We were happy to have him as a Yankee, and wish him well in his future career," MacPhail said.²⁶

Colavito retired having hit the third-most home runs for a right-handed batter in American League history. He was 15th all-time in averaging a home run every 17.4 at-bats. In all, he hit 524 home runs as a professional ballplayer, 374 in the major leagues and 150 in the minors. He also had 1,159 RBI, scored 971 runs, rapped 1,730 hits and had a .980 fielding percentage. Over a 162-game season, Colavito averaged .266 with 33 home runs and 102 RBIs, along with 84 walks, as one of the most-feared hitters of his era.

Colavito almost launched a comeback with the Indians the next year. General Manager Gabe Paul suggested he consider coming back, possibly with memories of him as a gate attraction in mind. But manager Alvin Dark discouraged the idea. "Alvin said, 'You're retired, and I think it would be smarter if you didn't,'" Colavito said. "He didn't say so emphatically—it was more like reading between the lines. I let the idea go, but I would have tried."

16

Outside the White Lines

Playing baseball was no longer a part of Rocky Colavito's life for the first time since he was a boy. The sport had consumed him since he began playing on the sandlots at the Bronx's Crotona Park. That feeling stayed with him when he signed with the Indians at age 17, and as he climbed the minor league ladder through stops in Daytona Beach, Cedar Rapids and Spartanburg, on up to Reading, Indianapolis, and San Diego. The feeling was there when he played in his first major league game at age 22, and for the next 13 years as he chased down fly balls, rifled throws to cut down baserunners, ran the bases, and blasted balls far beyond the reach of outfielders. Colavito did the same in Cleveland and Detroit and Kansas City, and back to Cleveland again, before brief stops at the end of his career with the White Sox, Dodgers, and Yankees. He was a star when baseball was still the national pastime, a household name in Cleveland and the White House, and a baseball and Italian-American icon. Millions across the country saw him play. The money he made throughout his career paled next to even the minimum salaries major leaguers drew decades later, but it still allowed Colavito, at 35, to have a financial cushion as he prepared for his next stage in life.

What that was going to be wasn't entirely clear. For starters, Colavito wasn't fully reconciled that his playing days were over, since he still felt he could perform at a high level. He also hadn't developed a plan for what to do when he was no longer a ballplayer. But Colavito had been leaving home to play baseball in the spring and summer since he was a teenager, and he looked forward to spending time at home with Carmen and their three children. He also wanted to help his father-in-law, Tavis Perrotti, whose health had been on the wane, with his mushroom business.

The mushroom-growing operation was about 300 feet from Perrotti's door, and a five-minute drive for Colavito, who rose at 4:30 a.m. to be there at 5. The mushrooms were grown in buildings that looked like greenhouses, with windows at both ends but otherwise little light. Colavito cleaned mushroom beds, sprayed for red mites, filled in holes around the mushrooms with dirt, and watered them. Mushroom growing was far from the world he was born into, but he worked at it. Even so, it was apparent to some that he was a fish out of water. "A friend of mine from the Bronx visited me once," Colavito recalled. "He saw what I did and looked at me—I'll never forget the look on his face—and said, 'This is not for you.' That's all he said. To me, I was on some sort of a mission trying to help my father-in-law and make it easier for him. His knees were bad, and he wasn't feeling all that great. He was really a pretty wonderful human being."

The Yankees came calling less than four months after Colavito played his last game. The team wanted him to be a roving minor-league instructor and special scout. He agreed as long as he was able to work around the mushroom harvesting schedule. Colavito visited Yankee farm teams, helping the managers in the lower rungs who didn't have coaches. He enjoyed working with young ballplayers and visiting former teammates and peers now managing in the minors. One was Bill Monbouquette, the former Red Sox 20-game winner who, like Colavito, played with the Yankees in 1968 before finishing his career that season with the Giants. Since he was based in Pennsylvania, Colavito was occasionally asked to scout National League teams playing the Phillies at Connie Mack Stadium. When the season ended, Colavito decided not to return. He also turned down Indians manager Alvin Dark's offer to be a minor league batting instructor and work in the promotions department. In 1969, Colavito was also named runner-up to pitcher Sam McDowell as the Indians' Player of the Decade in a vote conducted by the *Cleveland Plain Dealer*. He received 1,652 votes to McDowell's 2,308, despite playing only 2½ seasons for Cleveland in the 1960s. His point total was nearly double that of third-place finisher Max Alvis.

Colavito decided to try getting back into baseball in 1971 as a manager, coach, or broadcaster, contacting nearly every major league club. Colavito had offers to manage the Yankees' Manchester team in the Eastern League, the Senators' Denver farm club in the American Association, and the Indians' Sarasota club in the Gulf States (Rookie) League. He was interested in managing but turned the offers down, feeling he had earned the chance to start at the major league level.[1] Colavito asked Cleveland GM Gabe Paul about succeeding interim Indians manager Johnny Lipon, who had taken over after Dark was fired mid-season, but Paul showed no interest. Although Colavito never managed, he thought his personal communication skills could have made him successful. "Most former players know how to play the game, but managing is also handling the personnel, and I always got along with my fellow players," Colavito said. "I felt I knew how to treat them fairly and could have had discipline when I needed it without going overboard."

Baseball beckoned again in 1972 when Colavito was offered a job, with Paul's encouragement, as the TV color commentator on 48 Indians games broadcast on station WJW-TV in Cleveland. Colavito was paired with Harry Jones, former beat reporter for the *Cleveland Plain Dealer*. "When I first started I was a little nervous, but I played in the big leagues all those years," Colavito said. "I would just calm myself down and say all you have to do is talk about baseball." His insights and chemistry with his broadcasting partner impressed a critic at the *Cleveland Press*. "In my view, Rocky Colavito has been doing an utterly first-rate job as the color man on the WJW-TV broadcasts of the Indians' games," the writer said. "He knows what he's talking about; he has a sense of humor, and he meshes well with the excellent Harry Jones. It is one of the best baseball broadcast teams I have ever heard."[2] Colavito also helped as a batting instructor in spring training, and informally during the season for anyone who sought him out. "Rocky is a great coach," shortstop Frank Duffy said. "He has helped me a lot, in a lot of ways. I'm always glad when we're on television because then I know Rocky will be around."[3]

Colavito enjoyed the work, but Indians owner Nick Mileti had other ideas. Impressed by the former player's observations, he wanted Colavito out of the booth the next year and down on the field as a coach. Colavito took it as a compliment at first, but preferred staying where he was. The team didn't give him much choice. "Well, either you come down on the field, or you don't have a job," Colavito recalled Paul telling him. Before saying yes, he called the station's general manager and asked for a guaranteed two-year contract. "The station manager said—I'll never forget his words—'I wouldn't give my wife a two-year contract.' Sure enough, the guy was married five times."

Colavito returned to the field in 1973 as a first base coach and batting instructor under second-year manager Ken Aspromonte. Duffy, under Colavito's tutelage, had a career-best .263 average with eight home runs and 50 RBIs in 361 at bats. "I liked when I could help somebody like Frank Duffy," Colavito said. "I felt somewhat instrumental in helping him with his confidence. He didn't have much power, and I worked diligently with him, and he always appreciated it." Working with hitters had its share of frustrations as well as accomplishments. "You realize you can lead a horse to water, but you can't make him drink," he said. Colavito made $15,000 a year as a coach, a far cry from what he commanded as a player and too little, he found, when factoring the costs of commuting and having two kids in college. Aspromonte went to bat for Colavito with management at the end of the season to get him more money, but could only prod another $2,500 loose, triggering Colavito's resignation.

Colavito's father, who worked 35 years as a truck driver and strived to keep his family strong after his wife died when Rocky was a young boy, passed away in 1974. Back home, Colavito helped his father-in-law the next two years, but suggested it was time for a change for both. "I told him right out, 'Why don't you try to sell, and I'll try to get back in baseball. I know that better, I know it well,'" Colavito said. "It's not that I didn't think I could have run it, but it really wasn't my bag. I wasn't born and didn't grow up in that atmosphere. My friend from the Bronx said it exactly right."

Colavito was eligible for the Baseball Hall of Fame in 1974. Mickey Mantle and Whitey Ford were elected together, but Colavito drew just two votes. In 1975, he received one and was removed from the ballot. The poor showing hurt. "I would have loved to be voted in," Colavito said a half-century later.

> I see guys with fewer credentials than I had who were. It was a sore spot, it's still a sore spot, and it will always be a sore spot, because not only did I not get voted in, I didn't get a lot of votes. Some of the writers wanted you to kiss their ass, and I wouldn't do it. Ralph Kiner, who I played with and then for as a general manager, politicked. I had more home runs and RBIs, and he had a little higher batting average, but I don't think he did as well as me defensively or throwing. I told my wife that if I die, and they all of a sudden want to put me in, tell them they can stick it up their ass.

Colavito is still eligible to be considered by the Golden Era Committee, one of three 16-member committees appointed in 2010 by the Hall of Fame's Board of Directors to replace the Veterans Committee. It consists of eight Hall of Fame members, five executives, and three media members who meet every three years to consider players and others active from 1947 to 1972.

Colavito got his next baseball job at the December 1975 baseball winter meetings. He approached Cleveland's General Manager Phil Seghi, who had replaced Gabe Paul. Seghi suggested he talk to manager Frank Robinson, and the second-year manager and future Hall of Famer promptly made Colavito his batting and first base coach. "I was tickled to death that I went home with a job," Colavito said. At the suggestion of Indians President Alva T. "Ted" Bonda, and with Robinson's permission, Colavito combined his coaching duties with being a color man on Indians broadcasts once again, paired this time with play-by-play announcer Joe Tait. Sometimes Tait would go over to radio, and Herb Score, Colavito's teammate-turned-broadcaster and best friend, would call the game with him. His routine included splitting batting practice with batting coach Harvey Haddix, watching and instructing hitters. Then he went to the broadcasting booth to provide color commentary for the Indians' 40 televised games.

Although Paul was gone, Colavito had a low regard for Phil Seghi, the Indians' general manager for 13 years, ten of them losing seasons. "He was a minor-league player and manager cut from the Gabe Paul mode," Colavito said. "He was a braggart and turned out to be one real asshole. One time, he called me, the batting coach, up to his office and said when he played, he'd get two or three hits off left-handers. I was so tempted to say to him, 'Phil, if you were such a good fucking hitter, how come you never got past Double A?'"

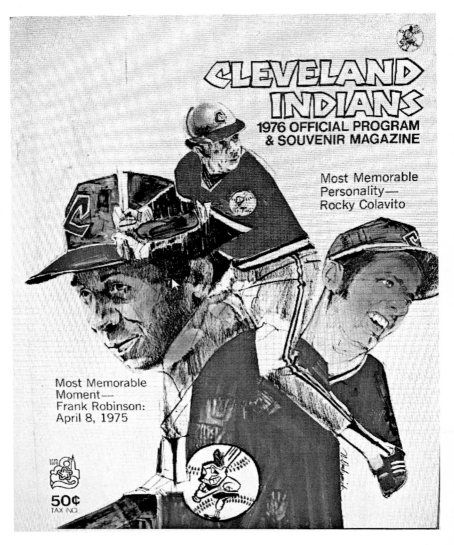

Indians coach Colavito, whose likeness is on a 1976 team program, was voted the team's all-time "most memorable personality" that year (Colavito's personal collection).

Frank Robinson had made baseball history the year before when the Indians appointed him to be the first black manager. A racial incident stood out for Colavito in 1976, Robinson's second year. "I remember one time in Oakland when Frank got on the seat where managers sat, the first one on the right, on a bus that was going to take us to the airport," Colavito said. "Frank said to the bus driver, 'OK, let's go.' The driver didn't go. Frank said, 'Let's go.' The guy didn't go. Frank got up, got real close to him, and started screaming, hot and heavy. One of the things he said was, 'Because I'm a black man, you're not thinking I run this ball club,' or something to that effect. He said, 'Let's go!' and the bus moved." Robinson's home run in his first-bat as the team's player-manager was voted "Most Memorable Moment" in the team's history in 1976. In the same poll, Colavito was voted "Most Memorable Personality," a testament to his enduring popularity. Colavito was chosen over Bob Feller, Lou Boudreau, Tris Speaker, and every other ballplayer who had at one time or another put on the Cleveland Indians uniform. "I thought it was a real honor, and I was thrilled," Colavito said.

Before the start of the 1977 season, Indians management told Colavito they only wanted him coaching, putting an end to broadcasting and the extra pay that came with it. In the middle of the season, Robinson, unable to get the Indians into pennant contention, was fired by Bonda and replaced by bullpen coach Jeff Torborg. "Bonda knew absolutely nothing about baseball and depended on other people," Colavito said. "He told me he was going to fire Frank before Frank knew it. Being loyal to Frank, I wouldn't ask for the job. Frank gave me a job, he was good to me, he respected me, and he treated me right. I have nothing but praise for Frank, so I wasn't about to say I wanted his job even though I would have loved to have it." Colavito coached under Torborg the rest of that season and in 1978.

After the season, he was fired along with Haddix and replaced by Dave Garcia and Chuck Hartenstein. Torborg told Colavito he had nothing to do with the decision, but Paul told the Hall of Fame Club at a luncheon after the season that Torborg wanted Garcia on his coaching staff. "I told Torborg to go ahead and contact Garcia, and when he finalized the arrangements for him to come to the Indians, Colavito had to go," Paul said.[4] Colavito, however, was skeptical, believing Paul put Torborg up to it. It fell to Seghi to tell Colavito he was out of a job. "When Seghi fired me, he said 'Rocky, I've got some bad news. We're going to let you go as a coach.' He told me I did a really good job, but they needed to make a change. I said, 'If I did such a good job, then why are you firing me?'"

"Rocky Colavito, perhaps the most popular player ever to wear an Indians' uniform, was fired along with pitching coach Harvey Haddix in a coaching shakeup long rumored," *The Sporting News* reported.[5] Colavito was credited with boosting the hitting of Andre Thornton, Duane Kuiper, and Tom Veryzer. All three had improved significantly at the plate in 1978. Colavito said in the article that he felt the team was headed in the right direction and expressed disappointment that he wouldn't be a part of the club's future. Carmen Colavito reacted with bewilderment. "Who knows what is going to happen in baseball? They make million-dollar mistakes and fire $20,000 coaches."[6]

Colavito's absence as batting coach was heavily felt the next season. The Indians' offense sputtered, and hitters who had developed a close working relationship with Colavito said they wished he was still there to turn to. That was particularly true for Andre Thornton, the team's power-hitting first baseman, who improved from 13 home runs and 35 RBIs to 33 homers and 105 RBIs with Colavito as batting coach. Thornton began the 1979 season 3-for-42, and with over one-fifth of the season gone was batting just .171.

> You don't feel like you're pressing, and Rocky's not here to notice if I am. We were so close the last two years.... Rocky made a big difference to me. He talked situations and he talked about the thinking aspects of hitting. He was a power hitter, too, and he knows how pitchers work and how pitchers think. I tried to get his number to call him, but if he didn't come down and see me, it would be difficult to help me.

Tom Veryzer also missed Colavito. "I can only speak for myself, but last year he saved my career," the shortstop said, noting that his average increased 74 points under Colavito's tutelage. "When you'd have a bad day, he'd come out with the reasons why, and you knew you were going to correct it the next day." Center fielder Rick Manning also felt Colavito's absence. "He was very important—as important as anybody," Manning said. "He helped a lot of us. He instilled a lot of confidence in people. He was a plus to the ball team. I wish he were still here. If we had any vote, we could say something about it, but we don't."[7]

It was the last time Colavito would work for the Indians. His abrupt departure, resentments over past treatment, and the little contact he would have with the team for years to come would leave Colavito feeling bitter toward an Indians organization he believed had discarded him.

17

Reconciliation

Rocky Colavito was done working as a coach with the Cleveland Indians, but his time in baseball was not over. There was one more team in his future, in a city he had played for in 1964. The Kansas City Athletics were now in Oakland, but the Kansas City Royals, which entered the major leagues the year after Colavito retired, came calling.

When Colavito lost his job with the Indians after the 1978 season, he turned a part-time job into a full-time one with Minute Men Temporary Health Service. The Cleveland company capitalized on the former player's celebrity by sending him and a partner on the road to visit companies. Colavito maintained an apartment in Cleveland, working two weeks on and two weeks off. He received an unexpected honor when he was inducted into the Ohio Baseball Hall of Fame in the summer of 1979 along with nine others, including former pitchers Mel Harder and Eppa Rixey, managers Fred Hutchinson and Miller Huggins, and owner Bill Veeck. Colavito was emotional as he thanked people who helped him throughout his baseball career, including Carmen, unable to be there due to illness. "I want to thank you from the bottom of my heart," Colavito said. "This is one of the greatest honors that could be bestowed on a person."[1]

He was also voted into the Chicago-based National Italian American Sports Hall of Fame in 1981, the same year the Colavito family moved into a new ranch-style home in nearby Bernville. The 3,600-square-foot, three-bedroom stone house had beautiful hillside views and came with a downstairs recreation room where Colavito put his pool table and career mementos. It was there, several months later, that Dick Howser, a former teammate of Colavito's and now the Royals manager, offered him a two-year contract as batting coach starting with the 1982 season. The job paid $35,000 a year, which Colavito planned to supplement with occasional off-season appearances at card and memorabilia shows. "I played with Rocky at Cleveland and he was the best two-strike power hitter I ever saw," Howser said in explaining his selection of Colavito. "No pitcher could get him out pitching from the middle of the plate in."[2]

Comments made by Charley Lau, the former Royals batting coach whose hitting philosophy was famously adopted by future Hall of Famer George Brett, put a damper on the announcement. Lau expressed concern that Colavito would try to convert the Royals' young ballplayers into long-ball hitters. Colavito, a teammate of Lau's at Kansas City in 1964, took sharp exception to the comments. "I help somebody with what they could do best, and I thought that was unkind of him to say because I always treated him decently," he said. Colavito used his 1958 season as an example of how a power hitter does more than hit home runs. "If I hit 41 home runs and get 148 hits, that means 107 hits weren't home runs. I think a player should go up to the plate with the intention of hitting the ball hard, but he should also know his limitations. I knew my limitations, and that helped me. I had a lot of baseball wars within myself, you know, slumps. What I want to do so badly is try to save these players from some of the mistakes I made."[3] Brett gave some credit to Colavito for the 19-game hitting streak he opened the season with in 1982. "Basically, Rocky's not trying to get me to pull any more than Charley [Lau] did, but Rocky's making me use my hands a lot more," Brett said. "I'm still hitting the ball to left field and still getting some hits, so everything's worked out."[4]

One of the players Colavito took under his wing was Hal McRae, who responded with a career year at age 36. The designated hitter saw his home runs jump from seven to 27 and his RBIs from 36 to 133, to go with a .308 batting average. "I'm Rocky's robot," McRae said. "He tells me what to do, and I go out and do it. I can't explain the fast start. I owe a lot to Rocky. He's the guy who made me a dangerous hitter…. Rocky noticed my hands were dragging and that it was taking away my power. When he started working with me, I was hitting about .200. Then my average started going up, and I was hitting the long ball."[5]

Catcher John Wathan also praised Colavito's coaching. "I'm sure no one pre-judged Rocky, but we all knew he was a power hitter, and because of that we were wondering if he'd fit in. Well, he has, and he's doing a great job," Wathan said.[6] Colavito was surprised at how some of the players knew little or nothing about baseball's past. One player had never heard of Babe Ruth and didn't know that Joe DiMaggio, then a pitchman for Mr. Coffee, had played baseball.

Colavito and Howser received unwelcome treatment from the Kansas City Police Department that summer. It began with Colavito driving his station wagon from the ballpark about an hour after an August 19, 1982, game against the White Sox. Howser was in the passenger seat, and Steve Colavito, now a teenager, sat in the back. Rocky made an illegal left turn from a stadium exit around 11 p.m., resulting in a minor traffic accident, according to the police account. Colavito and Howser argued with the 19-year-old driver of the other car, who was arrested and charged with driving while intoxicated. Officer Michael Paschal claimed that Colavito pushed him when he stepped between them. A second officer, Roy Callahan, became involved, and Howser jumped on his back, the policemen said, leading another officer to radio for assistance. Colavito and Howser were charged with hindering and interfering with an officer, and Colavito was also cited for a traffic violation.[7] Both Colavitos and Howser were taken to jail in a paddy wagon and released a short time later.

Colavito's interpretation of events—and the officers' testimony in Kansas City's Municipal Court—differed greatly from what was initially reported. Colavito said he hadn't made an illegal turn, and the other driver drove into his car. He denied having contact with a police officer, and Howser had heeded his advice not to get involved, let alone attack an officer. During an 80-minute hearing, Callahan told Judge Leonard Hughes that he put Colavito in a headlock because he thought he had raised an arm to strike Paschal. Colavito said the policemen were belligerent, grabbed him, and pushed him to the ground without warning or cause.[8] "I kept telling the cops I wasn't doing anything and wasn't offering any resistance, so why were they doing this," Colavito said. "When they got me down, the one I argued most with put his boot on my neck. When I felt like I was being choked, I got my strength and shoved them all off."

Colavito said he was afraid they might draw their guns and was especially concerned about his son's safety. Colavito and Howser were found guilty and sentenced in October to 90-day jail terms, plus a $250 fine for Colavito and $100 fine for Howser. A county circuit judge overturned the jail terms and the fines four months later, replacing them with six-month probation sentences. Colavito was glad the original sentences were overturned but he was still furious, believing the policemen's actions amounted to "police brutality." He felt vindicated when a policeman came up to him at the ballpark and apologized. "'Rocky, I hope you're not going to hold that against all of us, because we're not all like them,'" the policeman told him. Colavito told reporters he was "thoroughly disappointed" in Royals owner Ewing Kauffman and others in the front office for not backing up their manager and coach.[9]

Colavito found himself in the middle of another fracas the following season, which came to be known as "the Pine Tar incident." The controversy occurred in a July 24, 1983, game at Yankee Stadium, after Kansas City appeared to take a 5–4 lead in the ninth inning over the Bronx Bombers on George Brett's two-out, two-run homer. An umpire ruled that Brett used an excessive amount of pine tar on his bat and called him out. Brett burst out of the dugout upon learning the decision and went ballistic, leading teammates to restrain him. Colavito went on the field to try to cool things down. "I went out as a peacemaker trying to get George from getting thrown out of the game," he said. "I also grabbed the bat and gave it to Gaylord Perry, who ran it down the runway and into the clubhouse. It was a game bat, and I didn't want the bat to be confiscated because Brett homered with that bat." Colavito said the umpire's call didn't make sense because pine tar would have curtailed the ball's flight rather than aiding it. Also, players routinely put pine tar above the handle and toward the end of the bat to get some stickiness if the pine tar wore away from the handle. "The 'pine tar game' was a hell of a game. George went crazy after the umpire's decision, and he was 100 percent right to feel that way," Colavito said. American League President Lee MacPhail upheld the Royals' protest, reinstating what proved to be the game-winning home run and ordering the game to resume from where the umpires halted play. He also retroactively ejected Colavito, Howser, and Brett for arguing with the umpires, and Perry for giving the bat to the batboy.

After two years of coaching for Kansas City, Colavito resigned following the 1983 season. Traveling was getting harder, and he wanted to spend more time with his family. He got his baseball fix once a year participating in the Cracker Jack Old Timers Baseball Classic, which ran from 1982 to 1990. The games were played first in Washington, D.C., and later in Buffalo. Players were paid $1,000 plus expenses. Colavito played in all the games but the first one and had his share of success. He homered off the left field scoreboard in the first inning against Warren Spahn in the 1985 game, held at Buffalo's War Memorial Stadium, and later tripled to the wall in right. Colavito homered again the following year in a game held at Washington's RFK Memorial Stadium, where he played with former teammates Bob Feller and Roger Maris of the Indians, Dick McAuliffe and Bill Freehan of the Tigers, and Steve Barber of the Yankees. The manager was none other than Harvey Kuenn. The 52-year-old Colavito brought fans to their feet a second time in Washington with a strong throw from deep right field that hit the third baseman's glove on one bounce.[10]

After the 1988 game, Colavito joined several other players in meeting Vice President George H. W. Bush, who had been the captain of his baseball team at Yale University, at the residential Blair House. Colavito had one last Cracker Jack hurrah in the 1989 game in Buffalo, when he pounded a pitch in the first inning that was backhanded by Dick Allen on the warning track. Colavito spoke that day for the last time with Joe DiMaggio, who regularly attended the Cracker Jack games but never played. The only other players Colavito felt in awe of were Ted Williams and Stan Musial; he considered the marquee players of his day, such as Mickey Mantle, Willie Mays, and Hank Aaron, his peers. Before leaving, the "Yankee Clipper" inscribed a ball to Colavito that read, "To Rocky, a great talent." Colavito cherished it. "Imagine him writing 'a great talent,'" Colavito said, sounding star-struck almost 30 years later.

In 1984, Steve Colavito, who at six feet and 165 pounds was three inches shorter and 20 pounds lighter than his father's playing weight, was taken by the Baltimore Orioles in the 24th round of the June draft. Steve was a switch-hitting centerfielder and more of a line-drive hitter than a power hitter like his dad. He excelled defensively. "He was an exceptional outfielder. I know, and I've seen them," Rocky said. Steve played 65 games his first two seasons with the Bluefield Orioles in the rookie Appalachian League, and a third season with the non-affiliated New York-Penn League's Batavia Clippers. Steve's struggles at the plate kept him from getting regular playing time with both teams. His father, he said, was a constant comfort. "I always called my dad when I played ball and things were not going that good. I could always rely on him," he said. The following year, Rocky asked the Indians to give his son an opportunity, and Steve was signed to a Class A contract with the Waterloo Indians in the Midwest League. But the opportunity proved to be short-lived, and he was released after playing 34 games, something Rocky would hold against the Indians. "I never wanted any favors," Steve said. "I just wanted a chance to play, but I never had more than 19 at-bats in a row." He went to spring training with the Rangers in 1988 with little success to show for it, and again in 1989 with the Cubs. Jim Piersall, Rocky's former teammate, served as a minor league outfield instructor, but Steve received little attention from him and had few opportunities to play, much to his and his father's disappointment. That experience put an end to his minor league career, in which he hit a combined .167 in 276 at-bats over four seasons.

Steve and his sister Marisa McGrath, the middle child, live near their parents, while Rocky, the oldest sibling, lives in Las Vegas. Steve often goes hunting with his dad. He was only two years old when his father retired, so he has no memory of him as a ballplayer. "I've always been proud of my dad, but not just for the baseball playing," he said. "The biggest thing with my dad was that he always made time for me. Even when he was a coach, and he'd get back from the ballpark late at night and be tired, he would still throw to me in the morning. He never denied me. He always showed a lot of love to me and to his family."[11]

Marisa McGrath said faith is an essential part of her father's outlook. Growing up, the family often attended church, and they said prayers before meals and before bed.

My dad's faith is very quiet, but our religion is the basis and the foundation for who we are as a family. I've always admired him for his strength and his can-do attitude. He is very positive, and he sees the glass as half-full. I was never made to feel that being a female should get in my way, or that I couldn't do anything. My mom is equally as strong, and I think you would have to be because of the lifestyle of being a ballplayer's wife. She was supportive and loving, and I never felt like she stood behind my dad but alongside my dad. She was very capable, and she held down the fort.

Colavito (left) and Herb Score at Municipal Stadium, circa early 1980s (Nancy Score's personal collection).

Because of her father's fame, McGrath said she learned to share him with the world. "People always wanted time with him, and he would always acknowledge them, kids especially. He has such an appreciation for other people, and I've always admired that. He is still that person. My parents always did things selflessly, and their lesson was to treat people the way you would want to be treated."[12]

Colavito was in the running in 1985 to be a color commentator once again for Tribe telecasts but couldn't reach an agreement on salary. The following year, his brother Dom died from an illness. "He was my brother, and I couldn't have loved him more," Colavito said. "He always looked out for me, and I never forgot it." In 1988, Harvey Kuenn, the ballplayer who after the 1960 trade would forever be linked with Colavito, passed away at age 57. Kuenn had managed the Milwaukee Brewers to a pennant in 1982, after taking over in June from Bob Rodgers when the club was 23–24. The team finished 95–67 and overcame a 2–0 deficit against the California Angels to make it into the World Series, before losing to the Cardinals in seven games. He was dismissed the following year when the team finished fifth in the AL East with an 87–75 record.

In 1989, Colavito wrote a letter to his local newspaper, the *Reading Eagle,* to express his admiration for Brooklyn and Los Angeles Dodgers outfielder Carl Furillo upon his death. Colavito met Furillo, an Italian-American who was born and died in Stony Creek Mills, five miles from Reading, when the former Dodgers great worked in town as a security guard. Colavito wrote that he had admired Furillo as a player and thought he deserved greater local attention and better treatment from Major League Baseball.

> Carl was tough-minded, but he was honest and humble about his God-given talents, and worked hard at honing his skills. He gave a lot to baseball and should have been allowed to give a lot more through scouting, coaching, or as a hitting instructor. It's a pity that this yesterday's ballplayer, who was justifiably outspoken about management, was blacklisted, when today's ballplayer is rehabilitated from and even pardoned for drug abuse. He could have taught today's ballplayer so much. Baseball lost one of its best. He will be missed.[13]

In August 1990, Colavito and Harmon Killebrew, the co-home run champs in 1959 who squared off in December 1960 in the TV competition "Home Run Derby," reprised their competition at a park in Spencer, MA. Former first baseman Walt Dropo and pitchers Jim Lonborg and Gene Conley also made appearances. Killebrew had edged Colavito by one home run in the televised contest 30 years earlier, but this time Colavito trounced the former Senators and Twins star, 14–2, driving ball after ball over the cozy outfield dimensions that measured 300 feet down the line and 350 to center. In 1992, the Colavitos built a three-bedroom, ranch-style house to serve as a hunting camp on 83 acres of forest north of their Bernville home. That same year, Colavito had his first serious health issue, beating prostate cancer.

In 1994, Colavito's name appeared in the title of Cleveland sportswriter Terry Pluto's book, *The Curse of Rocky Colavito: A Loving Look at a Thirty-Year Slump.* The title referred to the 34 years in a row in which the Indians failed to contend for a pennant after Colavito's initial departure. The period of futility began in President Dwight Eisenhower's second term and continued into President Bill Clinton's first term, nine presidents in all. The phrase intentionally recalled "The Curse of the Bambino," which blamed the Boston Red Sox trade of Babe Ruth to the Yankees for the club's failure to win the World Series from 1918 to 2004. Since the Indians became a charter member of the American League in 1901, Cleveland has won just two World Series. The team began as the Bluebirds, changing its name shortly afterward to the Bronchos and then the Naps, for second baseman Napoleon Lajoie, before becoming the Indians in 1915. In 1920, the Indians beat the Brooklyn Robins, which didn't change its name to the Brooklyn Dodgers until 1932, behind Stanley Coveleski's three Series wins. In 1948, the Indians triumphed over the Boston Braves behind 31-year-old player-manager Lou Boudreau, who batted .355 during the season. The team lost its next four World Series appearances, in 1954 and, after the long drought, in 1995, 1997, and 2016. The Indians' latter loss to the Chicago Cubs pushed the team's losing streak to 68 years, the longest in the major leagues.

Some fans blame the "curse." "Rocky was awesome, and the reason that Cleveland was so bad in all sports until recently was because of what they did to him," Clevelander Larry Russ said. "I believe in the curse. Tell me anything else that would account for it."[14] Colavito, however, saw the catchy phrase as a way to sell some books, while throwing some unexpected attention his way. If there was a curse, he said, the blame lay elsewhere. "I never put a curse on anybody. As much as I hated the trade, I just didn't do that," he said. Was it the curse of Frank Lane? "I think that would be pretty accurate."

Municipal Stadium gave way to Jacobs Field in 1994, a new state-of-the-art ballpark with a 19-foot-high left field wall. President Clinton was on hand to throw out the ceremonial first pitch. The Indians were in the thick of the pennant race in what would be a strike-shortened season, but the team went on to win five consecutive division titles and two pennants before the decade concluded. The stadium was renamed Progressive Field in 2008, and Colavito is featured on one of 11 murals that surround the ballpark on the mezzanine level behind home plate. The others are Cy Young, Tris Speaker, Herb Score, Frank Robinson, Joe Sewell, Stanley Coveleski, Elmer Flick, Napoleon Lajoie, Early Wynn, and Adrian Joss. The five players featured on statues are Bob Feller, Larry Doby, Robinson, Boudreau, and Jim Thome. Retired uniform numbers seen over the right field grandstand were worn by Boudreau, Doby, Feller, Earl Averill, Bob Lemon, Mel Harder, and Thome.

Colavito's supporters have long urged the retirement of the No. 6 he wore in the 1950s, on his first tour of duty with the team. They also want his importance to the Indians commemorated with a statue, whether showing him holding his bat up high as he waited for a pitch, pointing his bat at the pitcher, or stretching in the on-deck circle, a bat behind his back. Indians executive Bob DiBiasio said the dividing line for such honors has been membership in the Hall of Fame. (Harder, who pitched 20 years for the Indians and had his uniform number retired without being in the Hall of Fame, is an exception. Thome's statue was erected in advance of Hall of Fame balloting, with the certainty of his future admission that occurred in 2018.) "There is a true fine line when it comes to honoring achievement in an Indians uniform," DiBiasio said.

> There is no question that for a certain generation or two, Rocky is one of the most popular players to ever wear an Indians uniform. When talking statues and retirement of numbers, you need to look deeper into on-field achievement. Because of our rich history, we begin the statue/retired uniform discussion at Hall of Fame induction. Is the player a member of the National Baseball Hall of Fame? Strict standards for sure, but when you have been around as long as we have, strict standards are needed to guide the process.[15]

Colavito resurfaced in the news in 2005, after several ballplayers were hauled before a Congressional committee over the use of steroids. Mark McGwire, Sammy Sosa, and Rafael Palmiero all denied that steroids were responsible for the dramatic boost in their home run numbers. Other players under a cloud of suspicion, the most notorious being Barry Bonds, also professed innocence. Colavito said he had lost all respect for ballplayers who turned to steroids and performance-enhancing drugs.

When Mark McGwire said in the hearings that he took that shit, and it didn't help him, it made me want to throw up. I don't like anybody that lies like that. Bonds was a good player, but he was a slender kid in Pittsburgh when, all of a sudden, his neck and head are big, and he looks like a bulldog. That was the same with McGwire and Sosa. There's no logic to Bonds and Sosa becoming great home run hitters late in their careers except if you take performance-enhancing drugs.

Colavito feels players who took performance-enhancing drugs have no place in the Hall of Fame. "They cheated. You do that, you should pay the price," he said. "Why should you be in with the guys who never did it, and be compared to them? Ruth never used anything. Gehrig never used anything. Mantle never used anything. Maris never used anything. Williams, the greatest hitter ever, never used anything. DiMaggio, Musial, Foxx—all of those guys put up great numbers and never used anything."

Colavito believes players in the decades since he retired have enjoyed enormous advantages over ballplayers from his generation.

I don't know how you can compare eras. They have a livelier, tighter ball today, shorter fences, and bats made from oak and maple, which allow the ball to come off the bat harder. I have taken a ball apart, and the ball in the middle that used to be cork is like a super ball. You can bounce it and hit the ceiling. I think they changed the ball when the players went on strike, and the fans were backing off. They figured more home runs would bring them back, and that's exactly what happened. All those things considered have a definite advantage. I bet I hit 25 to 30 balls close to the fence in a year, and many of those balls would have been home runs with today's bats and balls.

In 2003, Colavito had a second health scare when he needed quadruple bypass surgery after suffering a heart attack. One artery was completely closed, one was 90 percent closed, and a third was 75 percent blocked. Despite his serious heart condition, Colavito made a full recovery. He would later be diagnosed with and take non-insulin medicine for type two diabetes. In 2015, a circulation problem from the disease that began in a big toe led to a portion of Colavito's right leg being amputated below the knee. He was fitted with a prosthesis and remains active despite needing a wheelchair. He was deeply touched by the response from fans after Terry Pluto wrote a column informing *Cleveland Plain Dealer* readers of Colavito's plight. "I got over 200 cards from all over, but especially the Cleveland area. I read every one, and it picked me up," Colavito said. His son Steve marveled at how his father never complained about the curveball he was thrown. "I don't know how many people would have handled the situation with his leg the way he has," he said.[16] Ironically, Kuenn would also have quadruple bypass surgery and have his right leg amputated below the knee. Like Colavito, he was also classified 4-F for military service, in his case due to a knee injury suffered in football rather than for flat feet.

"One thing I feel good about is that I gave my very best every day," Colavito said, reflecting on his career.

> I knew no other way. I also felt good about setting an example for some of the kids coming up to the majors. I always treated them well, because when I came up, the stars of the team kept you at a little bit of a distance until you started showing you were a big leaguer. There were also some beautiful days and some heartburn-churning days, where you left a guy on base or struck out with the bases loaded. But I always tried to feel that the good ones overshadowed the bad ones. My favorite accomplishment was hitting four home runs, without a doubt. How many guys do that? I was lucky enough to be one of them. Winning a big league game as a pitcher was another thrill. So was my 35th home run in 1958, after I had told my manager that if I played regularly I would hit 35 home runs, changed that to 30, and he still told the press 35. My biggest regret was that I didn't play on a pennant-winning team and in the World Series. I wanted to be on a winner. I was on winners in 1953 and '54, in the minors, and it was a good feeling. We came so damn close a couple of times, and just didn't get there. That's always been a thorn in my side.

Colavito continues to root for the Indians and has particularly enjoyed the play of shortstop Francisco Lindor. "I like his attitude and his talent," Colavito said. "He always has a smile on his face, he hustles, he makes good plays and has some power." Colavito took exception with the team's decision in 2018 to retire Chief Wahoo, which critics have called a racist caricature. He fondly recalled the Indians mascot that was worn on his left sleeve when he played. "I like the logo, and I don't think the team should have given in," Colavito said. He cheered for Lebron James and the Cleveland Cavaliers in 2016, when the team won the first major sports championship in Cleveland since the Cleveland Browns won the NFL title game in 1964.

Despite being one of the Indians' most popular players ever, Colavito's involvement with the franchise was practically non-existent for years. It began with his firing as a coach in 1978 and lasted until the mid–1990s. That didn't go unnoticed by DiBiasio, the senior vice president of public affairs for the Indians who, for 40 years, has held what he calls "the best job in the world." DiBiasio, a Cleveland native, said his favorite player growing up was Rocky Colavito. "Everybody in my generation, not just the Italians, imitated Rocky when we were in the on-deck circle," DiBiasio said. "We imitated Rocky when we got in the batter's box and pointed the bat. In every sandlot in Cleveland where kids our age played Little League, he was our hero."[17]

DiBiasio's whole family embraced Colavito. "I remember my parents, my older brothers, everyone gravitating to Rocky," he said. "Rocky was in my house from day one." His mother cried when Rocky was traded the first time, and he can remember his own excitement at age ten when the ballplayer returned to the Indians. "He was iconic," DiBiasio said. "He had striking good looks, and there was that perfect aspect to him that I think people were drawn to. There was a class to Joe DiMaggio in the way he dressed and the way he acted, and I think Rocky emulated that. He was very classy. From the end of the '50s through the late '60s, I think our town would tell you that that period belonged to him." But DiBiasio was aware some distance had grown between Colavito and the Indians organization over the years. "The warm feelings may have

The Cleveland Indians Hall of Fame induction ceremony reunited Colavito (top) with close friend Herb Score (Marvin Fong/Barcroft Media).

cooled a bit," he said.[18] Frosty was more like it. Colavito credits DiBiasio for breaking the ice.

The Indians' popular goodwill ambassador asked Colavito to throw out the first pitch before Game 5 of the 1995 American League Championship Series against the Seattle Mariners. Colavito received a standing ovation when he stepped onto the mound and threw the ceremonial first pitch to catcher Sandy Alomar, Jr. "I got such a fantastic reception and greeting," Colavito recalled. "It was a wonderful feeling to know that they didn't forget me." He sat four rows behind home plate and cheered the Indians on to victory. Colavito returned to Cleveland six years later in 2001 as a member of the Indians' All-Century Team, in which he was named one of the team's 100 greatest players. "There were 43 players there for a pregame ceremony, and he got as big an ovation as any of the other players, including current players," DiBiasio recalled.[19]

The next step in rebuilding Colavito's connection to the Indians came in 2006, when he was inducted into the Cleveland Hall of Fame along with Herb Score, Sam McDowell, Addie Joss, Al Lopez, Al Rosen, and Ray Chapman. It was the first time the team added players since 1959, a span of 47 years, and Colavito was honored to be included. The plaque read:

> Electrified fans with power bat and strong throwing arm. "The Rock" tied major league record with four consecutive HR June 10, 1959 at Baltimore. Hit 300 homers faster than all but four players in the history of baseball. Led American League in HRs in 1959 with 42. Led A.L. in RBI with 108 in 1965. Among Tribe All-Time Leaders in home runs and slugging percentage. The three-time American League All-Star with Tribe was voted most memorable personality in club history in poll conducted in 1975.

The Baseball Heritage Museum in Cleveland commemorated the 50th anniversary of the infamous April 17 trade anniversary in 2010. "It was a time to reflect on Rocky and on the Harvey Kuenn trade, that trade that sent Rocky away from Cleveland for the first time," said Morris Eckhouse, the museum's special projects coordinator. "The trade was a touchstone moment for a lot of the people in the room. It was a combination of celebrating Rocky's status in Cleveland baseball history and reflecting on the pros and cons of what happened, and how it affected the Indians."[20]

Colavito, 84, sits at the kitchen table with a scrapbook of his playing days open in his Bernville, PA, home on April 22, 2018 (Mark Sommer).

A celebration put on by the Indians for Colavito's 80th birthday was held at the ballpark on August 10, 2013. DiBiasio presented his idea to Carmen Colavito first, to help make plans. The gathering was held in the stadium's Terrace Club. Hundreds of assembled guests serenaded the Indians' legend by singing "Happy Birthday." The remembrance meant a lot to Colavito, and he signed autographed baseballs for everyone in attendance. He also took part in a televised "Indians Alumni Roundtable" that weekend moderated by DiBiasio. Colavito appeared with Gary Bell, a teammate in the

1950s and 1960s, and Max Alvis, whom he played with in the 1960s. The Indians' legend walked out onto Jacobs Field on his birthday that Saturday to a stirring reaction. "When he came off the mound throwing the first pitch, it was Niagara Falls. It was special," DiBiasio said, suggesting there wasn't a dry eye in the house. "I think he always felt connected to the franchise, but I think that just really cemented it."[21]

Colavito was able to share the moment with his family, which in addition to Carmen, Rocky Jr., Marisa, and Steve, included spouses, five granddaughters and one great-grandson. "My birthday was extra-special. They took care of my whole family and did everything first-class, and that endeared them to me," Colavito said of the Indians. "It was a cleansing. They wiped out all the animosity I ever felt toward the old regimes I felt didn't treat me fairly."

Some of the lingering hurt had never gone away. "The Cleveland Indians, starting with Frank Lane and then on to Gabe Paul—but never, never the town—didn't treat me and a lot of the other guys right," Colavito said. "I always thought Detroit took care of Al Kaline, who was a great player. It just didn't seem to be the right way to treat a guy who was as loyal as I was to them. I was raised in that organization. I belonged there. I always rooted for Cleveland, and I always will. The city of Cleveland loved me, and I loved them."

Appendix:
Reconsidering the
Hall of Fame

Rocky Colavito's career ended decades before advanced metrics were used to measure a ballplayer's value and performance. To re-examine Colavito's worthiness for the Hall of Fame, two practitioners were asked to evaluate his career using advanced metrics.

Adam Darowski created the Hall of Stats, an alternate hall of fame determined by a mathematical formula. He also chairs a committee of the Society for American Baseball Research on overlooked 19th-century ballplayers. He lives in Peterborough, NH. Brian Heise is a former editor and senior staff writer for the Cleveland Indians content site Fansided.com. He lives in Blacklick, OH. While each reached a different conclusion regarding Colavito's worthiness for the Hall of Fame, career longevity was seen by both as the biggest hurdle to election.

Here's what Adam Darowski found

I use a metric I developed using Baseball-Reference's Wins Above Replacement and Wins Above Average to rank every player in baseball history. There are 226 players in the Hall of Fame strictly based on their MLB playing career. The Hall of Stats removes everyone from the Hall of Fame and replaces them with the top 226 players by rating. The result is that about 31 percent of Hall of Famers (70/226) are replaced with players outside the Hall of Fame. They ranged from obvious picks, like Roger Clemens and Barry Bonds, to others currently on the ballot, such as Curt Schilling and Larry Walker, to generally overlooked players, past and present. A Hall Rating of 100 represents the Hall of Fame borderline. That's where we get to Rocky Colavito.

Colavito's Hall Rating is 83, meaning statistically he falls short. A Hall Rating of 83 ranks exactly 400th all-time. The 399th is Hall of Fame right fielder Harry Hooper, and the 409th is Hall of Fame right fielder Sam Rice. So, while Colavito doesn't quite stack up statistically, he's still within the range of possible induction. In fact, he ranks ahead of 33 Hall of Famers by the Hall Rating. The right fielders that rank behind him include Rice, Ross Youngs, and Tommy McCarthy.

So, how does Colavito arrive at that 83 Hall Rating? The inputs used were Wins Above Average, a statistical framework that takes a player's batting, fielding, base-running, and position into consideration and converts it to how many wins a player is worth above an average player; and Wins Above Replacement, which works similarly but also gives a player credit for longevity. Wins Above Average is more important in a Hall of Fame or historical significance context because it better captures dominance over the league average. Colavito's 21.1 Wins Above Average put him near corner outfielders like Hall of Famer Chuck Klein, Babe Herman, Darryl Strawberry, Jesse Barfield, and Roy White.

I also looked closely at Colavito's batting average, on-base percentage, and slugging percentage—but compared to the league average rather than just taken by itself. Colavito's BA/OBP/SLG was .266/.359/.489. The league average during his career was .259/.330/.397. So, while Rocky's batting average wasn't that much above the league average, he starts to distance himself with OBP thanks to a good eye and even more with his power. Between 1956 and 1966 (Colavito's 11-year peak), only Mays, Aaron, Mantle, and Frank Robinson hit more homers. Only Mantle and Eddie Mathews drew more walks. About 60 players had a better batting average (minimum 3,000 plate appearances). When combining OBP and SLG into OPS, Colavito ranks 13th for the era. He ranks 13th by OPS+ (which takes OPS, compares it to the league average, and adjusts based on ballpark factors).

Colavito also rates as an excellent defender according to WAR. He was particularly strong in his 20s, rating at 77 runs above average. He slowed in his 30s, rating at 18 runs below average. In his 20s, only Al Kaline and Roberto Clemente rated ahead of him among right fielders. Hank Aaron wasn't far behind.

What hurt Colavito was, of course, his lack of longevity. Colavito was done at age 34, so he only played in 1,841 games and fell short of many statistical milestones. At age 34, he hit only .211 with 8 home runs in 79 games while drawing 29 walks. Those numbers look lousy on the surface, but when compared to the league average they look much better. That was 1968 and nobody could hit then. His offensive production was 12 percent above the league average. Similarly, Mickey Mantle hit .237 with 18 homers that year (his final year). But his offensive production was 43 percent above league average.

I also looked at whether Colavito deserved to win a Most Valuable Player Award during any of his best seasons: According to the Wins Above Replacement framework, Covalito's best seasons as a hitter were:

1958	(5.9 oWAR—that's WAR without fielding included)
1961	(5.9)
1964	(4.9)
1965	(4.4)
1962	(4.1)
1959	(3.6)

It just so happens those are the six years when he received MVP votes, too. While he hit at a better rate in 1958 vs. 1961, he played more in 1961, which evens things out. Defense is tricky. A lot of people don't trust advanced defensive metrics because they can fluctuate. A big reason why that happens is the smaller sample sizes. It's easier to stabilize your performance across a larger sample (like 600 trips to the plate). Colavito had strong defensive numbers in 1961, 1962, and 1959. He was basically league average in 1958 and a bit below average in 1964 and 1965. Worth noting is that Colavito rated as a much better left fielder than right fielder, so in the years he played left more, he tended to grade better. That all said, here's where WAR totals end up once you factor in his defense:

1961:	7.6
1958:	5.8
1962:	5.7
1959:	5.3
1964:	4.1
1957:	3.6 (this one sneaks on the list due to strong defense)
1965:	3.2

I've written about the average MVP having 7.62 WAR. So, that 1961 season is really the only one that puts Colavito on that level. Colavito ranked 4th in the AL in WAR that year. He was even third on his own team. Mickey Mantle (10.5), Norm Cash (9.2), and Al Kaline (8.4) were ahead of him. Of course, it was Roger Maris who ended up winning the award. The next year Colavito had 5.7 WAR but ranked third among position players, just a fraction of a win off the leader (Frank Robinson, 6.1). It wasn't Colavito's flashiest season because he only hit .273, but he did lead the league in total bases and graded as a great left fielder. In 1958, he also finished 4th. behind Mantle (8.7), Kaline, and Bob Cerv. In 1959, he finished 7th but just a little over a win behind the leader (Mantle, 6.6).

While Colavito had some great seasons, I don't think he was particularly robbed of any MVP awards. He easily could have won an MVP in 1961, but several players had great seasons that year, partly because it was an expansion year. Also, if he had one of his better fielding years in 1958, he would have had a great case as well.

Brian Heise reached another conclusion

For Rocky Colavito, the numbers that Hall of Fame voters have traditionally looked at certainly seem to provide support for Hall of Fame induction. Over the course of his 14-year career, Colavito amassed a .266 batting average, 374 home runs, and 1,159 RBI. Compare that with the averages of all currently inducted players. Per Baseball Reference's Hall of Fame Register, the average Hall of Fame inductee batted .302 with 223 home runs and 1,227 RBI. In addition to these traditional statistics, Colavito was also elected to six All-Star teams, finished three times in the top five of MVP vote getters and four times in the top ten. He was runner-up in the 1956 AL Rookie of the Year voting.

During the ten-year period in which Rocky Colavito would have been eligible for induction by the Baseball Writers Association of America, these are numbers they would have seemed to have looked at favorably. Instead, Colavito received only two votes during his first year of eligibility and one vote in his second and final year on the ballot. The most surprising thing and what's really stuck with me after looking at his numbers is just how little consideration he received and how few votes he got, especially when you consider some other players that hang around on the ballot year after year. That's what I would be most upset about if I were Colavito.

Do modern metrics look at Colavito more favorably than baseball's traditional statistics? Did he deserve more Hall of Fame consideration than originally received?

The first and most obvious modern metric to look at, the Holy Grail in our current baseball lexicon, is Wins Above Replacement (WAR). What WAR is intended to tell us is a player's total contributions to his team, in other words, his value. It does this by comparing the player in question against an average replacement with a baseline of 0. The higher this value for the aforementioned player, the more value or contribution to wins they have over the replacement or any other player they are being compared against. There are two universally agreed upon calculations for WAR, Fangraphs (fWAR) and Baseball Reference (bWAR), with minor differences between the two.

With Baseball Reference, Rocky Colavito accumulated a career wins above replacement total of 44.5. When compared to other Hall of Fame members, this is a fairly modest number. Players in the upper echelon typically have career Wins Above Replacement totals in the low to mid–100s. Even Baseball Reference's Hall of Fame registry has the average Hall of Famer at 69 Wins Above Replacement, creating a sizeable gap of 25 Wins Above Replacement between Colavito and the average.

For some, this could be cause enough to dismiss Colavito's case for Hall of Fame induction. Baseball Reference also pinpoints the average Hall of

Famer's career length at 18 seasons. Compare this to Colavito's 13 seasons and some cracks form in that argument. Remove the final two seasons of decline and subpar performance and that leaves Colavito with only 11 seasons of prime performance. And while one can argue career longevity, or lack thereof, as a reason against enshrinement, ultimately the decision should come down to what that player did in those prime seasons—and Colavito was great.

From 1956 to 1966, Colavito slashed .270/.363/.502. Had he slugged .502 for the entirety of his career, he would have finished in the top 100 sluggers of all time. Even so, his career slugging percentage of .489 is good enough for 139th all-time. During this time period, Colavito averaged 36 homers and 108 RBI per 162 games, numbers nothing short of incredible.

Digging deeper, Colavito's career OPS+ of 132 meant he performed 32 percent better than the league average, tying him with several players at 142nd on the all-time rankings, among them first-ballot Hall of Famer Tony Gwynn.

One additional modern statistic that weighs favorably for Colavito is Weighted Runs Created Plus (wRC+). This is a measure of how well above average a player was able to create runs while also taking into account park effects. Colavito's wRC+ of 132 tells us that he helped create runs for his teams 32 percent better than the league average over his career. This places him in the same company as first-ballot Hall of Famers Ricky Henderson, George Brett, Rod Carew, Wade Boggs, and Tony Gwynn. Fan Graphs roughly estimates anything above 140 wRC+ as great, a number Colavito is close to.

One thing not evaluated that WAR takes into account is defense and base running ability As a center fielder, for example, Mantle would have an automatic edge in terms of value since it's a more demanding position with more responsibility that ultimately helps save more runs than right field. It's just hard to really quantify or examine with older players because we don't have the defensive information available that we do now.

Do modern metrics help bolster his Hall of Fame argument by showing he may have been worthy of more American League honors?

In 1956, Luis Aparicio of the White Sox was a near-unanimous pick for AL Rookie of the Year. He received 22 out of 24 total votes. However, while Aparicio put together a solid .266/.311/.341 slash line in 152 games with a .653 OPS while accumulating 1.5 bWAR, Colavito slashed .276/.372/.531 with a .903 OPS and 2.4 bWAR in 101 games. Colavito's 21 home runs and 65 RBI also dwarfed Aparicio's three home runs and 56 RBI in 211 fewer at-bats. By this measure, Colavito was the better player and more deserving of the honor.

When it comes to MVP awards, Colavito finished third in 1958 while putting up one of his finest statistical seasons, slashing .303/.405/.620 with 41 home runs and 113 RBI. From a traditional statistical standpoint, he may well have been the best player. For the season, Colavito was responsible for 6.0 bWAR. He was certainly a worthy contender for the honor, but finished third in the voting behind Jackie Jensen, 4.9 bWAR, and Bob Turley, 3.5 bWAR. Mickey Mantle was the most deserving of the title. His 8.7 bWAR made him by far the most valuable player in the American League in 1958. It wasn't even close.

The following season, 1959, saw Colavito once again belt over 40 homers and drive in 100 runs. However, his .257/.337/.512 slash line was not up to the level of his 1958 season. As a result, his value took a hit. And while his 42 home runs and 111 RBI were impressive, when combined with the slash line and other peripheral numbers, his bWAR was only 5.3. Nellie Fox won the award with a 6.0 bWAR, but the most deserving player may very well have been Washington's Camilo Pascual, who finished 19th overall. With a 17–10 record and 2.64 ERA in 30 starts, he was the clear frontrunner with an 8.6 bWAR. In terms of position players, Mickey Mantle was once again at the top of the mountain with a 6.6 bWAR. Meanwhile, Colavito was the seventh-place finisher based on wins above replacement alone. In addition, he may have finished fourth due to competition. Teammate Tito Francona finished fifth and may have robbed Colavito of votes. And while those lost votes would not have won him the award, they may have helped him finish higher.

Speaking of bad luck, 1961 may define the term for Rocky Colavito. It was Colavito's finest season as a professional, but he finished only eighth in voting. He slashed .290/.402/.580, hit 45 home runs, drove in 140 runs, and accumulated 7.6 bWAR. In terms of production, it's hard to be better than that. Unfortunately for Colavito and many other deserving players, 1961 was the year of Roger Maris. So, while Mickey Mantle (10.5 bWAR), Norm Cash (9.2 bWAR), Al Kaline (8.4 bWAR), and Colavito (7.6 bWAR) all provided more value than Maris (6.9 bWAR), it was the pursuit of history that won him the award. Maris's 61 homers set a new major league single-season record, surpassing Babe Ruth, and in the process overshadowed anyone and everyone else.

In the following season, 1962, Colavito was great once again. His .273/.371/.514 slash line, 37 home runs and 112 RBI had become automatic at this point. It was proof yet again that Colavito was among the most consistent hitters the game had seen up to this point. For his efforts, Colavito finished 16th in the AL MVP race. Mickey Mantle took home the award with 5.9 bWAR, but Colavito was right behind him with 5.7 bWAR, placing him fifth behind Camilo Pascual's 6.2 bWAR. So, while Colavito may not have deserved the award in terms of wins above replacement, an additional top-five finish would have looked a lot better on his resume than 16th.

Finally, 1965, Colavito's fourth and final time finishing in the top ten of MVP vote-getters, was another strange season, to say the least. Colavito finished the season with a respectable line of .287/.383/.468 with 26 homers and 108 RBI, and MVP voters rewarded his performance with a fifth-place finish.

However, Colavito's 3.2 bWAR placed him barely in the top 20 among vote-getters, 19th overall.

So where does that leave Rocky Colavito? Well, while Colavito neither won an MVP award nor deserved to win one based on today's understanding of value, it does help shine a light on how he was viewed at the time. Despite not being in the Hall of Fame, Colavito's performance on a nearly annual basis put him in the company of many players who are in. He was their peer and their equal in many regards even if he remains on the outside looking in.

One final item to consider relates to value and Wins Above Replacement. Jay Jaffe, a writer for SI.com, has become an authority on the Baseball Hall of Fame, who should be in and who should not thanks to his development of the Jaffe Wins Above Replacement Score (JAWS). This metric compares players at a given position against those who are already enshrined. It does this by averaging a player's career Wins Above Replacement with his seven-year career peak (seven best seasons). It is a statistic new to the Hall of Fame argument, but one that has gained favor in many circles.

The average JAWS score for a Hall of Fame right fielder is calculated as 57.8. Rocky Colavito's JAWS score rounds out to an even 40.0. While this score is not favorable to Colavito's case for induction, there are a few things worth noting that may help sway the argument, or at least put it into the proper context.

Colavito's 40.0 is right at the tail end of the JAWS range for Hall of Fame right fielders. His 40.0 JAWS is good enough for 34th all-time among right fielders. Kiki Cuyler and Chuck Klein are both in the Hall of Fame with JAWS scores of 40.8 and 40.2, respectively. In addition, several Hall of Fame members have JAWS scores below that of Colavito, including Sam Thompson (38.7), King Kelly (37.7), Ross Youngs (31.3) and Tommy McCarthy (17.6).

Second, career length certainly plays a role in determining a player's JAWS score, fairly or unfairly. Several Hall of Fame right fielders—Tony Gwynn (54.9), Dave Winfield (50.8), and Vladimir Guerrero (50.2)—have JAWS scores well above Colavito's 40.4. However, their seven peak seasons are within a reasonable range to Colavito's 35.4 bWAR—Gwynn (41.1), Winfield (37.7), Guerrero (41.1). Their advantage was career longevity. Colavito's 13 seasons paled next to Gwynn (20 seasons) and Winfield (22 seasons), and was less than Guerrero (16 seasons). It's no surprise some of the highest JAWS scores belong to players who played 20-plus seasons.

So, what conclusion are we to make from all of this? Is Rocky Colavito a Hall of Famer or not? I think the answer is yes. In terms of overall ability, career numbers, and modern statistical data he measures up with other Hall of Fame players, even if those achievements seem overshadowed by a lack of career longevity. Rocky Colavito was a Hall of Fame-caliber talent and performed up to the standard of a Hall of Fame player during the majority of his career.

Career Statistics

Year	Tm	G	PA	R	H	HR	RBI	BB	BA	OBP	SLG	OPS	OPS+
1955	CLE	5	9	3	4	0	0	0	.444	.444	.667	1.111	192
1956	CLE	101	380	55	89	21	65	49	.276	.372	.531	.903	135
1957	CLE	134	544	66	116	25	84	71	.252	.348	.471	.819	122
1958	CLE	143	578	80	148	41	113	84	.303	.405	.620	1.024	180
1959	CLE	154	664	90	151	42	111	71	.257	.337	.512	.849	133
1960	DET	145	616	67	138	35	87	53	.249	.317	.474	.791	108
1961	DET	163	708	129	169	45	140	113	.290	.402	.580	.982	157
1962	DET	161	707	90	164	37	112	96	.273	.371	.514	.885	132
1963	DET	160	692	91	162	22	91	84	.271	.358	.437	.795	119
1964	KCA	160	681	89	161	34	102	83	.274	.366	.507	.873	137
1965	CLE	162	695	92	170	26	108	93	.287	.383	.468	.851	140
1966	CLE	151	614	68	127	30	72	76	.238	.336	.432	.767	119
1967	TOT	123	436	30	88	8	50	49	.231	.317	.333	.651	95
1967	CLE	63	216	10	46	5	21	24	.241	.329	.366	.695	104
1967	CHW	60	220	20	42	3	29	25	.221	.306	.300	.606	85
1968	TOT	79	235	21	43	8	24	29	.211	.311	.373	.683	112
1968	LAD	40	129	8	23	3	11	15	.204	.295	.310	.604	89
1968	NYY	39	106	13	20	5	13	14	.220	.330	.451	.781	141
14Y	14Y	841	7559	283	21	374	951	880	.266	.359	.489	.848	132
162	162	162	665	85	152	33	102	84	.266	.359	.489	.848	132

Chapter Notes

All quotations attributed to Rocky Colavito are taken directly from interviews conducted with the author between February 2017 and August 2018, except where other sources are cited.

Introduction

1. Tony DeMarco, *Sporting News Selects 50 Greatest Sluggers* (St. Louis: Times Mirror Magazines, 2000), 56–57.

Chapter 1

1. Author's interview with Sheldon Green, March 2018.
2. Author's interview with Gary Stromberg, April 2018.
3. Author's interview with Thomas Rudar, Jr., April 2018.
4. Charles Ferroni, "Encyclopedia of Cleveland History: Italians," Case Western Reserve University (online), https://case.edu/ech/articles/i/italians.
5. Carol Poh Miller and Robert A. Wheeler, *Cleveland: A Concise History, 1796–1996* (Bloomington: Indiana University Press, 1997), 82.
6. *Ibid.*, 82.
7. *Ibid.*, 103.
8. *Ibid.*, 131.
9. Ferroni, "Encyclopedia of Cleveland History: Italians."
10. Miller and Wheeler, *Cleveland*, 113–115, 129.
11. Peter Chakerian, *Pop Goes Cleveland! The Impact of Cleveland (and Northeast Ohio) on Pop Culture* (Cleveland Landmarks Press, 2009), 34–35.
12. Lawrence Baldassaro, *Beyond DiMaggio: Italian Americans in Baseball* (Lincoln: University of Nebraska Press, 2013), xii, xxix.

13. David A. Taylor, "During World War II, the U.S. Saw Italian-Americans as a Threat to Homeland Security," Smithsonian.com, February 2, 2017.
14. Author's interview with Basil Russo, April 2018.
15. *Ibid.*
16. Warren Corbett, "Frank Lane," SABR Biography Project, https://sabr.org/node/40756.
17. Edward Linn, "Why Cleveland Loves Colavito," *Saturday Evening Post*, July 25, 1959, 25.
18. Frank Gibbons, "Lane Proves He Has Guts of a Burglar," *Cleveland Press*, April 18, 1960.
19. Vance Lauderdale, "The Russwood Park Fire," *Memphis* magazine, May 1, 2013.
20. Harry Jones, "Colavito Stunned by Lane Trade," *Cleveland Plain Dealer*, April 18, 1960, 33.
21. Joe Falls, "Nobody Is Safe Now," *Detroit Free Press*, April 18, 1960, 1.
22. "Tribe Gets Kuenn in Colavito Trade," *Cleveland Plain Dealer*, April 18, 1960, 1.
23. Gordon Cobbledick, "Plain Dealing," *Cleveland Plain Dealer*, April 18, 1960, 33.
24. "Tribe Gets Kuenn in Colavito Trade," 1.
25. Debbie Gilbert, "The Night Russwood Park Burned," *Memphis* magazine, January 1992.
26. *Ibid.*

Chapter 2

1. "The Bronx—A Historical Sketch," Bronx County Historical Society, http://bronxhistoricalsociety.org/about/bronx-history/.
2. *Ibid.*
3. *Ibid.*
4. Author's interview with Jerry Muro, August 2018.
5. Hal Lebovitz, "Everybody Loves Rocky Colavito," *Sport*, April 1959, 13.

6. Author's interview with Joan Smith, June 2018.

7. Edward Linn, "Why Cleveland Loves Colavito," *Saturday Evening Post*, July 25, 1959, 25.

8. Gordon Cobbledick, *Don't Knock the Rock: The Rocky Colavito Story* (New York: World Publishing, 1966), 42.

9. *Ibid.*, 43.

10. "Why Cleveland Loves Colavito," 25.

11. Cobbledick, *Don't Knock the Rock*, 43.

12. *Ibid.*, 44.

13. Joe Trimble and Joe O'Day, "Colavito Slams 4 Homers," *New York Daily News*, June 11, 1959.

14. Cobbledick, *Don't Knock the Rock*, 45.

15. Linn, "Why Cleveland Loves Colavito."

16. *Ibid.*

Chapter 3

1. Bernard Kahn, "'Nice Guy' Colavito Comes into Own as Tribe Star," *Daytona Beach News-Journal*, June 14, 1959, 21.

2. Author's interview with Joe Altobelli, October 2017.

3. "Highlights of Lower Minors," *The Sporting News*, August 22, 1951, 40.

4. Bob Talbert, "Visit with Boyhood Hero Stirs Memories," *Detroit Free Press*, May 19, 1976, 13.

5. Lester Koelling, "The Bullpen," *Indianapolis News*, May 6, 1954, 16.

6. Author's interview with Carmen Colavito, January 2018.

7. *Ibid.*

8. *Ibid.*

9. Gordon Cobbledick, "Plain Dealing," *Cleveland Plain Dealer*, May 22, 1954, 25.

10. Tommy Fitzgerald, "American Association," *The Sporting News*, July 21, 1954, 29.

11. *Ibid.*, 27.

12. Russell Schneider, "Colavito Rapped 3 Homers Playing with Sore Elbow," *Cleveland Plain Dealer*, March 28, 1965.

13. Jackie Freers, "Rocky's Biggest Hit," *Indianapolis Star*, June 22, 1954, 37.

14. Author's interview with Carmen Colavito, January 2018.

15. Harry Jones, "Tribe Rookie from Bronx Likes Looks of Stadium," *Cleveland Plain Dealer*, January 12, 1955, 28.

16. *Cleveland Plain Dealer*, January 16, 1955. Caption as published: "Rocky and Carmen Colavito get their first look inside Municipal Stadium."

17. James A. Toman, and Gregory G. Deegan, *Cleveland Stadium: The Last Chapter*, (Cleveland Landmarks Press), 1997.

18. "Rookies to Watch in '55," *Sport*, February 1955.

19. Harry Jones, "Indian Rookies will get Extensive Trials," *Cleveland Plain Dealer*, March 1, 1955, 25.

20. *Cleveland Plain Dealer*, March 2, 1955, "Rocky Colavito and Ralph Kiner pose for pictures in advance of the 1955 season." Caption as published: "A Couple of Clouters—Kiner and Colavito."

21. Cobbledick, *Don't Knock the Rock*, 77.

22. Author's interview with Jim Kaat, September 2018.

23. Harry Jones, "Wynn Signs for $40,000 Bonus," *Cleveland Plain Dealer*, March 7, 1955, 33.

24. Harry Jones, "Colavito Raps Homer as Tribe Triumphs, 8–2," *Cleveland Plain Dealer*, March 26, 1955, 25.

25. Cobbledick, *Don't Knock the Rock*, 62.

Chapter 4

1. Richard Goldstein, "Herb Score, 75, Indians Pitcher Derailed by Line Drive, Dies," *New York Times*, November 11, 2008, B19.

2. Terry Pluto, *The Curse of Rocky Colavito* (New York: Simon & Schuster, 1994), 32.

3. Ira, Berkow, "McDougald, Once a Quiet Yankee Star, Now Lives in Quiet World," *New York Times*, July 10, 1994, 84.

4. Hal Lebovitz, "Score Ribs Pals Colavito, Garcia on Hospital Visit," *The Sporting News*, May 22, 1957, 8.

5. Hal Lebovitz, "Score & Colavito: Mutual Admiration Society," *Sport*, August 1957, 20, 85–87.

6. Terry Pluto, *The Curse of Rocky Colavito*, 31.

7. Author's interview with Nancy Score, December 2017.

8. Harry Jones, "Score Wins 3–2 on Hamner Hit in 9th; Garcia is 6–3 Loser," *Cleveland Plain Dealer*, May 30, 1959, 33.

9. Gordon Cobbledick, "Plain Dealing," *Cleveland Plain Dealer*, April 19, 1960, 29.

10. Joseph Wancho, "Herb Score," SABR Biography Project, https://sabr.org/bioproj/person/1b133b89.

11. Goldstein, "Herb Score, 75, Indians Pitcher Derailed by Line Drive, Dies," 84.

12. Author's interview with Sonny Siebert, November 2017.

13. Joseph Wancho, "Herb Score."

14. Author's interview with Bob DiBiasio, April 2017.

15. Author's interview with Nancy Score, December 2017.

Chapter 5

1. Harry Jones, "Indians Win 2, Clinch Second," *Cleveland Plain Dealer*, September 25, 1955, 1C.

2. Harry Jones, "Rocky Aims to Make Grade this Year Despite Curves"; "Colavito Raps 2 Home Runs; Chico Arrives," *Cleveland Plain Dealer*, March 4, 1956, 1-C.

3. Rocky Colavito, as Told to Furman Bisher, "What You Learn in the Big Leagues," *Sport*, July 1961, 9.

4. Bob Addie, "Bob Addie's Atoms," *The Sporting News*, May 30, 1956, 16.

5. Oscar Ruhl, "From the Ruhl Book," *The Sporting News*, February 22, 1956, 15.

6. Colavito, as told to Bisher, "What You Learn in the Big Leagues," 9.

7. Jimmy Dudley, quoted in Jimmy Jemail's "Hot Box," *Sports Illustrated*, April 9, 1956, 12.

8. Harry Jones, "The Witness Box: Take the Stand, Emily Fitzgibbons," *Cleveland Plain Dealer*, January 24, 1957, 25.

9. Author's interview with Barbara Warny, March 2018.

10. *The Official Rocky Colavito Fan Club News*, Vol. 1, No. 5, December 1956.

11. *Ibid.*

12. Bill Jenkinson, *Baseball's Ultimate Power: Ranking the All-Time Greatest Distance Home Run Hitters* (Guilford, CT: Lyons Press, 2010), 296.

13. "Colavito Eyes Record Throw," *San Diego Union*, June 27, 1956. Advertisement promoting Rocky Colavito throwing exhibition, July 1, 1956.

14. "Colavito Pegs Ball 435 Feet, but Misses Throwing Mark," *The Sporting News*, July 11, 1956, 37.

15. Jenkinson, *Baseball's Ultimate Power*, 295–297.

16. Edward Linn, "Why Cleveland Loves Colavito," *Saturday Evening Post*, July 25, 1959.

17. Harry Jones, Batting Around, *Cleveland Plain Dealer*, July 29, 1956, 3-C.

18. Author's interview with Barbara Warny, March 2018.

19. Emily Fitzgibbons, "Do More than Buy Gum," *The Sporting News*, October 2, 1957, 2.

20. Author's interview with Barbara Warny, March 2018.

21. Author's interview with Emily Toth, March 2018.

22. Hal Lebovitz, "Rocco-Socko Raps for A.L. Rookie Prize," *The Sporting News*, September 5, 1956, 7.

23. Harry Jones, "Colavito is Kirby's No. 1 Fan: Gives Tribe New Pilot Credit for Building His Confidence," *Cleveland Plain Dealer*, February 20, 1957, 31.

24. "Spink Foresees Another All-NY Series," *The Sporting News*, April 17, 1957, 2.

25. Chuck Heaton, "Rocky's Slugging Outburst Rewards Patient Farrell," *Cleveland Plain Dealer*, May 13, 1957, 33.

26. Author's interview with Barbara Warny, March 2018.

27. Staff special, *Cleveland Plain Dealer*, November 20, 1957, 29.

28. Hal Lebovitz, "Trade Posies Spur Lane to Bigger Deals," *The Sporting News*, December 18, 1957, 22.

Chapter 6

1. Talmadge Boston, *Baseball and the Baby Boomer: A History, Commentary and Memoir* (Houston: Bright Sky Press, 2009), 174–177.

2. Terry Pluto, *Our Tribe: A Baseball Memoir* (New York: Simon & Schuster, 1999), 179.

3. *Ibid.*, 181.

4. Tom Clavin, and Danny Peary, *Roger Maris: Baseball's Reluctant Hero* (New York: Touchstone, 2010), 70–71.

5. Daniel Dullum, "Roger Maris and the Indians,"*Batting Four Thousand: Baseball in the Western Reserve*, ed. Brad Sullivan (Cleveland: Society for American Baseball Research, 2008), 31.

6. *Ibid.*

7. *Ibid.*

8. *Ibid.*

9. Harry Jones, "Take the Stand, Emily Fitzgibbons," *Cleveland Plain Dealer*, January 24, 1957, 25.

10. Pluto, *Our Tribe*, 181.

11. *Ibid.*, 182.

12. *Ibid.*

13. Clavin and Peary, *Roger Maris*, 97.

14. Peterson, *Kansas City Athletics*, 277.

15. Larry Middlemas, "Seers Who Stumbled Over Crystal Ball," *The Sporting News*, January 4, 1961, 7.

16. Bob DiBiasio, email, July 6, 2017.

17. Pluto, *Curse of Rocky Colavito*, 63.

18. Milton Gross, "Last Chance for Roger Maris," *Sport*, April 1966.

19. Clavin and Peary, *Roger Maris*, 296.

20. *Ibid.*, 294.

21. *Ibid.*

22. *Ibid.*, 296.

23. Peter Golenbock, *Dynasty: When Rooting for the Yankees was Like Rooting for U.S. Steel* (Englewood Cliffs, NJ: Prentice-Hall, 1975), 302.

24. *Ibid.*

25. *Ibid.*

26. Clavin and Peary, *Roger Maris*, 360.

27. *Ibid.*, 370.

28. Mark Sommer, "Redemption in Pinstripes," *Topeka Capital-Journal*, January 25, 1994.

29. Author's interview with Ralph Terry, July 2017.

30. Pluto, *Curse of Rocky Colavito*, 39.

Chapter 7

1. Mark Kram, "Would You Trade with This Man?" *Sports Illustrated*, August 26, 1968, 30–35.
2. Bob Vanderberg, *Frantic Frank Lane: Baseball's Ultimate Wheeler-Dealer* (Jefferson, NC: McFarland, 2013), 4.
3. Clavin and Peary, *Roger Maris*, 93.
4. *Ibid.*
5. Plain Dealer Special, "Colavito Keeps his Muscles as limber as Mushrooms," *Cleveland Plain Dealer*, February 11, 1958, 26.
6. Gordon Cobbledick, "Plain Dealing," *Cleveland Plain Dealer*, March 30, 1958, 2-C.
7. *Ibid.*
8. Will Grimsley, Batting Around, *Cleveland Plain Dealer*, April 1, 1958, 26.
9. *The Sporting News*, May 28, 1958, 5.
10. *The Sporting News*, March 5, 1958, 6.
11. *The Sporting News*, May 7, 1958, 20.
12. "Here Come the Kids," *Time*, August 24, 1959, 54.
13. Bob Vanderberg, *Frantic Frank Lane*, 87.
14. Hal Lebovitz, "New Wobbles Put in Wigwam Infield by Injury to Avila," *Cleveland Plain Dealer*, June 18, 1958, 13.
15. *Associated Press*, January 23, 1959.
16. Bobby Bragan and Jeff Guinn, *You Can't Hit the Ball with the Bat on Your Shoulder: The Baseball Life and Times of Bobby Bragan* (Fort Worth, TX: Summit, 1992), 223.
17. Harry Jones, "Batting Around," *Cleveland Plain Dealer*, August 22, 1958, 37.
18. Edward Linn, "Why Cleveland Loves Colavito," *Saturday Evening Post*, July 25, 1959, 64.
19. Harry Jones, "Tribe Falls," *Cleveland Plain Dealer*, August 30, 1958, 19.
20. Harry Jones, "Colavito Nearing 35 Homer Goal," *Cleveland Plain Dealer*, September 10, 1958, 2-C.
21. Hal Lebovitz, "But Rocky's Sure Doing OK So Far," *Cleveland News*, September 27, 1958.
22. Hal Lebovitz, "Everybody Loves Rocky Colavito," *Sport*, April 1959, 57.
23. Harry Jones, "Colavito Fans 5 in Two Innings," *Cleveland Plain Dealer*, July 2, 1958, 21.
24. Hal Lebovitz, "Reminiscing About Rocky: The Night He Became a Pitcher," *Cleveland Plain Dealer*, January 25, 1965, 33.
25. Linn, "Why Cleveland Loves Colavito," 25.
26. Lebovitz, "Reminiscing About Rocky," 33.
27. Hal Lebovitz, "Everybody Loves Colavito," 57.
28. "Boost for Colavito," Voice of the Fan, *The Sporting News*, December 24, 1958, 32.
29. Hal Lebovitz, "McLish, Colavito, Power Tribe Entries in MVP Race," *The Sporting News*, September 24, 1958, 10.
30. Lawrence Stolle, "Rocky Slugging for In-dians as Ambassador of Goodwill," *The Sporting News*, February 18, 1959, 22.
31. Les Biederman, "Murtaugh Hailed by 1,300 Fans at Pittsburgh Party," *The Sporting News*, February 18, 1959, 24.
32. "Knife and Fork League," *The Sporting News*, January 7, 1959, 27.
33. Alpert Katz, "Beef Box," *The Sporting News*, February 11, 1959, 16.
34. "Semi-Pros Surprise Nieman's All-Stars," *The Sporting News*, October 29, 1958, 25.
35. Information supplied by collector Steven Pierce.
36. John Steadman, "Atlanta-to-Majors Move Given Boost," *The Sporting News*, January 10, 1962, 19.
37. Author's interview with Cindy Yost, June 2018.
38. Hal Lebovitz, "Heap Big Tribe Turnover Under Lane as Top Chief," *The Sporting News*, December 24, 1958, 2.
39. Hal Lebovitz, "Everybody Loves Rocky Colavito," *Sport*, April 1959, 57.
40. Dan Daniel, "Weiss is Braced for Yankees' Contract Squabbles," *The Sporting News*, January 21, 1959, 5.
41. Bob Vanderberg, *Frantic Frank Lane*, 91.
42. Gordon Cobbledick, "Cleveland's Soft Rock," *Cleveland Plain Dealer*, April 26, 1959, 16.
43. Lois Lichtenstein, Voice of the Fan, "Rocky the Rifleman," *The Sporting News*, May 13, 1959, 40.
44. Hal Lebovitz, "Colavito Shows Certain Parties," *Cleveland News*, September 22, 1959.

Chapter 8

1. Munsey and Suppes, https://ballparks.com/baseball/index.htm.
2. Jamie Turner, "When Rocky Rolled: 50 Years Ago, Colavito's Four Homers Flattened the Orioles in Baltimore," *Cleveland Plain Dealer*, June 10, 2009.
3. Hal Lebovitz, "Best Bet to Beat Bambino's 60?" *The Sporting News*, June 10, 1959, 3.
4. Research on home run distances by baseball historian Bill Jenkinson.
5. Hal Lebovitz, "Reminiscing About Rocky: The Night He Hit Four in a Row," *Cleveland Plain Dealer*, January 24, 1965, 4-C.
6. Jamie Turner, "When Rocky Rolled: 50 Years Ago, Colavito's Four Homers Flattened the Orioles in Baltimore," *Cleveland Plain Dealer*, June 10, 2009.
7. *Associated Press*, June 11, 1959, *Cleveland News*, 57.
8. Bob Vanderberg, *Frantic Frank Lane*, 96.
9. Jamie Turner, "When Rocky Rolled."
10. *Associated Press*, "Colavito Ties Record; Clubs Four Homers," June 10, 1959.

11. Gordon Beard, *Associated Press*, June 10, 1959.

12. *Associated Press*, "Colavito Ties Record; Clubs Four Homers," June 10, 1959.

13. Joe Trimble, and Joe O'Day, "Colavito Slams 4 Homers," *New York Daily News*, June 11, 1959.

14. "The Colavito Shift," *The Sporting News*, August 19, 1959, 7. Created by superimposing an image of Orioles outfielder Gene Wooding on a shot of the left field stands, where some of Colavito's homers had landed, the illustration ran under the line, "Well, Those Orioles Can Dream, Can't They?"

15. "You Can't Beat the Money," Blade Pictorial, *Toledo Blade*, August 6, 1961, 8.

16. Jamie Turner, "When Rocky Rolled: 50 Years Ago, Colavito's Four Homers Flattened the Orioles in Baltimore," *Cleveland Plain Dealer*, June 10, 2009, https://www.cleveland.com/tribe/index.ssf/2009/06/when

17. "Caught on the Fly," *The Sporting News*, July 1, 1959, 37.

Chapter 9

1. Larry Claflin, "Red Sox Almost Landed Rocky—Lane Backed Off," *The Sporting News*, December 7, 1963, 38.

2. "Several Exciting Angles in A.L. Race," *The Sporting News*, June 24, 1959, 12.

3. Tim Cohane, "The Indian War Club," *Look* magazine, July 21, 1959, 84.

4. Author's interview with Thomas Rudar, Jr., April 2018.

5. "Boy, 8, Dies Watching Tribe Game," *Cleveland Press*, June 24, 1959.

6. Chuck Heaton, "Minoso to Play in 6th All-Star Game," *Cleveland Plain Dealer*, June 28, 1959, 4-C.

7. *The Sporting News*, July 15, 1959, 18.

8. David Vincent, *The Midsummer Classic: The Compete History of Baseball's All-Star Game* (Lincoln: University of Nebraska Press, 2001), 171.

9. Jenkinson, *Baseball's Ultimate Power*, 277.

10. "3 Home Runs for A.L. Make it a 'Great Day for Italians,'" *The Sporting News*, August 12, 1959, 7.

11. Hal Lebovitz, "We'll See if Sox Have My Number," *Cleveland News*, August 25, 1959.

12. "Annual Babe Ruth Challenge," *The Sporting News*, September 2, 1959, 25.

13. "Here Come the Kids," *Time*, August 24, 1959, 54.

14. Hal Lebovitz, "Worried by Own Hitting, Power Helps Sock Yanks," *The Sporting News*, July 1, 1959, 23.

15. Walter Bingham, "The Joys and Agonies of Frank Lane," *Sports Illustrated*, July 27, 1959, 31, 56–57.

16. Bob Vanderberg, *Frantic Frank Lane*, 105–106.

17. Gordon Cobbledick, "Colavito's New Goal is $45,000," *Cleveland Plain Dealer*, January 23, 1960, 21.

18. "Colavito Standing Pat, Lane Talks of Swinging Big Deal," *The Sporting News*, February 10, 1960, 17.

19. Pluto, *The Curse of Rocky Colavito*, 46.

20. *Ibid.*, 45.

21. Larry Middlemas, "Seers Who Stumbled Over Crystal Ball," *The Sporting News*, January 4, 1961, 7.

22. Vanderberg, *Frantic Frank Lane*, 105–106.

23. Joe Falls, "Nobody is Safe Now," *Detroit Free Press*, April 18, 2018, 1.

24. Author's interview with Lawry Babitt, April 2017.

25. Author's interview with Susan Grimm, April 2017.

26. Bob Vanderberg, "Piersall Doubts Lane Could Hack It Today," *Chicago Tribune*, August 31, 2005, 10.

27. Author's interview with Gary Bell, December 2017.

28. "Tribe Fans Angry Over Rocky Trade," *Oakland (CA) Tribune*, April 18, 1960, 39.

29. Robert Dolgan, "'Lane Chickened on Firing Gordon'—Dolin," *The Sporting News*, December 8, 1962, 19.

30. Red Foley, "Kuenn Only Second A.L. Batting Baron to Be Shipped Away," *The Sporting News*, April 27, 1960, 4.

31. Pluto, *The Curse of Rocky Colavito*, 54.

32. Russell Schneider, *Tales from the Tribe Dugout* (Champaign, IL: Sports Publishing, 2002), 103.

33. Harry Jones, "Indians Get Kuenn in Deal," *Cleveland Plain Dealer*, April 18, 1960, 1.

34. Steve Wulf, "Really Big Deals," *Sports Illustrated*, August 22, 1988, 25.

35. *Ibid.*

36. Russell Schneider, "'Veeck Wrecked Tepee, Not I,' Fumes Frankie," *The Sporting News*, December 19, 1964, 5.

37. Schneider, *Tales from the Tribe Dugout*, 144.

38. Larry Whiteside, "Lane Obtains Kuenn Again—and Nobody Fires Rocks," *The Sporting News*, February 20, 1971, 43.

39. Vanderberg, *Frantic Frank Lane*, 4.

40. Author's interview with Bob Fitzpatrick, April 2017.

41. Author's interview with Dale McMillan, April 2017.

42. Author's interview with Kent Reinker, May 2018.

43. Author's interview with Barbara Warny and Emily Toth, March 2017.

44. Author's interview with Tito Francona, October 2017.

Chapter 10

1. Rocky Colavito as told to Furman Bisher, "What You Learn in the Big Leagues," *Sport*, July 1961, 18, 87–89.

2. Joe Falls, "Opening Day…. It Even Tops the World Series," *The Sporting News*, April 10, 1971, 3.

3. Myron Cope, "Baseball's Biggest Trade Two Years Later," *Sport*, August 1962, 57.

4. Bruce Markusen, "Colavito Still the Rock Despite Recent Health Issues," Detroit Athletic Co. (website), October 4, 2015. https://www.google.com/search?q=Bruce+Markusen,+%22Colavito+Still+the+Rock+Despite+Recent+Health+Issue.

5. Joe Falls, "Nobody is Safe Now," *Detroit Free Press*, April 18, 1960, 1.

6. Jim Hawkins, *Al Kaline: The Biography of a Tigers Icon* (Chicago: Triumph, 2010), 110.

7. Author's interview with Al Kaline, March 2018.

8. Russell Schneider, "Batting Around," *Cleveland Plain Dealer*, April 20, 1960, 36.

9. Pluto, *Curse of Rocky Colavito*, 55.

10. "Kuenn Is Injured," *Cleveland Plain Dealer*, April 20, 1960, 35.

11. Myron Cope, "Baseball's Biggest Trade Two Years Later," *Sport*, August 1962, 57.

12. Lou Darvas, "Rocking the Dream Boat," *Cleveland Press*, April 25, 1960. A cartoon showing Frank Lane haunted in his dreams by ballplayers he traded away.

13. Hal Middlesworth, "Will Rocky Replace Kaline as No. 1?" *Detroit Free Press*, April 26, 1960, 31.

14. Author's interview with Christine Williams, April 2017.

15. Myron Cope, "Baseball's Biggest Trade Two Years Later," *Sport*, August 1962, 57.

16. Hal Lebovitz, "Dykes follows Mack's Words of Wisdom," *The Sporting News*, August 17, 1960, 5.

17. Dick Young, "Rocky Calls Dykes 'Greatest' Manager," *New York Daily News*, July 21, 1968.

18. Joe Falls, "Rocky-Talkie," *Detroit Free Press*, March 3, 1961, 45.

19. *Ibid.*

20. *Ibid.*

21. Watson Spoelstra, "I'd Do It Again—Colavito: Invades Stands to Rescue Father," *Detroit News*, May 14, 1963, 1.

22. Joe King, "Colavito Rockets into Stands in Answering Call of the Clan," *Sporting News*, May 24, 1961, 11.

23. Watson Spoelstra, "I'd Do It Again—Colavito: Invades Stands to Rescue Father," *Detroit News*, 1.

24. King, "Colavito Rockets into Stands in Answering Call of the Clan," 11.

25. *Ibid.*

26. *Ibid.*

27. Barney Kremenko, "'I Needed No Help,' Says Rocky's Dad," *New York Journal-American*, May 14, 1961, 20-L.

28. *Ibid.*

29. Author's interview with Jake Wood, March 2018.

30. Author's interview with Paul Foytack, March 2017.

31. David Vincent, et al., *The Midsummer Classic: The Complete History of Baseball's All-Star Game* (Lincoln: University of Nebraska Press, 2001), 191.

32. Watson Spoelstra, "Safe this Season," *The Sporting News*, August 2, 1961, 11.

33. Hal Lebovitz, "Wigwam Waiting for Kirkland to Ignite Fuse on Powder Keg," *The Sporting News*, May 24, 1961, 18.

Chapter 11

1. Author's interview with Jake Wood, April 2018.

2. Author's interview with Willie Horton, May 2018.

3. Warren Spoelstra, "Negroes Happy Over New Tiger Spring Quarters," *The Sporting News*, May 9, 1962, 17.

4. Hal Lebovitz, "Mel's Word Will Be Law to '62 Tribe," *The Sporting News*, January 31, 1962, 29.

5. "Hungry Rocky Burned Up Energy, Poked 7 Safeties," *The Sporting News*, July 7, 1962, 11.

6. John Milner, "June 24, 1962: Yankees Outlast Tigers in 22-Inning Game," in *Tigers by the Tale: Great Games at Michigan and Trumbull*, ed. Scott Ferkovich (Phoenix: Society for American Baseball Research, 2016), 96.

7. "Masters of Mayhem with Mace," *Sporting News*, August 11, 1962, 7. Caption as published: "Home runs from Leon Wagner, Rocky Colavito, and Pete Runnels, powered the A.L. to a 9–4 win."

8. Author's interview with Jim Kaat, September 2018.

9. Charles Dexter, "How Ballplayers Fight for Private Lives," *Sport*, October 1962, 15–16, 84.

10. Hawkins, *Al Kaline*, 212–213.

11. Author's interview with Paul Foytack, April 2018.

12. Author's interview with Al Kaline, April 2018.

13. Bob Sudyk, "Rocky Colavito's Biggest Challenge," *Sport*, July 1965, 13.

14. Bill Dow, "The Special Connection Between Rocky Colavito and Willie Horton," Detroit Athletic Co. (website), May 25, 2009. https://www.detroitathletic.com/blog/2009/05/

25/the-special-connection-between-rocky-colavito-and-willie-horton/.

15. Author's interview with Willie Horton, May 2018.

16. Joe Falls, "A Real Big Leaguer? Try John Hiller," *The Sporting News*, May 17, 1980, 19.

17. Joe McGuff, "Colavito Delighted by Deal; 'I like to Feel Appreciated,'" *The Sporting News*, November 30, 1963, 17.

18. "Deer Hunter Colavito Got News of Trade via Radio," *The Sporting News*, November 30, 1963, 18.

19. Arthur Daley, "Return of the Rock," *New York Times*, January 1965, 29.

Chapter 12

1. John E. Peterson, *The Kansas City Athletics: A Baseball History, 1954–1967* (Jefferson, NC: McFarland, 2003), 123.

2. *Ibid.*, 178–191.

3. *Ibid.*, 125.

4. *Ibid.*, 124.

5. Vanderberg, *Frantic Frank Lane*, 114.

6. Peterson, *Kansas City Athletics*, 126.

7. *Ibid.*, 187.

8. *Ibid.*, 194.

9. Joe McGuff, "Colavito Trade Denied," *Kansas City Times*, March 4, 1964, 13.

10. Jack McDonald, "Friendly Finley Made Cimoli 'Bonus Baby,'" *The Sporting News*, December 28, 1963, 11.

11. Peterson, *Kansas City Athletics*, 210.

12. *Ibid.*, 210–211.

13. D. L. Nelson, "The Reign of Finley," Athletics Nation (website), https://www.athleticsnation.com/2013/8/1/4576930/the-reign-of-finley.

14. Peterson, *Kansas City Athletics*, 204.

15. *Ibid.*

16. *Ibid.*, 205.

17. "Major Flashes: American League," *The Sporting News*, August 8, 1964, 29.

18. Joe McGuff, "Homer Circus in Kaycee; 43 in 11 Contests," *The Sporting News*, May 16, 1964, 12.

19. *Ibid.*, 131.

20. Joe McGuff, "Rocky Finds Home-Run Haven in Kaycee's Cozy Playground," *The Sporting News*, May 30, 1964, 8.

21. "New Manager McGaha Picks Colavito as Kaycee's Captain," *The Sporting News*, June 27, 1964, 7.

22. Joe McGuff, "Hat's Off: Rocky Colavito," *The Sporting News*, September 5, 1964, 21.

23. Joe McGuff, "Rocky Cashes in at Dish Like He was Rockefeller," *The Sporting News*, August 8, 1964, 19.

24. Author's interview with Jim Gentile, November 2017.

25. *Ibid.*

26. *Ibid.*

27. *Ibid.*

28. Joe McGuff, "300 HRS, 900 RBIs for Rocky on Same Swing," *The Sporting News*, September 26, 1964, 11.

29. Author's interview with Marisa Colavito, July 2018.

30. Max Rieper, "Losing a Sports Team: The Relocation of the Kansas City Athletics," Royals Review (website), https://www.royalsreview.com/2016/1/20/10761476/losing-a-sports-team-the-relocation-of-the-kansas-city-athletics.

31. Nelson, "The Reign of Finley."

32. Bob Sudyk, "Rocky Colavito's Biggest Challenge," *Sport*, July 1965, 13.

33. *Ibid.*

34. Russell Schneider, "Happy Rocky's Return Raises Cleveland's Hopes," *The Sporting News*, February 6, 1965.

35. Russell Schneider, "Fans Toast the Return of Rocky," *The Sporting News*, January 30, 1965, 13.

36. *Ibid.*

37. Joe McGuff, "A's Give Up Rocky to Bolster Defense," *The Sporting News*, January 30, 1965, 16.

38. Cobbledick, *Don't Knock the Rock*, 139.

Chapter 13

1. Russell Schneider, *The Cleveland Indians Encyclopedia*, 3d ed. (Champaign, IL: Sports Publishing, 2005), 350.

2. Bob Sudyk, "Rocky's Biggest Challenge," *Sport*, July 1965, 13.

3. Phil Pepe, "Talkative Tommy the Hottest Proper Noun in Big Town," *The Sporting News*, June 30, 1979, 3.

4. "Fans Shout: We're Glad the Rock is Back," *Cleveland Plain Dealer*, January 21, 1965, 66.

5. "Colavito Glad Tepee is Open," *Cleveland Plain Dealer*, January 21, 1965, 65.

6. Author's interview with Bill Jonke, April 2017.

7. Author's interview with Sam McDowell, January 2018.

8. Bob Sudyk, "Wagner Sees Big Future for 'Me and Rock,'" *Cleveland Press*, April 22, 1965, 1F.

9. Bob Sudyk, "Rocky Colavito's Biggest Challenge," *Sport*, July 1965, 13.

10. Chuck Heaton, "Rocky's Influence Paves Wags' Road," *Cleveland Plain Dealer*, April 22, 1965, 57.

11. Hal Lebovitz, "Did You Enjoy the Opener?" *Cleveland Plain Dealer*, April 22, 1965, 57.

12. Editorial, "Indian Fans Meet a Challenge," *Cleveland Plain Dealer*, April 22, 1965, 18.

13. "Fruit Peddler," *Cleveland Plain Dealer*, April 22, 1965, 58.

14. "Nuns Have to Be Rocky Fans," *Cleveland Plain Dealer*, June 2, 1965, 14.

15. Russell Schneider, "Rocky Raps 14th to Win," *Cleveland Plain Dealer*, June 19, 1965, 35.

16. Chuck Heaton, "Long Homer Thrills Rock," *Cleveland Plain Dealer*, June 19, 1965, 35.

17. Author's interview with Bill Jenkinson, June 2018.

18. *Ibid.*

19. Author's interview with Ida Pocci, February 2018.

20. "Colavito Gets Another Fan With Advice to Conigliaro," *The Sporting News*, July 31, 1965, 29.

21. Author's interview with Jerry Michalek, April 2018.

22. Russell Schneider, "Whitfield Belt Wins Again," *Cleveland Plain Dealer*, September 24, 1965, 35.

23. Author's interview with Sam McDowell, January 2018.

24. John Hall, "Meet the New MVP," *Cleveland Plain Dealer*, July 19, 1965.

Chapter 14

1. Advertisement, *Cleveland Plain Dealer*, May 15, 1966.

2. Author's interview with Duke Sims, May 2018.

3. Russell Schneider, "Batting Around," *Cleveland Plain Dealer*, July 9, 1966, 36.

4. Author's interview with Max Alvis, January 2017.

5. Author's interview with Luis Tiant, December 2017.

6. Author's interview with Joe Azcue, December 2017.

7. Author's interview with Larry Brown, January 2017.

8. Author's interview with Sonny Siebert, December 2017.

9. Author's interview with George Culver, May 2018.

10. Baldassaro, *Beyond DiMaggio*, 313.

11. Author's interview with Duke Sims, April 2018.

12. Carroll Conklin, *Indians Pride: The Story of the Cleveland Indians in the 1960s* (Lewis Center, OH: Bright Stone, 2016), 295.

13. Dick Zunt, "Two 4-Homer Sluggers Clash in A.L. Contest First Time," *The Sporting News*, April 27, 1963, 25.

14. Staff Special, "Experiment Angers Wags," *Cleveland Plain Dealer*, March 23, 1967, 53.

15. Chuck Heaton, "Plucky Adcock Defies Critics," *Cleveland Plain Dealer*, April 11, 1967, 37.

16. Ross Newhan, "Nightmare of 1967 Over; Now Hinton is Delighted Angel," *Sporting News*, March 16, 1968, 4.

17. Author's interview with George Culver, May 2018.

18. Author's interview with Sonny Siebert, December 2018.

19. Author's interview with Duke Sims, May 2018.

20. Author's interview with Vern Fuller, January 2018.

21. Russell Schneider, "Rocky Sniffs at Pot of Gold at the End of Injun Trail," *The Sporting News*, August 12, 1967, 11.

22. Author's interview with Gerry Nesmeth, April 2018.

23. Author's interview with Brent Kecskemety, February 2018.

24. Chuck Heaton, "Indians' Colavito Goes to Chisox," *Cleveland Plain Dealer*, July 30, 1967, 6-C.

25. *Ibid.*

26. *Ibid.*

27. Author's interview with Joe Azcue, December 2018.

28. Author's interview with Max Alvis, January 2018.

Chapter 15

1. Milton Gross, "Boyer and Colavito: The Castoffs' Last Fling," *Sport*, November 1967, 40–43, 90.

2. Jerome Holtzman, "Boyer's Homer Inspires Chisox to Pennant Talk," *The Sporting News*, August 12, 1967, 10.

3. Dan Coughlin, "Rocky Pays His 1st Dividend," *Cleveland Plain Dealer*, August 1, 1967, 27.

4. *Ibid.*

5. Author's interview with Tommy John, May 2018.

6. Author's interview with Ken Berry, June 2018.

7. "Boyer and Colavito: The Castoffs' Last Fling," 40–43, 90.

8. Joe Falls, "Doctored Baseballs—How White Sox Did It," *The Sporting News*, September 30, 1967, 6.

9. Mark Liptak, "J.C. Martin Interview," *Baseball Almanac* online, 2005. http://www.baseball-almanac.com/players/jc_martin_interview.shtml.

10. Author's interview with Ken Berry, June 2018.

11. Falls, "Doctored Baseballs," 6.

12. Dan Hafner, "Dodgers Buy Colavito in Deal with Chisox," *Los Angeles Times*, March 27, 1968, 37.

13. *Los Angeles Times*, "Colavito Not Worried Over Dodger Park," March 21, 1968, H3.

14. *Ibid.*

15. "Yankees Sign Colavito; Downing Sent to Farm," *New York Times*, July 15, 1968, 45.

16. George Vecsey, "Bittersweet Return of the Native," *New York Times*, August 11, 1968, S3.

17. Author's interview with George Vecsey, June 2018.

18. Author's interview with Marty Appel, March 2018.

19. Bill Ryczek, "The Day Rocky Pitched," Our Game (blog of MLB Historian John Thorn), https://ourgame.mlblogs.com/the-day-rocky-pitched-c3fb4bc62179.

20. Author's interview with Robert Mc-Carthy, July 2018.

21. Bill Ryczek, "The Day Rocky Pitched," Our Game (blog of MLB Historian John Thorn), https://ourgame.mlblogs.com/the-day-rocky-pitched-c3fb4bc62179

22. Author's interview with Phyllis LaVietes, January 2018.

23. Email by Joe Pepitone to the author, May 2018.

24. Leonard Koppett, "Stottlemyre Gets 21st Victory as Yanks Split with Indians," *New York Times*, September 25, 1968, 50.

25. Jenkinson, *Baseball's Ultimate Power*, 290.

26. Thomas Rogers, "Yanks Drop Colavito, Buy Pitcher: Outfielder is Made a Free Agent at His Request," *New York Times*, October 1, 1968, 54.

Chapter 16

1. Dennis Lustig, "Visit with Rocky," *Cleveland Plain Dealer*, May 18, 1971, 1-E.

2. Dennis Lustig, "Colavito Wants to Manage," *Cleveland Plain Dealer*, October 27, 1971, 1-D.

3. Russell Schneider, "Duffy's New Specs Aid His Contact at Bat," *The Sporting News*, August 19, 1972, 8.

4. "Bell-for-Harrah Swap is Defended by Paul," *Cleveland Plain Dealer*, December 12, 1978, 4-C.

5. Bob Sudyk, "Garcia, Hartenstein New Tribe Aides," *The Sporting News*, November 25, 1978, 50.

6. Dennis Lustig, "Disappointed: Coaches Colavito, Haddix Fired; Tribe Hires Garcia, Hartenstein," *Cleveland Plain Dealer*, November 7, 1978, 1-D.

7. Bob Nold, "Indians Miss Piece of 'The Rock,'" *Akron Beacon Journal*, May 20, 1979, C1.

Chapter 17

1. *United Press International*, "Former Baseball Greats Inducted," July 16, 1979.

2. Bill Althaus, "Colavito Big Hit as Royals' Coach," *Independence (MO) Examiner*, May 17, 1982, 1B.

3. Bill Althaus, "'Rock' Happy He's Back," *Independence (MO) Examiner*, March 9, 1982, 1B.

4. *Associated Press*, "Brett Explains his Hot Start: 'Kind of Trance,'" April 24, 1982.

5. Bill Althaus, "Colavito, Hard Work Lift McRae," *Independence (MO) Examiner*, June 19, 1982, 1B.

6. Bill Althaus, "Colavito Big Hit as Royals' Coach," *Independence (MO) Examiner*, May 17, 1982, 1B.

7. Eric St. John, "Howser, Colavito Arrested in Altercation with Police," *Washington Post*, August 21, 1982, D1.

8. Mike McKenzie, "Howser and Rocky Facing Jury Trial," *The Sporting News*, November 8, 1982, 32.

9. *Ibid.*

10. Thomas Boswell, "They Have More Paunch Than Punch, But They Know How to Play the Game," *Washington Post*, June 24, 1986, E3.

11. Author's interview with Steve Colavito, June 2018.

12. Author's interview with Marisa Colavito, August 2018.

13. Rocky Colavito, "Carl Furillo: 'One of the Greatest,'" *Reading (PA) Eagle*, February 5, 1989, C-11.

14. Author's interview with Larry Russ, June 2018.

15. Author's interview with Bob DiBiasio, February 2017.

16. Author's interview with Steve Colavito, August 2018.

17. Author's interview with Bob DiBiasio, February 2017.

18. *Ibid.*

19. *Ibid.*

20. Author's interview with Morris Eckhouse, March 2018.

21. Author's interview with Bob DiBiasio, February 2017

Bibliography

Interviews

Colavito Family: Carmen, wife; Marisa, daughter; Rocco, Jr., son; and Steven, son
Former Cleveland Indians players: Joe Altobelli, Max Alvis, Joe Azcue, Gary Bell, Larry Brown, George Culver, the late Tito Francona, Vern Fuller, Sam McDowell, Sonny Siebert, Duke Sims, Ralph Terry, and Luis Tiant.
Former teammates: Paul Foytack, Willie Horton, Al Kaline, and Jake Wood of the Detroit Tigers; Joe Pepitone of the New York Yankees; Jim Gentile of the Kansas City Athletics; and Ken Berry and Tommy John of the Chicago White Sox.
Indians fans: Brian Berg, Bob Fitzpatrick, Sheldon Green, Susan Grimm, Dan Gugliotta, Dale McMillin, Jerry Michalek, Gerry Nemeth, Brent Kecskemety, Ida Pocci, Kent Reinker, Allen Richardson, Thomas Rudar, Jr., Gary Stromberg, and Christine Williams.
Others: Marty Appel, former public relations director, New York Yankees, and author; Marc Bona, reporter, *Cleveland.com*; Lawrence Baldassaro, historian and author; Bob DiBiasio, senior vice president of public affairs, Cleveland Indians; Bill Jenkinson, baseball historian and author; Jim Kaat, opposing pitcher, Senators (1959–1960) and Twins (1961–1968); Phyllis LaVietes, founder, Facebook Rocky Colavito Fan Club; Jerry Muro, close childhood friend; Basil Russo, president, Italian Sons and Daughters of America; Nancy Score, widow of Herb Score; Joan Smith, childhood friend; Emily Toth, co-founder, Rocky Colavito Fan Club; George Vecsey, sportswriter; Barbara Warny, co-founder, Rocky Colavito Fan Club; Cindy Yost, daughter of sporting goods salesman Duke Zilber.

Books

Baldassaro, Lawrence. *Beyond DiMaggio: Italian Americans in Baseball*. Lincoln: University of Nebraska Press, 2013.
Boston, Talmadge. *Baseball and the Baby Boomer: A History, Commentary and Memoir*. Houston: Bright Sky Press, 2009.
Bragan, Bobby, and Jeff Guinn. *You Can't Hit the Ball with the Bat on Your Shoulder: The Baseball Life and Times of Bobby Bragan*. Fort Worth, TX: Summit, 1992.
Chakerian, Peter. *Pop Goes Cleveland! The Impact of Cleveland (and Northeast Ohio) on Pop Culture*. Cleveland Landmarks Press, 2009.
Clavin, Tom, and Danny Peary. *Roger Maris: Baseball's Reluctant Hero*. New York: Touchstone, 2010.
Cobbledick, Gordon. *Don't Knock the Rock: The Rocky Colavito Story*. New York: World Publishing, 1966.

Conklin, Carroll. *Indians Pride: The Story of the Cleveland Indians in the 1960s.* Lewis Center, OH: Bright Stone, 2016.

DeMarco, Tony. *Sporting News Selects 50 Greatest Sluggers.* St. Louis: Times Mirror Magazines, 2000.

Golenbock, Peter. *Dynasty: When Rooting for the Yankees was Like Rooting for U.S. Steel.* Englewood Cliffs, NJ: Prentice-Hall, 1975.

Hawkins, Jim. *Al Kaline: The Biography of a Tigers Icon.* Chicago: Triumph, 2010.

Jenkinson, Bill. *Baseball's Ultimate Power: Ranking the All-Time Greatest Distance Home Run Hitters.* Guilford, CT: Lyons Press, 2010.

Miller, Carol Poh, and Robert A. Wheeler. *Cleveland: A Concise History, 1796–1996.* Bloomington: Indiana University Press, 1997.

Peterson, John E. *The Kansas City Athletics: A Baseball History, 1954–1967.* Jefferson, NC: McFarland, 2003.

Pluto, Terry. *The Curse of Rocky Colavito.* New York: Simon & Schuster, 1994.

_____. *Our Tribe: A Baseball Memoir.* New York: Simon & Schuster, 1999.

Schneider, Russell. *The Cleveland Indians Encyclopedia,* 3d ed. (Champaign, IL: Sports Publishing, 2005), 350.

_____. *Tales from the Tribe Dugout.* Champaign, IL: Sports Publishing, 2002.

Toman, James A., and Gregory G. Deegan. *Cleveland Stadium: The Last Chapter.* Cleveland: Landmarks Press, 1997.

Vanderberg, Bob. *Frantic Frank Lane: Baseball's Ultimate Wheeler-Dealer.* Jefferson, NC: McFarland, 2013.

Vincent, David, et al. *The Midsummer Classic: The Complete History of Baseball's All-Star Game.* Lincoln: University of Nebraska Press, 2001.

Newspapers

Akron Beacon Journal
Chicago Sun-Times
Chicago Tribune
Cleveland News
Cleveland Plain Dealer
Cleveland Press
Daytona Beach News-Journal
Detroit Free Press
Detroit News
Independence (MO) Examiner
Indianapolis News
Indianapolis Star
Kansas City Star
Kansas City Times
Los Angeles Times
New York Daily News
New York Journal-American
New York Times
Oakland Tribune
Philadelphia Inquirer
Reading (PA) Eagle
San Diego Union
Toledo Blade
Topeka Capital-Journal
Washington Post

Magazines

Baseball Digest
Baseball on the Western Reserve. Cleveland: Society for American Baseball Research
Look
Memphis
Saturday Evening Post
Sport
The Sporting News
Sports Illustrated

Online Sources

Baseball Almanac, www.baseball-almanac.com. An encyclopedia of year-by-year information and statistics, including Rocky Colavito.
Baseball-Reference.com, www.baseball-reference.com. A comprehensive repository for information and statistics on every major league player, including Rocky Colavito.
Corbett, Warren. "Frank Lane," SABR Biography Project, https://sabr.org/node/40756.
Ferroni, Charles. "Encyclopedia of Cleveland History: Italians." Case Western Reserve University, https://case.edu/ech/articles/i/italians.
Markusen, Bruce. "Colavito Still the Rock Despite Recent Health Issues," Detroit Athletic Co. https://www.detroitathletic.com/blog/2015/10/04/colavito-still-the-rock-despite-recent-health-issues/.
Nelson, D. L. "The Reign of Finley." Athletics Nation, https://www.athleticsnation.com/2013/8/1/4576930/the-reign-of-finley.
Rieper, Max. "Losing a Sports Team: The Relocation of the Kansas City Athletics." Royals Review, https://www.royalsreview.com/2016/1/20/10761476/losing-a-sports-team-the-relocation-of-the-kansas-city-athletics.
Ryczek, Bill. "The Day Rocky Pitched." Our Game (blog of MLB Historian John Thorn), https://ourgame.mlblogs.com/the-day-rocky-pitched-c3fb4bc62179.
Taylor, David A. "During World War II, the U.S. Saw Italian-Americans as a Threat to Homeland Security." Smithsonian.com, https://www.smithsonianmag.com/history/italian-americans-were-considered-enemy-aliens-world-war-ii-180962021/.
Wancho, Joseph. "Herb Score," SABR Biography Project, https://sabr.org/bioproj/person/1b133b89.

Index

Numbers in *bold italics* indicate pages with illustrations